DIVER
EQUITY&
INCLUSION
FOR TRAINERS

MARIA MORUKIAN

PRESS

Alexandria, VA

ATD Press is an internationally renowned source of insightful and practical information on talent development, training, and professional development.

ATD Press
1640 King Street
Alexandria, VA 22314 USA

Ordering information: Books published by ATD Press can be purchased by visiting ATD's website at td.org/books or by calling 800.628.2783 or 703.683.8100.

Library of Congress Control Number: 2021948271

ISBN-10: 1-953946-05-4
ISBN-13: 978-1-953946-05-8
e-ISBN: 978-1-953946-06-5

ATD Press Editorial Staff
Director: Sarah Halgas
Manager: Melissa Jones
Content Manager, L&D: Eliza Blanchard
Developmental Editor: Kathryn Stafford
Production Editor: Hannah Sternberg
Text Design: Shirley E.M. Raybuck
Cover Design: FaceOut Studio
Printed by BR Printers, San Jose, CA

Dedication

For my future peace teachers, Rosalie and Lilia, and my past peace teachers, Joni and Val. From one generation to the next, you inspire me every day to make the world a little bit better than I found it.

Contents

Introduction

If there was ever an example of the adage, "looks can be deceiving," my father was it.

Varujan "Val" Morukian was short in stature with thinning gray hair, wire-framed glasses, and a creased olive-skinned face that looked vaguely "ethnic" to most people in the suburban Detroit neighborhood where I grew up. He walked around with a friendly smile and a vague look in his eyes. He was hard of hearing, and between that and his foreign accent people often assumed he didn't understand them or was not "all there."

The truth was that my father was paying very close attention to everything. His intellect was sharp. His curiosity was endless. His life story could have been a script for an epic movie. What people "saw" was by no means representative of the courageous, complex human underneath.

My family were Armenians who were forced to flee Turkey in the 1920s. As refugees they settled in Cuba, where my father was born. He was raised by an incredible, resilient single mother and two older sisters. In Havana he often sat in the plaza with the old-timers while they played dominos and spun stories. He visited with Blanca, an old Afro-Cuban woman who practiced Santeria. She was feared by the other neighborhood kids as a *bruja* (witch) but was loved by my father. After coming to the US, he served in the army as a sniper in the Korean War, earning the Bronze Star for his valor. He worked as a bartender and a bowling alley attendant, and on one eventful night he stood in as a security guard for Jimmy Hoffa. He earned a graduate degree from the University of Michigan. He became a history teacher and changed the lives of thousands of struggling teenagers in Detroit public schools over his 30-plus-year career.

My father was an endless learner. He was continually curious about other people and saw beyond immediate impressions, finding something to admire about everyone. He showed genuine interest and compassion for everyone equally. In return, people were their best selves with him. Struggling students improved. Neighbors flocked to our house when they needed a coffee and confidential conversation. Grocery store clerks, waitstaff at restaurants, and auto mechanics greeted him by name with bright smiles, handshakes, and hugs. I learned from him that when we treat others with dignity and warmth, they typically respond in kind.

Why Diversity, Equity, and Inclusion?

Throughout my career, I have been drawn to exploring how our unique identities influence our work and personal lives, and how diverse combinations of people contribute to organizational success. I have also seen the corrosive effect of inequality and systemic oppression on organizations and society as a whole.

As a trainer and facilitator, my work has led me to believe deeply in the importance of challenging people to look at the world from various perspectives, not only to build connections with others but also to gain wisdom. As an organization development practitioner, I have learned that change only happens when DEI becomes a core part of the organizational structure and culture, when it is recognized by all as critical to the organization's sustainability.

Why This Book?

Diversity, equity, and inclusion work is incredibly complex. There is not a clear and well-worn path to follow for those who want to learn. Unlike more technical professions, DEI feels more amorphous. Many people in the space of DEI have had to forge their own way, learning as they went. Although there are now benchmarks for DEI success and best practices to follow, the field is continuing to evolve, and there is no centralized certifying body for DEI to ensure that practitioners have a shared set of skills and knowledge.

Our society is also at a turning point that demands individuals and institutions focus on DEI as an imperative for sustainability. Our population is more demographically diverse than ever, and social polarization has continued to push people into identity-based camps that foster distrust, disregard, and hatred.

I began outlining this book in early 2020, when the COVID-19 pandemic had just begun. While writing the book, I witnessed the aftermath of the murders of George Floyd, Ahmaud Arbery, Breonna Taylor, and countless others. Many White people started to wake up to the everyday oppression and terror that Black people experience. Marches and protests supporting Black Lives Matter took place all across the US and around the world. Books like Ibram X. Kendi's *How to Be an Antiracist* and Robin DiAngelo's *White Fragility* flew off the shelves as folks grappled (many for the first time) with the truths of White supremacy and racism in the US. Requests for DEI training and consulting surged. The year 2020 really pushed the "E" piece into high gear and prompted organizations to take a more serious look at themselves and what gaps they had in terms of diversity, equity, and inclusion. Many of the leaders I have encountered in the last year have had a wake-up call and realized they have to prioritize DEI in a more systemic way than just a one-off workshop. Employees' voices have grown louder, as have the voices of consumers, pushing leaders to engage in more genuine efforts to address systemic inequalities.

This awakening has been both encouraging and frustrating to many veterans of DEI work. On the one hand it brought a renewed energy and focus, with more of an invitation to engage in uncomfortable conversations around identity and inequality than has been tolerated in the past. However, it has also been frustrating for three reasons:

- **DEI work isn't new.** Racism, sexism, and systemic oppression didn't disappear and suddenly reappear in the last few years. People of color feel frustrated with White people who appear shocked that racism still exists. They have been trying to get White people's attention for years to point out this is happening, only to be dismissed or ignored. Women are fed up with hearing that the reason they are not promoted is because they lack confidence, when in reality they are consistently judged by a different set of expectations than their male colleagues. Although progress has been made, people from marginalized identity groups continue to face challenges in their organizations and society.
- **DEI work takes years of learning and practice.** A lot of very caring, well-intentioned people who want to be part of the solution are trying to get into DEI training without developing the skills necessary to do the work well. Some may have deep training experience but have never done DEI training. Some have been involved in social justice activism but have never facilitated dialogues on DEI issues. This is the equivalent of assuming a dentist can perform heart surgery. One set of skills simply won't transfer and can do more harm than good.
- **DEI work requires a commitment to self-reflection.** DEI training can become problematic when a trainer has not taken the time and effort to explore their own understanding of and relationship with DEI issues. Even seasoned DEI practitioners can experience emotional reactions in a training session, which if not handled well may disrupt or even derail the learning experience. Beyond developing the knowledge and skills to train others in the core concepts of DEI, practitioners must do their own work. DEI work requires you to continuously reflect on your own beliefs and blind spots. It's deeply humbling work in which you have to be willing to acknowledge your own individual privilege and biases. You have to be willing to make yourself

vulnerable to others, sharing your personal stories and owning your mistakes. You have to be open to challenging and changing your perceptions.

What to Expect in This Book

This book will guide you through the process of developing your skills as a DEI trainer, with a focus on embedding DEI into the broader organizational fabric. Each chapter includes reflection questions and worksheets to support your ongoing learning and development.

Chapter 1 provides an overview of core concepts related to DEI, a brief history of the evolution of DEI work, and different philosophical underpinnings.

Chapter 2 explores processes for assessing the need for DEI training, including methods for data gathering and analysis to provide relevant training solutions.

Chapter 3 provides guidance on how to design and develop effective DEI-specific training, considering the elements of the organizational culture and external forces influencing DEI. This chapter also explores a continuum of awareness and skills related to DEI to help customize training for specific audience needs.

Chapter 4 discusses how to embed DEI practices and content into any training program, regardless of subject matter. This includes designing representative, inclusive, and accessible content, as well as ensuring the training delivery accommodates the needs of diverse learners.

Chapter 5 explores the complexities of delivering DEI training, and provides guidance on how to facilitate dialogues on DEI and handle challenging situations.

Chapter 6 lays out ways to promote continuity and collaboration to ensure a sustainable outcome, including practices for strategy, continuity, and accountability.

Chapter 7 explores DEI from a global context, providing insights and recommendations for ensuring DEI training is relevant in different cultures and regions.

Chapter 8 provides trainers with an opportunity to engage in their own DEI self-exploration. It is imperative that DEI trainers continuously reflect on and refresh their learning.

The DEI field needs more skilled practitioners who can provide high-quality training and help embed DEI into organizations in a meaningful way.

My hope is that this book will serve as a road map for those who are interested in becoming DEI practitioners, as well as those who are charged with integrating DEI principles into organizational training programs, to provide education that cuts through the noise and gives people space for honest dialogue.

Chapter 1
Overview of the DEI Landscape

As the daughter of educators, I felt like I was receiving a lesson in every moment spent with my parents. If I asked my mother for help with an essay, she pulled out a dictionary, a thesaurus, and a red ballpoint pen. Hours later, my essay would be covered in red lines with suggestions for better word choices in the margins. There would be several rounds of edits before she was satisfied with the final product. If I had to study for a history exam or write a paper on a particular historical event, my father would settle into his green wingback chair, adjust his glasses, and begin, "Well, to understand the Korean War we really need to go back a few hundred years to understand Chinese–Korean relations . . ." I would emerge with pages of notes and a dazed look on my face after a marathon history lesson from my dad, wondering how I was going to fit all the stories he wove together into a consolidated report. As a kid, I found these home lessons tedious, and sometimes wished I had never opened my mouth to ask for help. I just wanted to do the assignment as quickly as possible and go back to watching TV.

But from those evenings of study with my parents I learned two overarching lessons that have forged my path and purpose in life.

From my English-teacher mother, I learned the **power of words**. They can be used to inspire, illuminate, and elevate. They can be used to inflict pain, dismiss, and destroy. They can incite movements of compassion or hate. They can promote intellectual and emotional growth or regression. Words can bring forth laughter, tears, love, fear, rage, or diffidence. They can raise us up or shut us down. The absence of words when we stay silent can also be powerful, especially when the power of our words is needed to support others who have been silenced. Words are to be chosen with great care and intention.

From my history-teacher father, I learned the **power of stories**—the stories we hear and the stories we tell one another—and the power held by those whose stories are most often told. Our past serves as a window into the future. The further back we go and the more we explore human history, the clearer the patterns of our civilization become. To make sense of the present and to envision the future, we must delve into the past and explore history from multiple perspectives, especially from those who have been silenced or marginalized. The adage "History is often told by the winners" clouds our collective understanding of the past and does not accurately reflect the experiences of those who have been oppressed or victimized. Who writes the history books and whose stories do they choose to tell? How might we perpetuate lies and oppression by passing along stories that are one-sided?

Diversity, equity, and inclusion work starts and ends with the self. We have to be willing and able to explore the multiple dimensions that come together to create our unique identities. We must explore how words, our own and those of others, can create positive or negative reactions. We have to be open to challenging others' beliefs and be willing to have our own beliefs challenged.

DEI work requires an understanding of how history has shaped the way we experience the world. It requires a balance of strategy and storytelling.

How do you define diversity, equity, and inclusion?

This chapter sets the foundation for our study of DEI. First, we define the common terms of *diversity*, *equity*, and *inclusion*. We also introduce the newer concept of expansion, which is integral to progress in DEI work. We then cover a brief history of the evolution of DEI work, examine the challenges to making DEI efforts "stick," and outline key efforts to make DEI sustainable in our organizations. A worksheet at the end of the chapter can help prepare you to deliver DEI training.

Defining Core Concepts

Diversity encompasses all the dimensions of human identity that make us who we are. Diversity includes all characteristics that shape our identity "lenses"—our beliefs, values, worldviews, perceptions—which thus influence our communication, our behaviors, and ultimately our relationships with others.

Diversity includes characteristics like race, skin color, ethnicity, gender, national origin, sexual orientation, religion, physical or mental ability or disability, socioeconomic background, academic background, profession, family and relationship status, language, habits and activities, and personality traits.

There are dimensions of our identity, like race, gender, sexual orientation, or physical or mental disability, over which we may have little or no control, but which have a significant impact on how we are treated, how we live our lives, and how we perceive ourselves and others.

Other dimensions of our identity, like religion, geographic location, and socioeconomic status, which we may be born into, may change over the course of our lives.

Depending on the context, we may find certain dimensions of identity play a more prominent role in how we define ourselves, how we are perceived and treated, and how we engage with others. For example, we may be very aware of certain dimensions of our identity in the workplace that are not as much of a priority in our personal lives. We are often much more aware of specific dimensions of our identity when we are in the minority, or when we have less power or privilege because of that dimension of identity.

Equity promotes fairness by creating a level playing field for everyone. This means providing opportunities for people to advance in their careers, to receive fair compensation and credit for their work, and to provide input into decisions that impact them.

Imagine an oval racetrack. The outer lane is longer than the inner one. So the runners' starting points are staggered to ensure fairness. By placing the runner in the outer lane a few paces ahead, we're not giving them an unfair advantage; we're evening the race. If we placed everyone at the same exact point on the starting line, the person on the inside track has a greater advantage because they have a shorter distance to run.

Equity works in a similar way. It's not about giving unearned advantages to people. It's actually recognizing that some people already have unearned advantages simply by being part of a group that has held power and privilege in our society. When we are intentional, we ensure that we provide opportunities for growth, training, mentoring, and career advancement for people who perhaps have not been given those opportunities.

Research shows that often men will apply for a new position even if they don't have all of the existing qualifications, while women will not apply unless they have all those qualifications (Mohr 2014). As an example of equity, a leader may encourage a female colleague to apply for a position even if she doesn't have all the qualifications and provide advice on how to handle questions in the interview process.

In another example, it may be more difficult for an employee of color who is in a lower-level role to see themselves as capable of making a career shift, while a White employee may feel more empowered to take that risk or ask for professional development opportunities to be eligible for a different role. Equity in this case would be to encourage and provide time and resources for an employee of color to develop the new skills needed to shift to a new area of expertise.

Inclusion is the practice of creating an environment where everyone feels equally valued and respected for their individuality. Inclusive environments ensure that every person is able to participate fully in organizational life, and has equal opportunities to leverage their talents, skills, and potential.

All human beings want to both feel a sense of belonging with the group and be recognized for their unique qualities and characteristics. The term *optimal distinctiveness*, coined in 1991 by the social psychologist Marilynn Brewer, describes individuals striving to achieve the optimal balance between belonging and differentiation both within and across social groups. A core part of our human survival has been our reliance on group belonging.

In the context of the workplace, *inclusion* refers to practices, behaviors, and structures that promote a sense of belonging and inter-dependence of the collective and encourage divergent ideas, acknowledge unique skills and experiences, and value individual characteristics and identities.

Expansion is the practice of immersing oneself in the lived experiences of others, broadening one's social networks beyond the comfortable "us" group, and building community across the broad landscape of our differences.

I employ this term because of two trends I witnessed in my work:

- Often the individuals in positions of privilege and power have noble intentions but lack an understanding of the depth of work they need to do to truly enact change in their organizations and communities. A number of organizations' diversity, equity, and inclusion efforts only scratch the surface of the deep-seated problems around inequity and exclusion, often because the people who most need to change their attitudes and behaviors have the least incentive to do so.

- Our society has increasingly become polarized due to a variety of factors—political, economic, cultural, technological—that play into our instinctual human need to entrench ourselves in our "us" group. If we are to make progress not only in DEI but in all the complex challenges we face as a human civilization, we need tools to override our biases, make ourselves emotionally vulnerable to those we have been conditioned to perceive as the "other," and embrace new ways of thinking, communicating, and living with one another.

Expansion means seeking out new voices, divergent ways of thinking, and pushing oneself to challenge existing schemas. Expansion requires individuals, especially those in positions of privilege and power, to:

- Leave their comfort zone to immerse themselves in the experiences of those they perceive as "other." Human nature often drives us to seek out or stay in the spaces that feel safe to us. When we encounter people whose beliefs or behaviors are foreign, confusing, or in conflict with our own, our instinctual reaction is often to distance ourselves. Expansion requires us to do the opposite, to engage fully and listen openly when we encounter opposite viewpoints. This does not mean we must sacrifice our core values or beliefs. It simply frees us to explore and thus better understand the reasons people may see the world differently.
- Shift power to the voices that are often silenced. Expansion goes beyond superficial acts of inclusion, where we not only welcome people to our space, we leave our comfort zone behind and venture into spaces that are unknown to us. Accepting or inviting people to our proverbial table has an inherent power dynamic buried within. There is an implicit message of giving permission for others who are not part of the norm or majority. Expansion shifts the power from those who already had a seat at the table and requires us to leave our seat and maybe even leave the table itself to make room for people who have not historically had a seat. When practicing expansion, we have to be willing to temporarily displace ourselves from what is known and feels safe. We have to be willing to explore and engage with people in their comfort zones, where they have power.
- Challenge existing schemas and blind spots. Expansion is about bringing deep curiosity and a willingness to question our own mental models. We are willing to examine the way we've always done things and question whom the current structure and culture serves and whom it does not.
- Co-create a new culture with shared purpose and power. Expansion provides the unique opportunity to co-create a culture that works for everyone. Rather than expecting assimilation from those who have been underrepresented or sidelined,

we explore how to design a new way of working together that incorporates divergent experiences, values, and needs, and seeks to create a more balanced power structure.

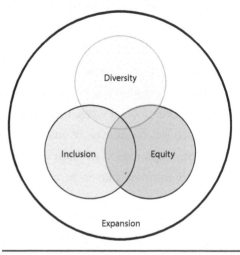

Figure 1-1. Diversity, Equity, and Inclusion

Diversity, equity, and inclusion are interconnected and interdependent (Figure 1-1). To enact long-term change, we need to explore these three concepts in a meaningful way. Expansion is the glue that binds them all together.

DEI: A Historical Perspective

Human history is rife with stories of inequality, oppression, and polarization. It is also rich with stories of compassion, intercultural communication, diplomacy, and social progress. Mark Twain purportedly said, "History doesn't repeat itself, but it often rhymes."

To more fully grasp the present-day context of DEI, it is important to have some knowledge of what prefaced the era in which we find ourselves. This is by no means a comprehensive history so much as a spotlight on the major themes that influenced how people viewed issues of diversity, equity, and inclusion during a particular period of time.

Civil Rights and Social Justice (Righting Wrongs) (1950s–'60s)

The 1950s and '60s brought an awakening to the US about the daily injustices racial minorities, women, and members of the LGBTQIA+ community experienced across the country. This era, rife with civil unrest, violence, and assassinations, culminated in significant societal changes as well as policy changes. There were a number of inflection points that contributed to the civil rights movement. Following are just a few of those inflection points.

In just a little over a decade, there were landmark decisions by the Supreme Court to outlaw segregation, and federal laws were passed guaranteeing equal employment and upholding voting rights. There were peaceful protests of all sizes, including the Montgomery bus boycotts, the Greensboro lunch counter sit-ins, the Delano grape boycotts in California to fight the exploitation of farm workers, the March on Washington, and the "Bloody Sunday" march across the Edmund Pettus Bridge. There was the incomprehensible loss of life, including icons like Malcom X, Martin Luther King Jr., and Robert F. Kennedy, as well as allies like Viola Liuzzo and James Reeb. The Stonewall Uprising in New York in June 1969 was a galvanizing moment for LGBTQIA+ activism, in which members of the LGBTQIA+ community took to the streets and confronted law enforcement to fight against endless discrimination and human rights violations. Powerful images of children and young people illustrate the heroes and martyrs of this time, from the photos of a tiny, six-year-old Ruby Bridges being escorted by National Guard as part of school desegregation, to the graphic images of young, peaceful protestors being attacked by law enforcement with fire hoses and dogs, to the unforgettable image of 14-year-old Emmett Till, whose mother insisted on an open casket after her son was violently murdered by two White men in Mississippi.

This was a time of reckoning, of fury, hope, violence, and social change.

DEI Training Implications

The impact of this period on our history as it relates to DEI is immeasurable. Although many Americans are familiar to a certain degree with the titans of the movement like Martin Luther King Jr, Rosa Parks, Malcolm X, and John Lewis, there are innumerable stories that are not taught universally in American classrooms and not discussed in American families. To truly comprehend the vast, systemic oppression and terror that has been the lived experience of Black citizens in the US, we must revisit this part of our country's history with open eyes and hearts.

It is also critical to acknowledge that these movements were successful in enacting systemic change because they united people from diverse backgrounds in a common cause. The ability to engage in coalition building not only within each "us" community, but between communities of different racial, ethnic, religious, and socioeconomic backgrounds, was instrumental in creating the groundswell needed to disrupt systems of oppression and inequality.

The advent of what we now know as DEI-related training really took off in this era. However, it mainly focused on compliance with Title VII of the Civil Rights Act of 1964, prohibiting discrimination of employees based on sex, color, race, national origin, or religion. The remedy for organizations accused of discrimination or harassment was court-mandated compliance training for all employees.

Implementing Social Change (Filling the Gaps) (1970s–'80s)

The Civil Rights movement of the 1960s led to sweeping policy changes and a broader societal recognition of the discrimination and violence against people of color, members of the LGBTQIA+ community, and women. However, organizations and institutions struggled to uphold the new policies, and to create more diverse and equitable systems through affirmative action policies, including race and gender quotas.

There rose a backlash, mainly from Whites and males, who feared they were going to become the victims of "reverse discrimination," a term used to argue that any policies or practices that gave special preference or opportunities to right the wrongs of the past led to discrimination against members of the dominant or majority group. In 1978, the Supreme Court's ruling on *Regents of University of California v. Bakke* determined that the university's racial quotas were unconstitutional, but that a school's use of affirmative action to accept more minority applicants was permissible.

This era also saw an increase in women entering the workforce and a heightened focus on gender parity, anti-harassment policies, and pay equity. The Equal Employment Opportunity Commission (EEOC) received more than 50,000 complaints of sex-based discrimination in its first five years of operation. Title IX of the Education Amendments of 1972 ensured equal access for women to higher education and professional schools, which increased the number of women enrolling in historically male-dominated professions like medicine, law, and engineering. The number of girls and women participating in athletics increased exponentially due to Title IX as well. The Equal Rights Amendment to ensure equality for all sexes was finally passed by Congress in 1972 (50 years after it was introduced) and sent to states for ratification; however, to date, it still lacks the ratification by three-quarters of states that is required for the amendment to be added to the US Constitution.

Disability rights activists also celebrated progress during this time, as they lobbied Congress and marched on Washington to demand civil rights. The Rehabilitation Act of 1973 mandated equal opportunities for employment in the federal government for people with mental and physical disabilities. The act also established a governing body to ensure compliance with laws requiring equal access to public services for people with disabilities. The 1975 Education for All Handicapped Children Act guaranteed equal access to education for children with disabilities. In 1990, after decades of advocacy, disability rights activists were successful in getting Congress to pass the Americans With Disabilities Act (ADA), which guaranteed equal treatment and access to employment opportunities and public accommodations.

This era saw a global rise in advocacy for LGBTQIA+ rights, with the first out gay minister ordained by the United Church of Christ in 1972. The 1980s brought the HIV/AIDS epidemic, which took a horrendous toll on the gay male population. During this time, there were both societal and political efforts to demonize the LGBTQIA+ community as well as an outpouring of public advocacy supporting LGBTQIA+ rights.

Training and Development Implications

DEI training during this time continued to focus mainly on compliance with EEOC regulations. There was some effort by organizations to focus on teaching beyond compliance "dos and don'ts," yet many of the training efforts fell short of motivating people to change attitudes and behaviors or to value diversity. There was not yet a focus on changing organizational culture to be a workplace that was inclusive and inviting for a diverse employee population.

Often, affirmative action debates may arise in a DEI training conversation. Trainers should know the history and evolution of affirmative action policies to a certain degree in order to manage such debates effectively. A few talking points to consider regarding affirmative action:

- The origins of affirmative action stem from the Civil Rights movement and can be traced back to John F. Kennedy's 1961 executive order on equal rights for all races. Thus, affirmative action at its core is intended to right the injustices of the past that have held back racial minorities (mainly Black Americans) and women. Ironically, research shows that White women have benefited the most from affirmative action policies but have also become some of the fiercest opponents of affirmative action policies (Crenshaw 2006).

- Over the years, the courts have defined affirmative action more clearly, ruling quotas unconstitutional but not the use of affirmative action practices to strengthen diversity of marginalized populations. There continues to be some controversy surrounding who "wins or loses" with affirmative action policies.

- Forcing quotas is not necessarily the best solution to diversifying the workforce. On the other hand, research indicates that organizations that make no intentional efforts to diversify their workforce end up with homogenous teams, especially at the executive leadership and board levels (Dixon-Fyle et al. 2020). Bias continues to drive decisions that leave qualified women and racial and ethnic minorities out of senior positions.

- Organizations that are committed to DEI engage in policies and practices to mitigate bias in recruiting, hiring, and promotions. They take active and visible actions to hire and promote diverse teams at every level.

Managing Diversity (Making It Work) (1990s–early 2000s)

The 1990s and early 2000s saw a continued upswing in diversity due to a combination of factors. EEOC and ADA policies had become a fixed norm within organizational life. Two-income households became more universal as both men and women entered and stayed in the workforce. The demographics of the US population were increasingly diverse, racially and ethnically. Our economy was more globally interdependent than ever, and organizations increasingly were doing business with overseas employees, clients, and vendors.

More organizations began to acknowledge the importance of valuing diversity and the peril of ignoring it. Offices devoted to EEO and civil rights had been the center point of DEI efforts, but some forward-thinking organizations began to hire chief diversity officers and build systems for training employees across the organization on working in diverse teams.

Although the focus started to shift beyond mere compliance of laws and policies, there was still more of a superficial approach. Many traditionally marginalized employees (people of color, women, people with disabilities, LGBTQIA+, and so on) were still expected to assimilate to the dominant cultural norms, which were traditionally built around a history of White cisgender males being in power.

Training and educational programs emerged that focused conversations on specific identity dimensions that were historically marginalized. Simultaneously, there was a rising trend in diversity training during this time that broadened the conversation to encompass all identity characteristics and not solely focus on race, gender, and the EEOC-protected classes. Some practitioners argued that this "watered down" the conversation and made it overly comfortable for those with the most power and privilege. Others argued for the broadening of the conversation, saying it was valuable in changing attitudes toward diversity and undoing the damage of the "blame and shame" approach that had turned off many White people and men in past diversity efforts.

We also saw some practitioners begin to use terms like "multiculturalism" and "cultural competence" to define the skills needed to manage diverse teams and organizations. The intent of these terms was to illustrate that everyone brings a set of cultural lenses and norms that dictate how they see the world and how they behave. It reinforced an approach that celebrated diversity as an asset and pushed the business case for diversity in terms of managing across diverse cultural norms and patterns of communication.

Although this approach helped to bring about more openness to exploring diversity and helped lessen the defensiveness of those in the dominant groups, some practitioners argued that it missed the mark in disrupting racism, sexism, and homophobia at their core and pushing people to talk openly about power and societal privilege, and thus it stopped short of ensuring accountability for upholding workplace cultures that were equitable and inclusive.

Training and Development Implications

Many participants in today's DEI training are likely to still see it through the lens of managing diversity. There is often a push by organizational leaders to spend time focusing on the business case for diversity and broadening the conversation to encapsulate diversity in all its forms, including diversity of thought.

Although it can be helpful to provide a research-backed rationale for why DEI is a strategic imperative, trainers should beware of overly focusing on the business case. People who have historically been marginalized are fatigued by having to state (or hear others state) why their voices and experience should hold equal weight to that of the dominant population.

Similarly, it is important to use a broad definition of diversity that encapsulates all the dimensions that make us who we are. This approach is valuable in that it:

- Creates an opportunity for every participant to feel they are a part of the conversation on diversity
- Breaks down the single-story stereotypes that narrow people's views of one another to one or two dimensions of identity
- Highlights the importance of exploring intersectionality and how multiple dimensions of identity can compound one's advantages or disadvantages

It is equally important to articulate when using a broad definition of diversity that the intent is not to dilute or distract from some of the dimensions that people find it more difficult to engage with, which in the US tend to be primarily race and ethnicity, gender and gender identity, and sexual orientation.

Diversity and Inclusion (Changing Behaviors) (2000s–mid 2010s)

In the early 21st century, diversity and inclusion work became more of a legitimate part of organizational strategy. During this time, there was an increase in the number of chief diversity officers and D&I departments, increasingly standing alone from HR functions. As more research showed the benefits of diversity in organizations, and as demographics in the US continued to diversify in terms of race and ethnicity, leaders began to take notice that the incoming workforce and the future pool of talent was not only more diverse but had a different set of expectations of what the workplace should be like and how divergent voices should be valued.

The rising popularity of research and books focusing on corporate culture change and leadership increased knowledge and appreciation of concepts like emotional intelligence and empathy. Research on neuropsychology, unconscious bias, and implicit associations began to show up in diversity training and provided people with new insights into how our brains are hardwired for prejudice and automatic judgment. Research on micro-expressions and micro-messages also invited people to think about diversity and inclusion not just in terms of preventing blatant acts of discrimination and harassment, but to acknowledge the small, subtle, daily indignities that many marginalized populations experience.

This era of training also solidified the interdependence of diversity and inclusion, as leaders in the field increasingly made the case for focusing not just on representation of diversity in organizations but on practices and policies that lead to a culture of inclusion. Training increasingly focused on providing people with skills to check their assumptions and behaviors, and to be intentional about valuing diverse voices and communicating with heightened sensitivity.

Global diversity and intercultural competence training continued to gain in popularity and practice during this time, as more companies expanded multinationally and outsourcing to overseas employees became more prominent.

During this time, many organizations began to integrate diversity and inclusion concepts within overall initiatives focusing on employee engagement, wellness, and belonging. There are pros and cons to this approach. On the one hand, diversity and inclusion are crucial for building healthy, thriving organizations. On the other hand, diversity practitioners argued that this approach was an avoidance tactic to not address systemic barriers for historically marginalized people.

During President Barack Obama's time in office, many leaders fell under the illusion that racism was no longer an issue that needed attention now that the US had elected its first Black and multiracial president. In 2013, the Supreme Court invalidated a key part of the Voting Rights Act of 1965, which then freed up states to change their election laws without federal approval. Chief Justice John Roberts wrote for the majority, "While any racial discrimination in voting is too much, Congress must ensure that the legislation it passes to remedy that problem speaks to current conditions" (Shelby County v. Holder 2013). Meanwhile, violence and disparate treatment against marginalized populations, especially Black people, continued. As graphic accounts and video evidence caught on smartphones spread on social media, the world was unable to ignore the injustices that continued. The stories of innocent citizens who were killed, many by police, including Trayvon Martin, Philando Castile, and Michael Brown, sparked the Black Lives Matter movement in 2013 to raise awareness of anti-Black violence and systemic racism.

The latter part of this period showed the juxtaposition between a desire to couch diversity and inclusion as a means to promote unity, wellness, and belonging alongside a burgeoning tide of frustration and anger at the injustice and inequity that continued to plague nondominant identity groups.

Training and Development Implications

The more pronounced focus during this time on inclusion and changing individual behaviors to build positive relationships was a shift toward fostering long-lasting culture change in organizations. More organizations built diversity and inclusion into their operations and hired professionals who specialized in it. D&I training became a regular offering in most organizations for managers and employees. D&I concepts also became core competencies in leadership and management training, and increasingly linked to performance evaluations for anyone in a supervisory or leadership position.

Concepts like unconscious bias, emotional intelligence, and micromessages continue to be a prominent part of DEI training today.

Progress, Politics, and Polarization (Disrupting Systems of Oppression and Injustice) (Mid 2010s–the present)

The late 2010s through the early 2020s appear to be revisiting the cycle of civil unrest and systemic disruption that we saw in the 1960s during the civil rights movement. The BLM movement has continued to grow, followed by the #MeToo movement that gained widespread attention in 2017 in the midst of multiple reports of sexual harassment and assault against women.

The ever-increasing polarization that exists not only in US society but also around the world has been worsened by a rise in populism, a deepening economic division between the haves and have-nots, and social media that caters to our human instinct for gravitating toward those in our networks and confirming rather than challenging our biases. The increase in use of social networks and streaming services as sources of news and information has made it increasingly easier for people to be manipulated by information that is either skewed to reinforce their pre-existing beliefs or is straight-up propaganda.

The COVID-19 pandemic further illustrated the inequalities that exist for nondominant groups, including women; Black, indigenous, and people of color (BIPOC); and people of lower socioeconomic status.

The fight for LGBTQIA+ equality has experienced progress, with the Supreme Court legalizing same-sex marriage in 2015 and declaring it illegal to fire someone because they are gay or transgender. Representation of same-sex couples and LGBTQIA+ people in the media and entertainment industry has risen, but when examined from an intersectional lens, the representation is still overwhelmingly White (Nielsen 2020). Furthermore, progress has stalled and in some cases been thwarted, in particular for the gender nonbinary and trans communities. The largest mass shooting in US history was a hate crime against the LGBTQIA+ community, which occurred in 2016 at the Pulse nightclub in Orlando, Florida. 2020 was the most violent year on record for crimes against trans and nonbinary people, with 44 reported fatalities (HRC 2021). A number of state legislatures are considering laws to ban gender affirming treatment for minors.

Although there has been significant progress toward inclusion for LGBTQIA+ employees in the workplace, the percentage of LGBTQIA+ employees who say they are closeted at work has only decreased slightly in the last decade, from 50 to 46 percent. More than half of LGBTQIA+ workers report hearing jokes about gay and lesbian people, and the top reason most LGBTQIA+ workers decide not to report such behaviors is because they don't believe anything would be done about it (HRC 2018). Additionally, supportive legislation and corporate policies have been put into place regarding parental leave, but these policies largely are built around a heteronormative focus on parenthood that excludes same sex male couples.

The cumulative result of these steps forward and back in terms of representation and fair treatment has been a heightened focus on disrupting systems of inequity and oppression. Increasingly, leaders and practitioners are adding the "E" (equity) to the "D" and "I" to symbolize an equal focus on ensuring fairness and equity for all. In fact, many are putting the "E" first in the acronym (EDI) to emphasize its importance. The language and focal point of a lot of diversity-related work have shifted toward challenging those with power and privilege to reflect and take action to right the wrongs of the past. In many ways, it feels like a resurgence of the 1960s civil rights era. There has been an influx of interest and urgency to engage in efforts to drive change for diversity.

Training and Development Implications

DEI training has received a renewed focus and demand, but this time many organizations are being pushed by their employees and even consumers and other outside stakeholders to go deeper than past training efforts, which may be perceived as too generic or superficial. Training is more likely to prioritize equity along with inclusion and belonging. Organizations are providing training that more explicitly focuses on issues of race, power, and privilege.

The value of these more frank conversations and learning experiences is that people with status and power are now examining societal and organizational systems of exclusion and oppression and taking action to disrupt them. The challenge is the inevitable backlash that comes with systemic disruption that causes some to react with anger, defensiveness, guilt, or shame.

Also, the increased attention and demand has led to many people who lack the proper training and experience to conduct such training being asked (or volunteering) to do DEI training. Conducting DEI training without experience is not only a recipe for disaster for the individual trainer; it also delegitimizes those who have devoted their careers to this type of work.

In a subsequent chapter, we will discuss how to do your own work as a DEI trainer and the appropriate steps to consider before hanging your shingle out to do DEI training.

Philosophies Underpinning DEI

There are six distinct but interrelated philosophies that underpin DEI work (Figure 2-1):

- Social justice
- Business results
- Compliance
- Advocacy and allyship

- Valuing differences
- Oneness and unity

Each philosophy and subsequent approach will influence the way a DEI initiative is designed and its results. There is not necessarily a "right" or "wrong" philosophy. It's important to consider how to include some elements of each of these concepts into the work. Yet, depending on the organizational culture and need, practitioners may find themselves leaning into some ideas more than others. Each approach also has a counterbalance. These are not necessarily opposing philosophies; rather, they can be considered centripetal, with DEI as the central body around which all six conceptual categories contribute energy.

Figure 1-2. DEI Philosophies

It is important to consider how much we rely on each of these tentpole ideas so we don't lose balance or momentum. Over-focusing on one or two may result in challenges, resistance, or setbacks.

Social Justice

"It's time to right the wrongs of the past."

Social justice is defined by the *Oxford English Dictionary* as "justice in terms of the distribution of wealth, opportunities, and privileges within a society."

The United Nations (2006) defines it this way: "Social justice may be broadly understood as the fair and compassionate distribution of the fruits of economic growth."

The social justice philosophy in terms of DEI work is strongly focused on equity. Social justice is centered around equal rights, equal access, and equal treatment. It's about acknowledging and working to right the wrongs of the past in terms of people who have been systematically marginalized, mistreated, or oppressed in society.

This philosophy is a powerful pillar for DEI work because it can move people to challenge and work to equalize the balance of power. It invites tough but necessary conversations around who in society has received unearned advantages and who has not. Without a focus on social justice, it can be challenging to overcome the deep, institutionalized barriers that have robbed so many people of the opportunities for success.

An underlying assumption in social justice philosophy is that people will recognize, understand, and agree with the notion that some populations have been historically (and continue to be) treated disparately. The social justice philosophy can also be challenging because it calls into question many people's beliefs, biases, and narratives about their world, especially those who have received unearned advantages because of some aspect of their identity. This philosophy can also be hard for people who are part of nondominant identity groups. They may be exposed to conversations that retraumatize them. They also may experience blowback from individuals who are resistant to giving up power.

The social justice philosophy may work best in organizational or societal cultures that deeply value equality, civil rights, and community building and a focus on collective versus individualized needs.

Business Results

"DEI makes good business sense."

The business results philosophy is about profit and productivity. It relies on research showing the financial gains of companies with more diversity at every level. The business results philosophy is backed up by years of research in organization development and behavior indicating that organizations with cultures that value DEI:

- Are more innovative
- Have more engaged employees

- Are able to hire and retain top talent
- Have teams capable of better complex problem solving
- Have higher financial performance
- Have fewer EEO complaints

This approach to DEI is the counterbalance to the social justice philosophy. An underlying assumption in the business results philosophy is that people will be not only intellectually but emotionally moved to action by the data showing the business case for DEI. The business results philosophy can be valuable in that it typically incites less active resistance or defensiveness because it's not calling people to question anyone's deeply held assumptions or beliefs, and it doesn't explicitly prioritize any deeply personal work. This philosophy may work well in highly capitalistic and individualist cultures, where there is a strong need to win over those in power by focusing on bottom-line results.

However, therein lies the challenge. This philosophy alone doesn't always yield true attitude and behavior change, and may result in superficial or short-term gains but a lack of sustainable culture change. For those who have been marginalized, oppressed, or abused because of their identity, this approach may feel hollow.

Compliance

"Follow the rules and we will have equity."

The compliance philosophy focuses primarily on following regulations, policies, and practices related to fair and equitable treatment. The US Equal Employment Opportunity Commission (EEOC) enforces federal requirements for organizations in the US. Although these requirements differ depending on the organization's size, sector, and other factors, most entities are prohibited in some way from engaging in discrimination on the basis of race, skin color, age, sex, religion, national origin, disability, or genetic information. Many organizations have additional rules and policies related to equal treatment that are enforced as well.

The compliance philosophy is valuable in that it provides a solid foundation of parameters that indicate what behaviors and practices are permitted and what is prohibited. Although there is often ambiguity in interpreting the law and identifying discrimination and harassment, decades of legal precedent provide pretty clear guidance for employers and employees on how to act. An underlying assumption of the compliance philosophy is that such regulations will lead to positive and proactive attitudes and behaviors that foster DEI. However, a challenge with focusing only on compliance is that many will feel they've checked the DEI box as long as they learn and follow the rules. In so doing, there is little effort to engage in the necessary work of co-creating a workplace where everyone feels a deep sense of belonging. Leaders may resist engaging in proactive culture change based on the argument, "We have few complaints of discrimination or harassment, so what's the problem?" Compliance alone does not yield a positive work environment for all; in fact it can sometimes have the opposite effect.

Advocacy and Allyship

"We each have to be a voice for others."

The advocacy and allyship philosophy is the counterweight to compliance. It is all about taking a proactive approach and refusing to settle for compliance as the entire solution. The advocacy and allyship philosophy embraces the notion that every individual bears an obligation to be a vocal proponent of DEI and actively challenge and disrupt the existing structures that impede DEI progress.

This philosophy is centered on individuals in dominant and nondominant groups advocating not only for their own needs but being visible allies for others who may be treated disparately.

This philosophy is valuable in that it engages individuals to take a stand for others, so the burden is not solely on those who are marginalized to always have to advocate for their own needs. It requires people to be willing to acknowledge individual power, status, and privilege, and to practice courage and take interpersonal risks by challenging behaviors or decisions that are not conducive to DEI. This philosophy can be challenging for just that reason, in that it requires individuals to be willing to sacrifice their status or their relationships within their identity groups. It often falls upon the shoulders of a small group of individuals to consistently be the standard bearers for DEI. It can be emotionally taxing to individuals and can create a drain on productivity, at least in the short term, as it does disrupt commonly held norms and practices that are deeply engrained in the organizational or societal culture.

Valuing Differences

"Our differences are what define us."

The valuing differences philosophy is rooted in the notion that our differences make us stronger. It centers around exploring divergent experiences, perspectives, and beliefs. It celebrates and calls forth uniqueness. This philosophy prioritizes the multiple dimensions of identity that make each of us different from one another.

The valuing differences philosophy can be powerful in that it encompasses all the different characteristics of identity and makes space for everyone to feel that their unique stories, talents, and styles are important. The valuing differences philosophy invites "creative abrasion," in which individuals are encouraged to challenge and debate one another (Hill et al. 2014). This philosophy works well in highly individualistic, innovative cultures.

The potential drawback to this philosophy is that it can overemphasize differences and uniqueness at the risk of ignoring the importance of building community or seeking harmony. It can also at times be so focused on individualized differences that it ignores or discounts the collective advantages or disadvantages that members of common identity groups experience. It can thus fail to challenge systemic barriers that impede opportunities for marginalized groups.

Oneness and Unity

"We're all in this together."

The oneness and unity philosophy is rooted in the notion that our common humanity binds us together. This philosophy focuses on emphasizing communal goals, highlighting basic human needs and behaviors over differences, and building harmony among individuals and groups.

This philosophy can be powerful in that it helps break down "us versus them" barriers and promotes a sense of interdependence.

The potential challenge with this philosophy is that it can minimize the important differences that define one's identity, or ignore how different identity groups have been treated in our society. This is where we fall into the trap of saying, "I treat everyone the same," "I don't see color," or, "If we just focus on what we have in common all the rest of our issues will disappear." An overreliance on this philosophy can actually make it very challenging for those who are not having an equitable or inclusive experience to feel safe coming forward and expressing dissatisfaction. It can also lead to groupthink or a lack of divergent perspectives if the culture is overly prioritizing harmony and agreement.

Why Do Some DEI Training or Organizational Change Efforts Fail?

Although there is much research indicating the importance of DEI training and development work for organizational success, many have argued that there has been insufficient progress made in truly changing cultures and systems to be more diverse, equitable, and inclusive. In fact, there are plenty of instances where DEI efforts not only failed but led to resistance and backlash.

Why do we see so many organizations struggle to achieve or maintain successful efforts for DEI? Here are some challenges that often hamper DEI efforts.

Over-focus on representation. Some organizations focus only on getting more diversity in their workforce without paying attention to the environment that those employees will be entering. This leads to high levels of turnover and disengagement if the workplace culture is not inclusive or equitable.

Focus on what's easy and comfortable. Leaders will often go for the low-hanging fruit with DEI efforts, which may include celebrations or social gatherings, or one-off training sessions on topics that don't tackle the very real day-to-day challenges underrepresented groups face. In fact, a worldwide study of diversity efforts in organizations found that

75 percent of employees from underrepresented groups did not feel they had benefited from their organization's diversity efforts (Krentz et al. 2019). The training is a way to check the box and doesn't foster a sense of commitment to change behaviors.

Conduct in conjunction with or by EEO compliance. When DEI is relegated to either Human Resources or EEO compliance, it is often much more difficult to engage in sustainable culture change. Compliance with policies and regulations will not alone create a culture of DEI. In fact, a focus on compliance alone can often yield resistance to a more proactive approach to disrupting the status quo, and fostering creative, thriving, inclusive environments for all.

Lack of accountability. Successful DEI initiatives require everyone to fully embrace the importance of diversity. All who participate need to see the importance of managing their own biases in decision making and interactions. And there must be a process of accountability at the individual and systems level to ensure people are experiencing equity and inclusion.

"Blame and shame" approach to training. There is a delicate balance between having frank, tough conversations about issues of inequity and exclusion with the intent to raise awareness and pointing the finger at those who have unearned privilege as the perpetrators of oppression. If the training does not take a constructive approach that invites everyone to learn and grow together, it can quickly erode trust and a sense of ownership on the part of those who can be the biggest and most necessary allies in this work.

Leaders avoid doing their own work. Leaders often delegate to others but don't participate actively or visibly in the initiative. Often I have found that senior leaders struggle to recognize that they need to do more than pay lip service to DEI. They must practice humility and an openness to learn, to engage in courageous conversations, and to apologize when they get it wrong. Leaders must set the tone and model inclusive and equitable practices for the DEI effort to stick.

Maintain status quo. DEI requires disrupting a system that has worked for those in positions of power, whether it's formal or informal power. Not only is it hard work to change the organizational culture, but it can be painful. Without realizing it, sometimes leaders of DEI efforts end up making a few small tweaks but largely leave the biggest barriers to DEI untouched.

Performative allyship. In the wake of recent violence and social unrest, there has been an increase in this kind of activity. Posting a statement or updating a website to say one is committed to diversity is not going to make true change happen. Also, if underrepresented groups see such statements but don't see them backed up by actual change, they will lose trust in such organizations.

Trainers don't do their own work. Facilitating DEI training is not easy by any stretch. Even seasoned trainers and facilitators may be hijacked by their own emotional reactions. Many DEI efforts fail when trainers have not had the proper training to facilitate DEI dialogues. They either don't know how to address the complex emotional issues that arise; they have not done deep enough research on key issues related to DEI from a historical, cultural, or psychological perspective; or they are emotionally triggered by something that occurs in the training environment and are no longer able to serve in a neutral capacity.

Questions for Consideration

- How does my organization define diversity, equity, and inclusion?
- What is my organization's history in the context of DEI work?
- How long has the organization existed?
- What was the organization's role or connection to different historical eras related to DEI?
- What, if any, "skeletons" do we need to pull out of our closet as an organization to give legitimacy to our DEI training?
- What DEI philosophies currently dominate our organizational conversations around DEI? What are the implications of that? What philosophies do we need to incorporate?
- What potential pitfalls do we need to avoid?

Summary

Diversity, equity, and inclusion are interconnected concepts, and expansion is the act of continuously exploring our learning edge. The goal of DEI work requires us to embrace the unique talents, experiences, and needs of different people, and to create workplaces that thrive because of their commitment to diversity, equity, and inclusion. To be effective, DEI training should be aligned with strategic organizational goals. It needs to create space for courageous conversations that acknowledge hard truths around systemic inequities and explore real issues that people face in their lives and at work. DEI training should be practical, continuous, and constructive. In chapter 2, we will explore how to assess the specific training needs of your organization to design a relevant and powerful learning experience.

Worksheet 1-1. Introduction to DEI Training

Use this worksheet as a preparation for your DEI training. Consider the people or groups with whom you should collaborate on answering these questions, or with whom you should share this information. Revisit this worksheet regularly to gauge progress and recenter your DEI efforts.

DEI Focus	What metrics are we focusing on (e.g., demographic representation, turnover rates, employee engagement scores, consumer satisfaction results)?
Reason for DEI Training	What is the explicit purpose of training (e.g., foster an inclusive environment and ensure everyone feels valued)? What is the implicit purpose of training (is this truly the intention or is it an attempt to appease marginalized groups or check the box)? Are the explicit and implicit reasons for training aligned? How will that affect the potential success of training?
Accountability	Who will be held accountable for applying the learning from this training? How will people be held accountable? How will leaders and people in positions of power be involved in the training (e.g., executive team, board, management)?
Philosophy	Which of the six philosophies are currently most prominent in your organization's discussions and approach to DEI training? • Social justice • Business results • Compliance • Advocacy and allyship • Valuing differences • Oneness and unity Which philosophy might you want to add to create balance?
Approach	What words or phrases do you hope people will use to describe the DEI training approach you are taking? (Avoid "blame and shame.")
Trainers	Who is conducting the training? What are their qualifications? Are they the appropriate fit for this training?

Chapter 2

Assessing the Organizational and Individual Need for DEI

I was working with a new client organization who had approached me to support an initiative focusing on diversity, equity, and inclusion. This was the first time the organization had done anything formally on DEI, so I recommended we begin with a culture audit to assess the current state and experiences people had in their everyday work lives.

I started by interviewing members of the leadership team. In those interviews I heard two common themes: "I have an open-door policy" and "We're just like one big family."

The minute I heard these comments my Spidey senses were activated. I wanted to put a big red warning label on the page where I was taking notes that said, "Challenges may be closer than they appear."

When I interviewed and surveyed employees across the organization, I heard frustration, anger, and disillusionment from them. Their response to leadership's supposed open-door policy was, "That door may be open, but I certainly don't feel safe walking through it to speak the truth." The notion of being a "family" was also problematic for many employees, particularly those who were part of minority identity groups. Although some employees expressed a sense of belonging and camaraderie, others felt like the cousins whom nobody invited to the picnic. And several employees said within the family dynamic they felt like the leadership acted like parents who had their favorite children while the others often went ignored.

When I shared this feedback with the leadership of the organization, they reacted with surprise, dismay, and some defensiveness. Although it took some time and effort, the leadership team accepted that their experience of the organization was not widely shared, and they committed to change their actions, to accept feedback from their staff more openly, and to create mechanisms for more inclusive decision making.

This trend is common in my assessments of organizations. In my experience, it is not because those in leadership are inherently uncaring. However, the more status and power we accumulate, the more disconnected we may become from what's happening on our organizational front lines. There is actually research that indicates that power may even impede our brain's ability to empathize (Useem 2017).

Moreover, particularly in hierarchical or top-heavy organizations, leaders have much more direct involvement in decision making. Employees with less visibility or input into decision-making processes may feel less engaged, less likely to share ideas or raise concerns, and less trusting in the organization's leadership. Furthermore, my assessments often uncover that certain identity groups have a more negative experience or perception than others, be it based on race and ethnicity, gender, sexual orientation, age, tenure, or job function.

However, it's impossible to make progress toward building a more diverse, equitable, and inclusive organization unless you know who is having a different experience. What often moves people most to commit to change is not always the numbers that come from the survey data; it's the stories. Listening to the testimonials or painful experiences that employees have shared is frequently eye-opening for leaders, who have been unaware of the challenges that their employees face. Following the ADDIE (assess, design, develop, implement, evaluate) model, this chapter begins with an assessment of the organization's needs. A worksheet at the end of the chapter can help you assess your own organization.

How do you assess DEI needs for your organization and its people?

Assessing an Organization's Needs

Although there are foundational concepts and skills for any DEI training, it is important to tailor the approach to the specific needs of the organization or team, as well as to the individuals who will participate in the program. Therefore, any training that is rolled out should be based on data gathered and analyzed in an assessment process. If you're working in talent development, you will most likely be collaborating with HR or DEI teams on the assessment process rather than conducting the assessment independently.

Here's how you can support the assessment process from your role in talent development.

Serving multiple purposes, the assessment:

- Provides baseline data, which helps determine the current state of the organization, team, and individuals in terms of knowledge, awareness, skills, and attitudes
- Indicates individuals' needs and expectations around DEI
- Indicates key areas for skill development for various populations to help customize the training
- Can be used to evaluate progress post-training
- Helps generate interest in and support for DEI training
- Provides anecdotal information to support the design of the training

When determining the approach and depth of the needs-assessment process, consider the following factors:

- **Alignment with organizational goals.** How is the data-gathering process aligned with overall organizational goals around DEI? The more you can demonstrate that the data you gather serves multiple strategic purposes, the more likely you are to gain buy-in and resources from leadership.
- **Organizational commitment.** What's the level of commitment and support across the organization for DEI training? How might that influence your ability to gather credible information or maximize participation? If there is a lack of trust in the organization

or if many people are demoralized or fearful, it can be harder to get honest feedback from folks.

- **Relevant and useful data.** What is it you need to know and from whom do you need to hear it? Consider the information that you need in order to build a relevant, robust DEI program. This requires you to gather data on the knowledge and skills individuals already have, the gaps in their knowledge and skills, their attitudes toward DEI and willingness or openness to learn, their level of comfort with the learning mechanisms that you will need to leverage for your DEI program, and what you and others will be accountable for in terms of people's behavior changes post-training.

- **What data you already have.** The assessment should incorporate existing benchmarks or information from previous assessments that provide valuable insights into the organizational culture. This will help determine what new information you need to gather so you don't reinvent the proverbial wheel and burn people out on feedback surveys.

- **Level of effort.** Consider the amount of resources and availability you and your team have for conducting the assessment process. This will help determine the most realistic approach for data gathering and analysis.

- **Timing.** Some assessment activities are speedier than others. It's important to have a clear timeframe, and then determine the appropriate data-gathering methods based on the amount of time they will take to complete.

- **Accessibility of data-gathering methods.** This will be covered in more depth in the descriptions of each method, but note that it is important to consider up front when developing your assessment plan who will be able to participate in different data-gathering methods and what accommodations you will need to make in terms of technology, language and translation, literacy level, and scheduling.

Methods for Conducting DEI Needs Assessment

There are a variety of methods to consider when conducting a DEI needs assessment. Not every method will be applicable or appropriate for your organization or your project. Select the method or combination of methods that will provide the results needed for your DEI training initiative or project. For example, if you are embarking on a multiphase organizational change initiative, it may be important to use a combination of these methods to build a strong baseline of the entire organizational landscape. If you are designing a DEI program for a division or team, it may be necessary to use only one method to gather enough data to customize the training.

Every method has its pros and cons, which are outlined here. Consider what will work best for your needs.

Benchmarking Study

A benchmarking study analyzes other teams or organizations similar in size, scope, or industry to compare their DEI efforts (Table 2-1). This can be a powerful method for identifying best practices that are specific to your team's or organization's needs. Benchmarking can also serve to win support and commitment from leadership in your own organization, who may be motivated to put resources and effort into an initiative once they see how competitors or other organizations in your industry are focusing on DEI and the results they achieve.

Table 2-1. **Pros and Cons of Benchmarking**

Pros	Cons
• Provides valuable information about DEI efforts similar organizations (or competitors) are undertaking • Identifies industry best practices • Creates a sense of competition that can incentivize people in your organization to take action	• Can be time consuming • May entice leaders to take a one-size-fits-all approach or neglect necessary customization for your particular organization's needs

Determine the type of benchmarking analysis:

- **Internal benchmarking.** Look at the practices and policies of other teams or organizations within your institution. This can be especially helpful in large, geographically dispersed, or very decentralized organizations, where often best practices are not shared across the enterprise.
- **Competitive benchmarking.** This is the benchmarking that most frequently comes to mind. Look for organizations that are similar in size and scope, perhaps those who represent the competition in your industry or field, and compare their DEI practices to yours.
- **Strategic benchmarking.** This type can be useful when you are interested in broadening beyond your industry to seek overall best practices in DEI. It can also drive more innovative approaches when you look outside your industry and its usual suspects. Inspiration often comes when we look beyond the horizon.

Determine criteria for selecting organizations to benchmark:

- **Sector.** Which sectors are you interested in comparing your organization to? For instance, if your organization is a federal agency, you may want to look at other federal agencies, but also contractors or private sector companies that are involved in similar work or have similar employee populations. You may also want to compare with similar agencies in other nations.
- **Industry.** Consider organizations in your industry as well as similar industries. You may also wish to select one benchmarking organization that is in a completely different industry to give a fresh perspective to your analysis.
- **Employee population.** Consider the size and demographics of employee populations in the organizations you wish to benchmark.
- **Revenue.** Look for organizations of similar size in terms of revenue.
- **Geographic region.** Consider organizations that are in the same geographic region. You may also wish to benchmark one or two

organizations in different regions (domestic or international) to broaden your data gathering and get a different perspective.

- **Organization age and history.** Consider organizations that have had a similar length of time in the marketplace or have a similar history in terms of how they evolved. For example, if your organization has recently graduated from a small business or start-up to a medium-size business or was recently bought by a larger corporation, consider organizations with similar stories to see how they have addressed DEI.

Identify organizations for the benchmarking study:

- **Number of organizations to include.** Ideally, you want to benchmark somewhere between three and eight organizations, although it depends on the timeframe, resources available, and purpose of the study. A minimum of three organizations will provide you with basic insights and trends. The more organizations you add, the clearer the trends, but the more time and effort required.

- **Availability of data.** Think about how easy or difficult it will be to gather information about each organization's DEI efforts. What is in the public domain? What will require deeper information gathering from within those organizations? How willing or able will each organization be to provide such data?

- **Your approach.** Think about how you can leverage existing relationships to gain access to the information you want. Consider your messaging. For example, asking a competitor to share their DEI data with you may not be received positively, but if you approach it from the perspective of wanting to learn from their best practices so that you can lift up the entire industry, that may go further. There also may be a way to leverage professional associations or intra-industry collaborations to gather best practices.

Implement the benchmarking study:

- **Conduct interviews with key players.** This may include the organization's DEI leadership (such as the chief diversity officer or the office of diversity and inclusion) or the individuals in either human resources or the EEO/office of civil rights where applicable.

- **Gather data** from the organization's website, press releases, and other public documents indicating the organization's DEI strategy, approach, and communication.
- **Request written information from the organization on its DEI efforts.** This may include asking for its DEI annual report, DEI strategic plan, or any other reporting information it is willing to share.
- Once you have gathered all the data, **identify key patterns and trends in terms of best practices and results**. Measure your organization's performance in comparison with these best practices.

Documents Review

A documents review is valuable in that it identifies the existing language, training, policies, and practices that either help or hinder DEI efforts in the organization (Table 2-2). The documents review can identify critical gaps that must be addressed in DEI training, as well as provide insights into broader organizational changes in terms of practices, policies, norms, and communications.

The documents review can be very broad or very specific, depending on the scope and need. The documents review is helpful not only in identifying actual policies and practices that exist, but also in determining misperceptions around policies and practices that may indicate a communication challenge. For instance, many DEI assessments uncover areas where employees believe there is a need for a policy that already exists. This can be frustrating for leaders and HR, but it is an indication that the policies are not well communicated or that the employee population does not trust the process will work for them. Conducting a documents review can provide clarity to the employee population about what already exists, and it can help leaders and HR professionals identify where they need to build understanding and trust so people leverage the practices and policies that are available to them.

Table 2-2. **Pros and Cons of Documents Review**

Pros	Cons
• Identifies existing policies and practices that support DEI • Identifies gaps or policies and practices that hinder DEI • Provides a comprehensive chronology of the organization's previous DEI efforts that contributes to determining the baseline from which to measure future progress • Clarifies disconnects in communication or trust in terms of employees leveraging policies that foster DEI	• Can be time consuming • Proper selection of appropriate and relevant documents requires adequate support from HR and leadership • Information may be incomplete • Data is restricted to what already exists, doesn't alone indicate how well people know or trust the process (this information would come from other data-gathering tools like interviews or surveys)

Documents to consider for review:

- **Employment policies and practices**
    - Equal employment opportunity policies
    - Whistleblower policies
    - Anti-bullying policies
    - Employee leave policies
    - Caregiver policies
    - Wellness programs and policies
    - Work flexibility (such as telework or flex schedule)
    - Reasonable-accommodation policies
- **Statistics**
    - EEO complaints and investigations
    - HR grievances
    - Hiring metrics
    - Turnover metrics
    - Exit interview data
    - Promotion metrics
    - Participation in career advancement practices (such as shadowing or mentoring programs)

- **Assessments and analyses**
  - Climate or culture surveys
  - Employee satisfaction or engagement assessments
  - 360-degree feedback
  - Previous DEI-related initiatives or assessments
- **Communications**
  - Onboarding materials for new employees
  - Website
  - Marketing materials
  - Customer communications
  - Leadership memos
  - Annual report
  - Board or executive meeting minutes
- **Training content**
  - DEI training
  - Leadership and management training materials
  - Leadership and management competency models
  - Communication skills training
  - Customer service training
  - Ethics training
  - Mentoring program training
  - Employee orientation training
  - Anti-discrimination, anti-harassment, EEO compliance, anti-bullying, and other trainings
- **Existing DEI Structures and Mechanisms**
  - Identify where DEI efforts live in the organization. Is there a DEI department or is it housed in HR or EEO/Civil Rights? What kind of staff and budget do they have and to whom do they report?
  - Identify if the organization has employee resource groups (ERG) and how they are leveraged; who leads and participates in ERG events?
  - Review documented strategic goals for DEI (if they exist). How are they aligned with the organization's overall strategic goals and funding?

- Is DEI linked to individual performance goals (for senior leaders, managers, and employees)?
  - How is DEI included in 360-degree feedback reports?

Conducting the Documents Review Process

- Determine which documents to review.
- Identify key informants and resource owners with whom to partner.
- Review all relevant documents. Identify key trends and patterns in terms of the following:
  - What currently exists that supports DEI?
  - What currently exists that does not support or hinders DEI?
  - Who has access to these documents and who does not?
  - Where are the gaps? (What is missing that is needed to support DEI more fully?)

Interviews

Individual interviews with a diverse selection of stakeholders provide insights into individuals' perspectives and experiences related to DEI in the organization (Table 2-3). They are a valuable tool for qualitative data gathering, and often provide rich stories from voices across the organizational landscape. Interviews offer participants a private, confidential, safe space to express their views with an outside source.

Table 2-3. Pros and Cons of Interviews

Pros	Cons
• Provide a safe space for candid conversations with individuals across the organization • Can clarify and probe deeper into responses for more comprehensive understanding of issues • Illustrate stories of experiences from diverse stakeholders • Can be used to create training content that is relevant and realistic	• Time consuming • Often only a small sample size of population participates (10–15 percent) • Some people may not feel comfortable being completely honest if they do not trust the interviewer or the process • Possibility of interviewer bias • More costly, requires an outside trained interviewer

Conducting Individual Interviews

Prior to interviews:

- Identify the stakeholder groups to be represented in the interview process (such as race, gender, ethnicity, age, tenure, management, division or work function, geographic region, or language).
- Determine the number of interviewees (consider 10–15 percent of employee population as a minimum sample size).
- Consider how to make the interviews as equitable and inclusive as possible.
  - Do you need to conduct any interviews in another language?
  - Do you need to provide alternative days or times to meet with an interviewee who works outside normal hours of business operation?
  - What technology access do interviewees need? Consider that not everyone has a home computer or access to the internet in their home.
  - How can you ensure the interviewee has access to a quiet, private space to conduct the interview?
- Send invitations to potential interviewees. Don't assume everyone you selected wants to be interviewed. Be clear in the invitation how the interviews will be conducted, what their purpose is, and how confidentiality will be maintained.
- Identify interviewers. It is strongly encouraged that you use an outside, neutral party that brings expertise in conducting qualitative data gathering. If you must use in-house interviewers, make sure they are not from the same division or work unit as the interviewees.
- Create an interview protocol so every interviewer uses the same approach and set of questions.
- Consider logistics in terms of where the interviews will take place (virtually or in-person), if the interviews should be recorded, and the duration of each interview.

- Consider whether it would be helpful to send the questions in advance to give interviewees time to think about their answers before you meet.

During interviews:

- Make sure you and the interviewee are in locations that are private and free from distractions.
- Introduce yourself, explain the purpose of the interviews, and assure the interviewee of confidentiality.
- Provide relevant definitions so the interviewee is familiar with key concepts, like diversity, equity, and inclusion.
- Start with questions that focus on the current state of the organization, then move to the interviewee's expectations for the future state of DEI at the organization.
- Start with questions that are less emotionally risky to build rapport, then move to higher-risk questions. For instance, it is often easier for people to talk about the organization as a whole before they are willing to share their personal stories of exclusion or unequal treatment.
- Listen deeply and take careful notes. You don't have to get every word, but you want to get the essence of the interviewee's responses. Consider repeating or paraphrasing the interviewee's answers back to them to gauge the accuracy of your notes.
- Pay attention to repetition of certain words or phrases, which may indicate the individual is eager to reinforce that particular message.
- Pay attention to what is not said. Listen for vocal tone changes, pauses, or nonverbal messages that may indicate a different meaning than what the interviewee says.
- Allow for silence. Some interviewees may need a few moments to reflect before answering, either because they are processing the question or because they are uncomfortable divulging something that is difficult or concerning. Silence can be a key data-gathering tool for you.

- Remain neutral but not devoid of feeling. You're a human and you're engaging with another human who is sharing their personal experiences. Listen with empathy and openness. Encourage further response but avoid falling into the trap of "leading the witness."
- At the end of the interview, summarize to make sure you have clarity on the interviewee's opinion. Thank them for their time and participation and explain the next steps in the assessment process.

Examples of Interview Questions

Low risk:
- What do you believe are the organization's biggest strengths in terms of DEI?
- What words or phrases come to your mind to describe the organization's culture in terms of DEI?

Medium risk:
- What do you think are some of the organization's biggest barriers or challenges when it comes to DEI?
- What is the single most important thing that needs to change for this DEI initiative to be successful?

High risk:
- Can you share a time when you personally observed or experienced being excluded or treated unequally because of some aspect of identity?
- How would you characterize your leadership's commitment to DEI? Your manager's? Your team's?
- How confident are you that the organization can make progress in DEI and why?

Focus Groups

Focus groups are another powerful qualitative data-gathering tool that provide rich stories and opportunities to explore people's perceptions of DEI in greater depth (Table 2-4). They also create a space for

Table 2-4. **Pros and Cons of Focus Groups**

Pros	Cons
• Provide opportunity to gather rich anecdotal data • Uncover themes and common or divergent experiences quickly • Offer opportunities for both heterogeneous and homogeneous groups to come together, both of which can yield valuable data points	• Can be hijacked by a few individuals who carry influence or power • If there is fear or distrust, people may not be candid in their responses • Can lead to groupthink • Can become emotionally charged and combative • More costly, require an outside trained facilitator and notetaker • Participants who are in the minority may not feel safe expressing opinions that are not aligned with the rest of the group

individuals to interact and exchange ideas and experiences, which can provide a thoughtful discussion and opportunity for learning as well as yield valuable data for the assessment.

When conducting focus groups:

- Determine the kind of focus group you want to gather data from:
  - Homogeneous groups offer people from the same identity dimension a safe space to share their stories with one another. They often illustrate the common perspectives and experiences of people from the same group.
  - Heterogeneous groups offer people from diverse identity groups the opportunity to come together and hear from one another. This can quickly show if people from some identity groups have a very different opinion or experience than others.
- Keep focus groups to between six and eight people. This ensures that everyone can participate fully and uncovers themes among participants in terms of their perspectives and experiences.
- Consider how to make the focus group equitable and inclusive:
  - Do you need to run any focus groups in another language or provide a translator?

- Do you need to run any focus groups outside the normal hours of business operation?
- If conducting the focus groups virtually, how can you ensure everyone has access to the technology needed to participate?
- If conducting the focus groups in person, what space will ensure privacy and safety? (For example, some participants may feel more comfortable and open if the focus group meets off-site.)

- Allot enough time to build a safe, confidential space for sharing and to ensure every voice is heard. Typically, focus groups should be 90–120 minutes long.
- If possible, it can be helpful to have a facilitation team that represents diversity. Similar to training, participants in focus groups may find themselves resonating with one or another facilitator's style differently and may feel safer sharing their experience if they see a facilitator that represents their identity in some way. For instance, POC participants may feel more comfortable divulging their opinion in front of a POC facilitator than a White one. Women may feel more comfortable talking about their experiences if one of the facilitators is a woman.
- Bring a notetaker to capture the responses or consider recording the session.
- Share a set of behavioral norms to ensure people are primed to engage in respectful dialogue.
- As with interviews, start with lower-risk questions and then move to higher-risk questions once people feel a sense of trust and rapport. Make sure everyone speaks early in the process, as it will make equal participation easier as the questions become more challenging.

Observation

Observation is a valuable tool for gathering data around organizational culture and climate, especially in terms of noticing the unwritten rules of a workplace (Table 2-5). Observation unearths the sometimes unconscious and often tacit group dynamics and behavioral norms that people become conditioned to engage in as part of daily organizational life.

Table 2-5. **Pros and Cons of Observation**

Pros	Cons
• Provides an opportunity to witness and analyze individual and team behaviors that either help or hinder DEI • Can provide measurable progress checks to see if the DEI training initiative is leading to behavioral changes	• People may be uncomfortable or inauthentic if they know they are being observed by an outside party • Can be time consuming, depending on how many events or interactions you need to observe

Conducting Observation Process

- Consider what types of interactions or events to observe:
  - What frequently held gatherings would provide insight into how people interact?
  - Where might you be able to gather data on how people are expected to behave and communicate?
  - How many times might you need to observe gatherings or interactions to accurately decipher behavioral patterns?
  - Are you observing only one division or team, or looking for patterns across working units in the organization?
- Be as inconspicuous as possible without being secretive. Think of a photographer at a wedding. Everyone knows the photographer is there, but they are so adept at moving through the crowd unnoticed that they are able to get natural shots of people interacting with one another.
- What to look for:
  - **Use of space.** How do people position themselves in the environment? Who sits where and with whom? How close together do people stand or sit?
  - **Time management.** When do meetings begin and end? How is time managed and by whom?

- **Verbal communication.** Who speaks first? Who speaks last? Who speaks the most? Who speaks the least? What is the volume of verbal communication? Do people speak one at a time? Are there multiple conversations happening at once? Do people interrupt one another and, if so, how frequently?
- **Intonation.** How do people speak? Do some people speak more declaratively and others use questions?
- **Nonverbal communication.** What do you notice in terms of facial expressions, eye contact, body language, posture, or use of hands?
- **Dress code.** How do people dress? Are there different degrees of formality in terms of dress? Do they dress differently based on any dimensions of identity? (For example, managers in suits versus employees in jeans, or older generations dressing more formally than younger.)
- **Roles and responsibilities.** Who takes notes? Who makes decisions? Who delegates tasks and to whom? Who cleans up after the meeting?

Survey

Surveys are a widely used assessment instrument, in large part because they are highly efficient to distribute to a large population and analyze (Table 2-6). Surveys are valuable because they provide an opportunity for everyone in the organization to participate in the assessment process. They provide "hard" data in terms of measuring perspectives and opinions. They can also provide valuable insight into variances by diverse demographic groups.

Surveys do not always tell the whole story. They are limited in that they do not necessarily provide opportunities to get the deeper story behind the opinion. They take away the human element, which can sometimes overcome data-gathering bias but also takes away the opportunity for participants to confide in another human about their perspectives. They also only provide data of individuals' opinions, not their observed behaviors.

Table 2-6. **Pros and Cons of Surveys**

Pros	Cons
• Efficient • Inexpensive • Potentially unbiased or less-biased data gathering • Provide quantitative results • Show statistically significant variances by demographic groups • Everyone can participate	• Don't get the stories behind the responses • Can feel less personal • No way to clarify responses that are confusing • Sometimes have low response rates, especially if there is apathy, fear, or lack of trust in how the data will be collected or analyzed

Conducting a Survey

- If possible, acquire the help of a professional with expertise in developing and analyzing survey data. There are specific practices in terms of how questions are created to yield the most statistically valid and reliable results. If the survey results are going to be shared widely with the organization to drive systemic change, it is imperative that the survey be conducted in a high-quality way.
- Clearly identify the issues the organization most wants or needs to address in terms of DEI. This may sound simplistic, but it is important to streamline the survey to questions you really need to know so participants feel like this is a good use of their time.
- Consider dividing the survey into sections related to different elements of DEI (such as diversity representation, equity practices, climate of inclusion and belonging, and expectations for the DEI initiative).
- Include a variety of data-gathering methods, such as Likert scale responses, importance vs. satisfaction comparisons, and open-ended responses.
- Consider the most equitable and inclusive way to distribute the survey and gather the data:
  - Do you need the survey translated into different languages?
  - Does the survey need to be distributed both online and in print form?

- Is the survey written in language that is clear and simple to understand for various literacy levels?
- Do individuals all have access to a computer to complete the online survey?
- If a print survey is used, how will the respondents submit their completed questionnaire? (Consider using self-addressed, post-stamped envelopes to ensure anonymity.)

- Communicate, communicate, communicate. The response rate of the survey is incumbent on clear communication and frequent reminders:
  - Send an initial communication out to all potential respondents outlining the purpose of the survey and encouraging responses. Include the link to the survey, the deadline for completion, and any other pertinent information to drive participation.
  - Send regular reminders to complete the survey. (Many commercial online survey platforms can send automatic reminders just to those who have not yet completed the survey.)
  - Post flyers around the office or work areas to remind people to respond. This is especially important for employees who do not regularly have access to email.
  - Ask supervisors and managers to remind employees to participate. You may even request that they allot time during work hours for employees to complete the survey.
  - Send a thank you note to those who have completed the survey.

The larger the organization, the more likely your response rate will be low. However, you can typically boost response rates by engaging in a communications campaign that reinforces the importance of each response. Although there is no agreed-upon standard response rate, ideally you want to try for a minimum of 50 percent.

Assessment Instruments

Consider any individual assessment instruments that may provide insight into the training and participants about their existing DEI-related knowledge, attitudes, and experience. Assessments can also provide insight into personal styles and preferences that impact how people work across differences.

You can design an assessment or inventory that is aligned with your organization's needs and objectives, or find off-the-shelf assessments from outside vendors. Your organization may also have 360-degree feedback instruments that include questions related to DEI.

Some commonly used instruments include:

- **Intercultural Development Inventory (IDI).** Provides insight into an individual's ability to accept, understand, and adapt to different cultural perspectives and behaviors.
- **Intercultural Conflict Style Inventory (ICS).** Explores four conflict styles that represent different communication styles and cultural identity values around emotional expression and directness.
- **GlobeSmart Profile.** A self-assessment tool that explores an individual's cultural identity based on five dimensions: egalitarianism, independence, risk taking, directness, and relationship orientation.
- **Inclusive Behaviors Inventory (IBI).** Assesses an individual's competence and comfort engaging and communicating across differences. It includes five dimensions: learning about bias, building key skills, working across boundaries, becoming a champion, and getting results.
- **Global Competencies Inventory (GCI).** Measures leadership and management skills in diverse settings. The GCI looks at three areas: perception management, relationship management, and self-management.

Comprehensive Data Analysis

Once the data-gathering process is complete, it is time to analyze the results:

- Bring together a data analysis team. Have a team of individuals review the findings. This may include anyone involved in the data gathering process, and additional individuals who may bring a fresh perspective when interpreting the results. This helps to mitigate any individual biases or blind spots that one person would bring.

- Identify common themes and patterns in the data. Look for repetition of words or phrases, or common themes that emerge:
  - Look across the findings to see if the same themes show up in more than one data-gathering method. For example, if a theme from the individual interviews was that women feel they are interrupted more frequently than men in meetings, did women have less-positive responses in the survey in terms of feeling valued for their input?
  - Look for discrepancies in results between data gathering methods. For instance, if the survey indicated that there is a perceived lack of adequate representation of diversity at the organization, but the documents review found there was an increase in hiring of POC and women candidates in the last year, this may be a flag that the organization needs to do a better job communicating its hiring efforts. It could also mean that the efforts to hire for diversity have not been sufficient in the eyes of employees or that employees are concerned about representation in certain job functions or management positions.

- Determine demographic variances. Are people from different groups having different experiences?
  - Look for divergent responses across demographic groups (such as race and ethnicity, age, gender, sexual orientation, and management status). This will indicate whether certain identity groups are feeling more or less valued and included.

Quite often, the respondents who are in privileged or dominant positions have more positive responses than those who are in nondominant or marginalized identity groups.

○ Look for common responses across demographic groups to indicate where there are general strengths or challenges of note.

- Treat neutral responses as a potential point of concern. If the survey yields a high number of neutral responses ("neither agree nor disagree" or "don't know"), this may not be a "passing grade." Consider what might draw a respondent to select a neutral response. Typically, people have opinions when it comes to DEI questions because they are based on personal experience, and those experiences can be emotionally fraught. If there are a high number of neutral responses, this may indicate apathy, fear, or lack of confidence. In any case, it should indicate room for exploration and growth.

- Create a set of recommended strategies to address the challenges identified. Consider how each strategy would help the organization make progress in that specific area. From a training perspective, consider the knowledge and competency gaps that need to be addressed for various stakeholder groups. For example, if the assessment indicates that there is a discrepancy in career development opportunities for women and POC employees, then consider training for managers and supervisors on how to mitigate bias and engage in equitable career development practices with all employees. Some common findings and training solutions are offered in Worksheet 2-1.

- Consider how to communicate with various stakeholder groups (leadership, managers, board, employees, customers). Too often, organizations do not adequately communicate results of their DEI assessments back to the respondents or the workforce in general. This can erode trust and commitment to the initiative. The more transparent you are with sharing the results, even if they are not pretty, the more you will win support for the initiative. People have taken the time to complete the assessment and some may even feel they took a personal risk in doing so. If they don't see the results of the assessment, or if those results are hidden or watered down to save the organizational leadership from embarrassment, those who have had more negative experiences will be frustrated and apathetic, and perhaps even demoralized or resentful. This doesn't mean you have to broadcast the details of every finding, but consider what needs to be communicated so people truly understand the importance of the findings and know what the organization plans to do next.

- Consider how to use this as benchmarking data further down the road.

Summary

Conducting an assessment is a crucial first step to designing effective training that is aligned with individual, team, and organizational needs. The assessment phase may be simple or comprehensive, depending on what data already exists. Consider what you need to know and whom you need to involve in the assessment process to gather sufficient information. With DEI assessments, it's important to gather not only opinions but stories. The personal experiences that people share can be a rich resource for case studies, scenarios, and testimonials that illustrate key concepts in the training you design.

The assessment process serves as a data-gathering tool and also can begin to socialize important concepts and build interest in DEI programming. Be sure to provide opportunities for diverse individuals to give input, so you gather a more well-rounded view of DEI perspectives, experiences, and needs from across the organization. After accomplishing this step, you're ready to approach training design and development, the subject of chapter 3.

Worksheet 2-1. DEI Organization Assessment Worksheet

Common Challenges	Possible Competency Gaps	Possible Solutions (both training and policy oriented)
Lack of adequate representation of diversity, especially in management positions	• Managing biases in decision making • Acknowledging societal privilege and systemic inequities • Expanding social networks	• Training for leaders and hiring managers focused on managing biases in decision making • Review and revise policies and practices to mitigate bias in employment practices
Lack of career development opportunities for nondominant employees	• Managing biases in decision making • Acknowledging societal privilege and systemic inequities	• Training for managers and supervisors focused on inclusive management • Equitable mentoring practices • Clearly written career development paths with guidelines for both prospective employees and managers
Inequities in promotions or delegation of career-enhancing tasks for nondominant employees	• Managing biases in decision making • Acknowledging societal privilege and systemic inequities	• Training for managers and supervisors to address and mitigate biases • Equitable mentoring practices • Clearly written career development paths with guidelines for both prospective employees and managers

Common Challenges	Possible Competency Gaps	Possible Solutions (both training and policy oriented)
Perceived lack of leadership or management support for DEI	• Comfort or ability to express commitment to DEI • Managing implicit biases • Culturally competent communication	• Leadership training and individualized coaching • Management training on fostering inclusive organizations and teams • Regular communications from leadership and management with consistent messaging supporting DEI • Link leadership and management performance to DEI mission and goals
Employees do not feel they have adequate input into decisions that impact them	• Inclusive decision making • Managing implicit biases • Trust building	• Leadership and management training that focuses on building psychological safety, delegation, and empowering the workforce • Practices that foster regular employee input (e.g., surveys, suggestion box, meetups with senior leaders)
Employees do not feel there is adequate transparency in leadership communications	• Inclusive decision making • Trust building • Inclusive communication	Create consistent communication mechanisms to provide rationale for decisions and gather feedback from the workforce

Common Challenges	Possible Competency Gaps	Possible Solutions (both training and policy oriented)
Nondominant employees do not feel comfortable being their authentic self at work	• Psychological safety • Acknowledging societal power and privilege • Inclusive communication • Managing micro-messages	• Leadership and management training that focuses on building psychological safety and leading inclusive teams • Review of policies and procedures to examine and revise with a DEI lens (e.g., culturally competent dress codes, gender-neutral facilities, inclusive holiday observances)
Employees (especially in nondominant identity groups) experience more micro-inequities or insensitive jokes	• Managing biases • Managing micro-messages • Inclusive communication • Accountability for exclusive actions	• Anti-bias training • Anti-bullying and anti-harassment policies with clear statements about disciplinary actions related to micro-inequities • Ombudsperson position or independent, confidential reporting mechanism for employees to direct complaints of exclusionary or toxic behaviors without fear of retribution

Common Challenges	Possible Competency Gaps	Possible Solutions (both training and policy oriented)
Nondominant employees report observing or experiencing discrimination or harassment	· EEO policies · Managing biases · Managing micro-messages · Inclusive communication · Accountability for exclusive actions	· Mandatory EEO training for all supervisors and managers · Mandatory EEO training for all employees · Include realistic scenarios to educate people on what discrimination and harassment may look like · Include scenarios of exclusionary behaviors that are not necessarily discriminatory by legal definitions but can still contribute to a disruptive or exclusive climate for nondominant employees
Leadership does not address diversity-related conflicts	· Conflict management · Accountability for exclusive actions	· Conflict management training for leaders and managers · Provide trained mediators (or ombudsman) to resolve conflicts · Provide and implement policies that prohibit exclusionary or hostile behaviors with clear disciplinary actions

Worksheet 2-1 (cont.)

Common Challenges	Possible Competency Gaps	Possible Solutions (both training and policy oriented)
Leaders and managers do not model inclusive behaviors	• Inclusive communication • Accountability for exclusive actions	• Training or coaching for leaders and managers on practices for inclusive leadership • Link leader and manager performance to DEI competencies
Respondents do not have confidence in the organization's DEI effort	Inclusive communication	• Create and communicate clear rationale for DEI and strategic goals. • Have representatives of diverse workforce serve on DEI committee or council or act as liaisons with leadership to provide input and support implementation of DEI strategy

Chapter 3
Designing and Developing Effective DEI Training

I've been a runner since childhood. I ran track in middle school and high school and have been running ever since. As an adult, I have run distance races, including a few marathons.

When it comes to preparing oneself for a long-distance race, there is a great deal of training required to build endurance—to prime our bodies, minds, and spirits to go the distance.

There are those who are avid runners, who have been training for months, maybe even years. They have probably been coached at various points to learn how to prepare themselves mentally and physically for the challenges of an endurance run. Along the way, they have learned lessons in how to select the best shoes for their feet, how to dress appropriately for different climates and weather, and how and what to drink and eat to maximize their energy use. Based on their conditioning, their training, and their nutritional intake, they are mentally and physically primed to endure the discomfort of a long-distance run, and capable of running farther and faster than many other people.

There are also those who perhaps have been more occasional runners, who are in decent shape and have done some training and conditioning. But they are more likely to need to go slower to finish the race. If you push them or challenge them to go faster, they may be able to speed up a bit or keep up with you for a mile or two, but in their current shape they are not conditioned enough to run as fast as the avid runners. Going too fast will result in side stitches, pulled muscles, or even a more serious injury. They may beat themselves up for not being able to keep up, or they may become angry or resentful for being pushed to go harder than they are able.

And then there are those who are not yet ready for a long-distance run. Some of them have never run a mile in their lives. Maybe they need to learn how to accept the discomfort they will inevitably feel as they train new muscles. However, there needs to be some oscillation between the stress and discomfort and recovery time. If you try to push them to run too fast or too far, they may not be able to keep up and will become frustrated. They may give up. They may even blame you or others for setting them up to fail. But if you are too easy on them, they may never learn to push their bodies to the next level of discomfort to find strength and growth on the other side.

It can be frustrating at times to run with someone who is not as prepared as you are. They may be more narrowly focused on their own pain and discomfort. They may move too slowly for you. They question whether this level of exercise is really all that good for anyone. They need to be frequently reminded to maintain the right posture and stay hydrated because otherwise they fall back into bad habits.

DEI work is kind of like training for a long-distance race.

What makes for an effective DEI training experience?

It is important to acknowledge that everyone is at a different stage of the journey of understanding themselves and others, with various levels of competence. We must manage our expectations for progress. If we make the training too simplistic or comfortable, people will not be suffi-ciently challenged to learn. They will fall back into habits that perpetuate the status quo without expanding their skills. If we try to push people too fast or too far into discomfort without giving them time and support to develop those new muscles, they may become defensive, resentful, or resigned to giving up.

Inevitably, as a trainer, you will see people at different stages of expo-sure and capability in the same learning environment, and it's important to create a training design that sets a foundation and a safe space to learn, yet still provides enough discomfort for everyone to experience new growth.

This chapter provides guidance on how to design DEI-focused training, including the major concepts that should be considered when designing a DEI training program. We explore some of the components to consider when building your playbook to best meet the needs of diverse participants who may require different training approaches to support their development. We begin, though, by examining organizational culture and how we are all influenced by a variety of external forces, such as political, economic, and environmental events, before we pivot to discuss your participants and how you design DEI training for them.

At the end of the chapter, I've included two worksheets for training design and participant analysis.

Organizational Culture

One of the primary considerations when designing your DEI training is the existing organizational culture and climate.

In his book *Organizational Culture and Leadership*, Edgar Schein (2010) defines culture as:

> *a pattern of shared basic assumptions learned by a group as it solved its problems of external adaptation and internal integration, which has worked well enough to be considered valid and, therefore, to be taught to new members as the correct way to perceive, think, and feel in relation to those problems.*

In short, *culture* refers to the way of being for people who belong to the culture. It provides a set of behavioral norms (either explicit or implicit) and a road map for how people should think, feel, believe, and act. Organizational cultures evolve over time, but many carry some lasting residue of their founding. The origin story of an organization can tell a lot about that organization's current culture. The formation and evolution of an organizational culture may change incrementally, often due to either external forces (social norm changes, technological advancements, policy and legislation) or internal forces that drive better functionality for daily life in the organization (interpersonal interactions, power dynamics, division of labor).

The concept of an organizational culture is quite abstract and may sometimes be hard to pin down, but it is of utmost importance to the way you design and deliver DEI training because often, DEI training is intended to make a fundamental change in the organizational culture. Changing an organizational culture is a monumental task, especially if the people in positions of power and influence in the organization are not motivated to change the culture. DEI training may be perceived (often unconsciously) as a threat by those who are in higher-status positions, who believe they gain more by maintaining the status quo. Even for those not in positions of power or influence, change can be perceived as difficult at best and threatening at worst. We become a product of our culture. Our beliefs, values, decisions, and actions are often driven by what is rewarded or punished in our culture. Our identity is inextricably tied to the culture. If the training challenges deeply held cultural beliefs, values, and norms or questions the organization's culture or status quo, the result can be denial, dismissiveness, resistance, or withdrawal.

Therefore, it is important to find ways to honor and maintain foundational components of the organizational culture while also challenging the aspects of the culture that need to change because they do not foster diversity, equity, and inclusion.

Components of culture to note:
- Symbols, artifacts, images
- Espoused values
- Lived and practiced values
- Distribution of power
- Common language
- Norms around communication, verbal and nonverbal (how do people interact with one another?)

- Approach to conflict
- Decision making

Not every member of the organization experiences the organizational culture the same way. Many cultures were either created to serve one subset of the population (for example, White cisgender males) or have not adequately evolved with changes in societal norms and expectations (for example, honoring gender nonbinary, trans, and genderqueer individuals).

There are often cultures within cultures in an organization. The larger the organization, the more likely there are subcultures that may interpret the culture of the organization differently or not subscribe to certain aspects of the macroculture. Subcultures may evolve based on a variety of dimensions of personal or professional identity. For example, engineering, accounting, and human resources may each be separate subcultures inside a large tech company's macroculture. Executives, middle managers, and individual contributors represent different subcultures that exist based on status and position in the organization's macroculture. Subcultures can also arise based on demographics like race, ethnicity, gender, and age. Many organizations' employee resource groups represent the subcultures that exist within the organization (such as ERGs for women, LGBTQIA+, Black, Latinx, and Asian American Pacific Islander employees).

Depending on the subculture or subcultures to which people belong, they may perceive the organization and their place in it very differently. They may possess their own shared set of beliefs, values, language, behavioral norms, and history, all of which can influence their perspectives and experiences in a DEI training environment.

When designing your DEI training program, consider the following questions:

- What are the aspects of the organizational culture that we need to explore or acknowledge?
- What strengths can we celebrate about the culture in terms of fostering DEI?
- What weaknesses or areas for improvement do we need to address?

- What subcultures exist and how might they perceive and engage with the organization differently?
- What information, activities, and language might resonate in this culture and what might not?

An organization with whom I worked had a long history and deep-seated traditions. It had a large, diverse, geographically dispersed workforce. It was not uncommon to meet employees who had spent their entire careers with this organization and were celebrating 30- or 40-year anniversaries. The loyalty to the organization and its mission was very strong. There was a central culture that had clear symbols and artifacts that were well known and loved by members of the workforce. There were also many unique subcultures within the organization, in terms of regional locations, work functions, and tenure within the organization. Each subculture had its own set of norms, written and unwritten, that influenced how people behaved. For example, the organization had an investigation branch that mostly consisted of people with military and law enforcement backgrounds. Their organizational culture was quite different from that of the customer service branch.

Across the different subcultures, one common trend we noticed was that the high-priority identity challenges were not so much race or gender bias (although those issues did exist), but bias based on age and tenure. New employees, including even people who had been with the organization for a decade, felt that their input was not given credence. They felt frustrated by the structure and culture of tradition that often squelched innovative ideas. Questioning why things were done a certain way was seen as disrespectful. More seasoned employees were frustrated with the influx of newer, younger employees coming in and not having the willingness to watch and learn. They experienced their new colleagues as unnecessarily impatient and entitled.

Our solution was to bring people together for leadership training, purposely mixing the classes to include people from different age groups and years in service. We conducted an activity where participants were asked to group by time in service and illustrate the culture of the organization with members of their group. The conversations that followed were enlightening for all the participants, as they were able to listen and understand the perspective of other groups rather than fall into stereotypical thinking or debate about what was good or bad about the organization. They found common ground and together as a large group identified practices that could help uphold parts of the culture that worked well for everyone while addressing some of the pain points they experienced.

External Forces

Context is critical to developing timely and relevant DEI training. DEI training is in a constant state of evolution, based on various events and individuals impacting the landscape of DEI work and our broader society and culture.

Political, Economic, Environmental, and Cultural Events

Major events that impact millions of lives not only shape our collective history, but also have a ripple effect at the community, organization, and individual level. Changes in political leadership and figures in power and shared achievements or catastrophes create an indelible imprint on our shared narrative about ourselves and our society. They also illustrate divergent perspectives or lived experiences of different populations in our country. Consider the terrorist attacks of September 11, 2001; Hurricane Katrina in 2005; or most recently the COVID-19 pandemic and the armed insurrection at the US Capitol on January 6, 2021. All these events had a significant impact on how we define ourselves in society and how we view issues of identity.

In the wake of 9/11, many US citizens felt a renewed sense of community and patriotism, rallying around one another in a shared sense of grief and desire to heal. However, a great number of people who were Muslim or of Middle Eastern descent, and even people of Indian and African backgrounds (Muslim or not), were targets of xenophobia and acts of hate. I recall a close friend of mine, Vineet, relating to me a terrifying moment following 9/11 when he was targeted. Vineet's parents are from India, but he grew up in the suburbs of Chicago. As he was riding the Metro home from his office one evening, a group of men began to verbally assault him, calling him a Muslim terrorist and telling him to go back to where he came from. I remember the heartbreak in his voice as he shared this story with me. As someone who deeply loves the US and was also significantly grieving the attacks on 9/11, he couldn't understand their misplaced hatred for him.

This elevated fear, misunderstanding, and aggression led to an increase in cultural competence training focused on raising awareness and understanding of Islam. Lobna "Luby" Ismail, a prominent advocate for cultural competence, has done a great deal of training for law enforcement and federal agencies. She described to me her approach:

> I had to bring my story because I could talk from my head but I needed to connect to [participants'] heart and that's where I began what I call my veil exercise.

In the veil exercise, Luby would enter the room wearing a hijab. She asked the participants to name all the stereotypes people had about women dressed like her.

Luby told me she often heard the following words: "submissive, anti-American, don't speak English, not from here, foreigner, radical, fanatic and . . . terrorist."

Then Luby would show written statements about herself to them:

> I am a former Miss Softball America pitcher.
> I am a Southerner.
> I am a soccer mom.
> I am a businesswoman.
> I am educated.
> I am an interculturalist.
> I am a former Girl Scout.
> I am Muslim.
> I am an American.

Rather than engaging in an intellectual discussion or presenting "facts" about Muslim identity, Luby chose to use herself and her story as a way to humanize and connect. This may sound simple, but it had a lasting impact on the participants.

A more recent example, in May 2020, is the aftermath of the grisly murder of George Floyd, who died when a police officer in Minneapolis, Minnesota held his knee on Floyd's neck while he pleaded for his life. George Floyd is one of countless unarmed Black citizens who have been killed by law enforcement. The Black Lives Matter movement (which arose from the 2012 death of Trayvon Martin, a Black teenager in Sanford, Florida, who was shot while walking to a family member's house) gained renewed attention in the summer of 2020, as videos of Floyd's death and other video clips of Black men and women being wrongfully accused, assaulted, or killed went viral on social media. Countless organizations, political leaders, and celebrities made statements of solidarity with the movement, and there was a tidal wave of requests for training and resources not only on general DEI skills but also with a focus on antiracism and addressing White fragility, White privilege, and White supremacy.

This trend has continued, with organizations and communities engaging in dialogues and ongoing learning to raise awareness, challenge systems that perpetuate racial prejudice and oppression, and hold individuals with status and privilege accountable for their actions in a more meaningful way.

Questions for Trainers

- What recent political, economic, environmental, and cultural events (in the last one to two years) may have influenced the organization's broader DEI efforts?
- What recent or current events (think front-page headlines in the last six months) are likely to be on people's minds in the DEI training environment?
- What different perspectives might people bring with them in relation to these events?

- How can we design content that reflects current and recent events?
- How might we prepare to address divergent perspectives or experiences in the live classroom environment?

Social Norm Changes

In the aftermath of such political, cultural, or economic events, we often see shifts in social norms that can have a positive impact on nondominant or marginalized groups. Nevertheless, these norm changes may coincide with resistance, pushback, and even aggression.

In the midst of the #MeToo movement, which came to widespread attention in 2017, there was backlash from men but also many women, who argued that calling men out for both egregious actions like sexual harassment and assault and subtle microaggressions was overkill. They argued that well-intentioned men were being unfairly punished and ultimately women would also suffer because men would be afraid to interact with them at all. Although those opinions still circulate, in a relatively short amount of time we have seen an increase in accountability for men who commit sexual assault and harassment as well as more subtle acts of sexism. "Mansplaining" is increasingly called out in more public ways, men are more frequently praised for elevating the voices of female colleagues, and more women are rising to positions of power and status in a variety of industries that have typically been dominated by men.

However, sexism and misogyny are not extinct by any stretch. The gender wage gap has remained relatively the same over the last 15 years. For every dollar earned by White, non-Hispanic men, White women earn 79 cents, Asian American women 85 cents, Black women 63 cents, Native American women 60 cents, and Latinx women 55 cents (National Partnership for Women and Families 2021). Women overall earn less in almost every occupation, even those that are typically female dominated. The COVID-19 pandemic further displayed the systemic barriers women face in terms of equity and inclusion. In fact, the International Labour Organization (ILO) warned in a recent report that "The bigger [women's] losses in employment during the lockdown phase and the greater the scarcity of jobs in the aftermath of the COVID-19 crisis, the harder it will be for women's employment to recover" (Lavietes 2020).

Another example that shows the complexity of social norm changes is LGBTQIA+ rights. In 2015, the US Supreme Court struck down all state bans on same-sex marriage, legalizing gay marriage nationwide. Although there has been some backlash to social norm changes related to same-sex marriage, by and large we have seen a social normalization of gay relationships and gay marriage even in less urban regions of the US. Organizations have also changed not only policies and practices to accommodate for and be more inclusive of gay employees (think paid time off for gay couples adopting children or going through the surrogacy process) but also in terms of general day-to-day interactions in organizations. Yet LGBTQIA+ individuals continue to face acts of exclusion and even aggression in the workplace and their communities.

As much as it is important to acknowledge and celebrate progress toward equity and inclusion, it is equally important to look at what has not changed in an organization, industry, or society.

Possible reasons for a lack of behavioral change in an organization include:

- Misalignment with organizational values
- Resistance from leadership
- Resistance from groups in power
- Slow rate of change in an organization
- Lack of active support for change
- Lack of implementation strategy
- Low representation of diversity of participants
- Lack of accountability for behavioral change

Questions for Trainers

- What are some social norm changes that we have seen as a result of recent political, economic, environmental, and cultural events?
- How have these social norm changes influenced organizations in our industry or sector?

- How have these social norm changes influenced our specific organizational culture? What behavioral norms have been adopted in the wake of these events?
- What has not changed? What are the implications of this stasis?
- How might the behavioral norm changes that have resulted from these societal events be received by different participants?

Science and Technology

Scientific and technological advancements can impact DEI work as well, sometimes in interesting and unexpected ways. Considering that DEI work involves humans, any scientific discoveries that change the course of how we view ourselves or make sense of humanity may influence DEI work. Furthermore, technological advancements can impact not only the content of DEI but also the platforms and methods we use in the training and learning.

The Human Genome Project was a monumental shift in DEI work, as it proved that our basic DNA construction is relatively the same regardless of race, ethnicity, or cultural background.

Research in neuroscience continues to uncover the ways in which our brains unconsciously process data and make meaning. For example, studies show how different parts of our brain are stimulated when we encounter a person whom we perceive as "like" us versus someone we perceive as "unlike" us. Our neural reaction to faces that represent otherness leads to a host of decisions that influence whom we build relationships with, whom we hire, whom we reward, and whom we trust (Banaji and Greenwald 2013).

Advancements in artificial intelligence (AI) have uncovered a whole new way in which bias exists, as AI is programmed by humans whose unconscious biases may filter into the programming, or AI is programmed to process data that is built from a prejudiced system and therefore may perpetuate biased beliefs or behaviors. For example, Amazon had to discontinue a promising new automated recruiting engine when it was discovered that the program was discriminating against women (Dastin 2018). The program was trained to vet applicants based on patterns in resumes over the previous decade, which has historically been dominated by men. Therefore, the AI taught itself that men were preferable candidates.

Technological advancements have also provided training professionals with a wealth of opportunities to leverage new ways of learning. Virtual or blended learning platforms can reach broader and more geographically dispersed audiences at a lower cost, thereby expanding the reach of DEI training. Additionally, augmented reality and virtual reality have advanced to be able to provide realistic and visceral scenarios in which people can walk in the shoes of those from another identity group. For example, the "I Am a Man" VR Experience is an interactive virtual reality experience that allows the participant to experience historic events of the Civil Rights Movement in the 1960s.

Questions for Trainers

- What new and relevant studies exist that are related to our DEI learning goals?
- What research would be most meaningful to the participants we are training?
- What reliable academic or professional sources could we draw from?
- What new technologies are available to us that could enhance the learning process?

Global Events

Events that occur in other countries and cultures can have an impact on DEI training, especially if you are designing training for an internationally focused or multinational organization.

With global access to news, information, and social media, we are much more aware about what is happening outside our national borders than before. Having an understanding of what global events are taking place that may impact participants in the organization for whom you are developing the training is instrumental to its success.

For instance, a company based in a fairly rural area in the US may be home to a migrant or refugee population that lives and works there. How might events taking place in that population's homeland be important to understand to best address their needs in the training? Think about this not only in terms of national origin but also race, religion, or minority cultural group. For example, small towns across the state of Nebraska have become home to increasing numbers of Karen refugees who were forced to flee Burma (Myanmar) due to religious and ethnic persecution. Karen refugees work predominantly in the region's food-processing industry, including meatpacking plants. During the COVID-19 pandemic, this translated to a heightened risk of exposure for members of the Karen community, not only because they worked in the plants, but also because the Karen community is very close knit. Moreover, Karen people worried they would face ridicule or even harassment as anti-Asian hate crimes increased in 2020 as a result of misconceptions about their role in the pandemic (Meigs and Baw 2021). Over all of this sweeps the ongoing violence in Myanmar, with the military seizing power in 2021. All these issues contribute to anxiety, uncertainty, and grief for the Karen refugee community in the US. Companies in Nebraska that employ members of the Karen community and public entities that serve populations where Karen people live need to understand the impact of these events and develop the cultural competence to best communicate with and support Karen employees and communities.

Questions for Trainers
- What world events are happening that could impact people affiliated with the organization, and how might they be impacted?
- How might global events have a ripple effect on the organization or its participants?
- What possible cultural tensions might present themselves?

Connecting With Your Audience
In addition to understanding cultural, structural, and societal forces that may impact the training design, it's of utmost importance to consider the individuals who will experience the training. DEI training should not be a one-size-fits-all approach.

In today's fast-paced organizational environments, where people are often juggling competing demands, it is imperative to make every moment of training count. The learning experience needs to be relevant to individual needs and motivations and delivered in a timely way when people are ready and willing to learn and act on their learning.

Furthermore, DEI training carries an extra level of sensitivity in terms of the subject matter and the emotional journey participants may take.

Although there may be foundational components that everyone in the organization needs to learn, there may also be specific groups of individuals that need a unique or slightly customized approach.

To connect with the audience, you should:

- Get a baseline of existing DEI knowledge, skills, and attitudes
- Consider past training, what it included, and how people responded to it
- Determine relevant DEI skills of participants
- Consider status and psychological safety
- Align with the existing learning and development structure

Get a Baseline

What is the existing level of DEI knowledge, skills, and attitudes of the participant groups?

Look to the results from the assessment to determine the key areas of knowledge and skills that different participants possess and those they lack. This will help you identify the learning topics universally needed for the organization, and specific knowledge or skills gaps to address with unique participant groups.

For example, the assessment results may show that:

- Employees do not feel comfortable speaking out if they see or experience offensive or inappropriate behaviors
- Employees have experienced managers making offensive or inappropriate comments to their direct reports
- Leaders do not consistently hold managers accountable for exclusionary behaviors

These results indicate that it would be best to provide general training to all employees on managing micro-messages and how to respond to exclusionary acts, as well as specific training to managers on practicing inclusive behaviors and specific training to leaders on how to hold people accountable for exclusionary acts.

Consider Past Training

Look at training that has been offered to participants that includes any relevant knowledge or skills. This might include formal training in:

- EEO compliance, anti-discrimination, anti-harassment, anti-bullying, ethics, and professionalism
- Communications or interpersonal skills
- Team building
- Conflict resolution
- Leadership and management
- DEI training

It could also include more informal or information-based experiences related to DEI topics, such as guest speakers, book clubs, employee resource group presentations, and dialogues.

Review the content covered in previous or existing courseware or informal experiences to gauge participants' understanding and skills levels. Be careful not to assume that just because training was offered in the past, it was done to the extent needed to achieve lasting behavior change.

For example, most organizations have some kind of mandated EEO compliance training, yet this will not necessarily include learning or skills practice for fostering inclusive teams, managing micro-messages, or addressing unconscious bias. Additionally, people may overestimate their level of knowledge and skills. Participants may incorrectly assume that they have all the tools they need to lead a diverse team because they participated in EEO compliance training, when in actuality they lack the skills to effectively manage their teams and need further training.

Reviewing existing or previous learning experiences is also instrumental in making sure you are building on existing knowledge and skills and challenging people appropriately. Depending on how long it has been since any previous training, a refresher of foundational topics may be helpful to reinforce key learning and ensure participants have the baseline they need to be successful in learning new topics. Yet you want to avoid being redundant, which potentially leads people to feel like the training is not a good use of their time.

Determine the DEI Knowledge or Skills Most Relevant to Each Group

A critical element in designing training is discerning who should be placed together in the learning environment. There may be foundational concepts or skills that everyone in the organization needs to share, and it would behoove you to create a training that is universally provided to all participants. However, specific groups may need separate learning experiences to gain the skills they need to perform their job more effectively.

Often, it is useful to provide separate training for people in executive leadership, midlevel supervision or management, and individual contributor roles. Each of these groups will likely benefit from having customized training that offers unique skills.

Additionally, think about custom training for different job functions or divisions in the organization. For example, human resource professionals may need specific training to manage potential biases in employment decision making. Marketing divisions may need training on how to use inclusive and equitable language and imagery. Sales departments may need training on how to interact inclusively with diverse customers and build relationships with customer groups that have been marginalized in the past.

It's also important to consider how participants' roles and responsibilities will impact their receptivity to various learning methods. Training for a group of engineers will need to look different than the training for educators, which will need to look different than training for firefighters and emergency services employees.

Consider conducting a participant analysis to identify the participant groups that will be part of the DEI training, outlining specific roles and responsibilities that may influence the training approach you take.

Determine participant group needs in terms of accessibility:

- What are their academic backgrounds?
- What are their literacy levels?
- What are their levels of language fluency?
- What access do they have to any technology required for the training?
- How accessible is the physical learning space—access to the facility as well as the classroom environment?
- Are there any physical ability accommodations that need to be considered?
- Are there any accommodations that need to be made for neurodivergent participants?

Consider Status and Psychological Safety

Who has status within the organization and how might that impact the level of safety people feel in sharing their personal experiences and opinions?

Nothing can derail a DEI training more quickly than an imbalance of power. When people feel they are on a level playing field, they are going to be more open to sharing and learning from one another. If there are people in the learning space whose status in the organization (due to their tenure, position, influence, or societal ranking) gives them significantly more power or advantages, then others may not feel comfortable or safe speaking candidly.

People tend to feel more powerful and have the capacity to leverage their power when they have a higher status in an organization. Status in an organization may be related to not only formal structures (level of leadership, job function, seniority) but also informal structures (access to people in power positions, knowledge or access to information). It may also be related to demographics that impact one's status in society (dominant race, ethnicity, gender group).

For example, I have experienced numerous training programs where even when we conducted separate training for managers and leaders, the individual contributor training sessions still contained power dynamics. Certain individuals were more outspoken, assertive, and willing to ask questions or challenge the content or the facilitators, while others barely spoke or engaged in the training. The more you know the power dynamics that exist in the organization, the better able you are to prepare for those dynamics showing up in the learning space.

Align With the Organization's Learning and Development Structure

DEI training is most effective when it is closely aligned with the existing learning and development structure in the organization. One of the first questions I ask my clients when designing training is, "How do you typically do training in your organization?" I want to know what works and what doesn't work.

This may relate to logistics like the length of the training, geographic location, and use of technology, but also to learning methods, images, language, and involvement by key participants.

It also provides an opportunity to look at existing practices or mechanisms to reinforce key concepts. For example, in replacement of or in addition to a DEI-specific training program, it may be more effective to embed DEI concepts into existing training programs in the organization. Some organizations have robust training and development structures in place, with consistent content and a regularly updated learning management system for ongoing development. Other organizations may have a more ad hoc approach, with training offered in response to an event or a determined need rather than on a regular basis. This is important information to help you determine how best to position the DEI training approach.

Questions for Trainers

- What is the existing infrastructure for learning and development?
- How often do people receive training and in what topics?

- Should the DEI training be added to or reinforced in any of the existing training and if so, how?
- What training approaches and methods are most widely used in this organization (such as "expert lectures" versus experiential activities)?
- What mechanisms are available in terms of both in-person and virtual learning? Are people accustomed and willing to do pre-work assignments, assessments, group projects, and so on?
- Who typically goes through training together?
- Who typically leads the training?
- How are senior leadership and management typically involved?

Know Your Training Environment and Resources

It's important to consider the technical capacity that is available to you for any training design. Consider the physical learning environment (classroom space, virtual platforms) as well as the resources available (funds for materials like articles or books, access to subject matter experts or key leaders or influencers to demonstrate commitment to DEI, and the number of dedicated staff to support the training effort).

Some DEI training programs are well resourced, with experienced staff to support the design, development, planning, and delivery of the training. Other programs are more shoestring, with limited financial resources and one or two people to bear the responsibility of developing and implementing the program. Know what you are dealing with up front to manage expectations or to make an informed request for what you need to successfully deliver an effective program.

Historically, DEI training has not been seen as a financial imperative by many organizational leaders. Thus, they offer the bare minimum of resources to check the box and say training was done. You may find yourself having to make a strong case for resources.

It is important to ensure the training environment is conducive to participants' ability to fully immerse themselves in the content without distraction.

Questions for Trainers

Regarding the physical training environment, ask:

- Is there a dedicated space in the organization's facilities?
- Is the space large enough to accommodate the number of participants who will attend the training?
- Does the space provide enough privacy to ensure candid conversations?
- Is the space free of distractions (such as proximity to noise, personal desks, or visual distractions)?
- Is the lighting and temperature amenable to learning?
- Is the seating comfortable?
- Is there adequate table space for people to put materials and personal items?
- What room setup is necessary considering the learning activities you plan to conduct?
- Are the AV and technology adequate?
- Are there any visual or audio barriers (columns, poor sound system, and so on)?
- Are there spaces for private small group conversations or individual reflection?
- Is there space for the facilitators to sit?
- Is there space for additional materials (books, supplies, snacks)?
- How close are the nearest accessible and gender-inclusive restrooms? Water sources? Food sources for snacks and meals?
- Where is the training location in proximity to people's workspace and how much distraction might you encounter?
- Are there windows or glass doors that might affect privacy?
- What security issues need to be considered (do participants need security badges or an escort to enter and exit the facility)?

In terms of the virtual learning space, consider:

- What type of learning platforms are approved or widely used?
- What security measures need to be taken into consideration (for example, secure registration process or password protected access)?

- What internet connectivity or bandwidth requirements need to be considered?
- What level of physical privacy is needed for individual participants to be able to participate?
- What considerations need to be made for those who have to call in by phone?
- What audio or visual disability considerations must be made (such as closed captioning or visual assistance)?

Follow the Intercultural Continuum

After considering the culture, the people, and the platforms available, now it's time to put this all together and consider the content you will deliver.

When it comes to DEI, every individual brings a unique vantage point based on their identity and life experience. However, there is a general path many of us experience when it comes to developing competencies around understanding and adapting to cultural identity differences. The degree to which we have been exposed to identity differences and the amount of advantages we have been afforded due to our status in society (which we will discuss in subsequent chapters) influence our willingness and ability to notice, understand, appreciate, and adapt to cultural diversity.

The Intercultural Development Continuum (IDC) (Figure 3-1), based on research by Milton and Janet Bennett and Mitchell Hammer, maps the developmental process individuals experience moving from a monocultural mindset toward an intercultural or global mindset. The IDC has been widely used not only in intercultural communication research and training but also in DEI work to illustrate the different orientations,

Figure 3-1. Intercultural Continuum

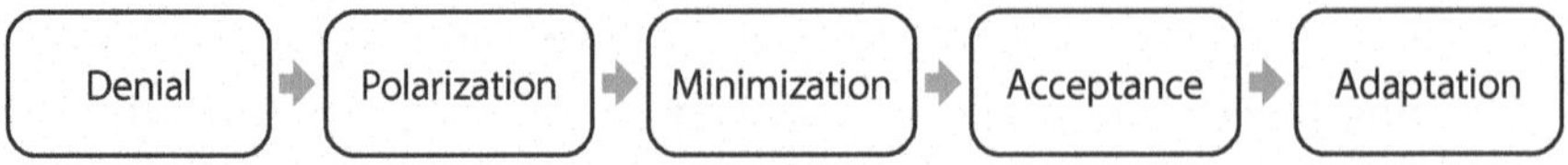

Denial ➡ Polarization ➡ Minimization ➡ Acceptance ➡ Adaptation

knowledge, skills, and attitudes people experience in their exposure to identity differences.

The IDC includes five unique mindsets or orientations:

Monocultural Mindset ➡ **Intercultural Mindset**

Monocultural mindsets are focused on preserving one's identity group or the dominant identity group as the "right" or true identity. Monocultural mindsets aim to maintain distance from the cultural "other" or to dismiss divergent perspectives and norms as wrong or lesser than one's own cultural group.

Intercultural mindsets are those that not only acknowledge cultural differences exist, but also appreciate those identities as equal in value to their own identities and are able to interact effectively across identity differences.

Let's explore the IDC's five unique mindsets and consider for each the implications for training design.

Denial

This mindset is generally oblivious to identity differences. This orientation to cultural differences is one of disinterest and avoidance, in which the individual has little to no ability to process or respond to differences. People who operate in the denial orientation have limited exposure to cultural difference and therefore tend to operate with stereotypes and generalizations of anyone they perceive as "other" than their cultural identity.

Many individuals who have a denial orientation are part of either the society's dominant identity group or a nondominant group that is isolated from mainstream society. Their orientation to identity and culture is limited because most of the people in their social orbit share the same cultural beliefs, values, norms, and characteristics. Although this is increasingly changing in our country as communities across the US become more demographically diverse, there are still many segments of the population where people from one identity group have little to no exposure to difference.

People in denial may acknowledge very superficial cultural differences, like food or clothing styles, but are limited in their understanding of deeper or more nuanced cultural identity differences, and therefore either dismiss them or are completely oblivious to them.

Training Implications

When working with an individual or group that is coming from a denial orientation, it is important to create a psychologically safe environment to explore differences without feeling threatened. Consider seeking ways to identify commonalities among identity groups, and to challenge stereotypes by exposing individuals to the multidimensionality of each person's identity. Have patience as these individuals begin to open themselves, perhaps for the first time, to other ways of seeing and being in the world. It may be disorienting, and they need to develop a foundation of understanding that differences exist and different does not mean dangerous.

Polarization

The polarization mindset is, true to its name, one that seeks to divide one identity group from another, typically with a value judgment applied where one identity group is superior to the other (or to all others). This can show up in a couple of different ways.

Defense is a form of polarization in which one's identity group is seen as the superior one. Individuals in the defense orientation acknowledge that other cultures or identities exist, but dismiss them as lesser or see them as threatening. Their exposure to identity differences is often still limited to negative messages, images, and interactions.

The most extreme versions of the defense orientation are violent actions like hate crimes and genocide. However, defense orientation is seen in much more subtle but equally insidious ways, such as in how religious, ethnic, and racial minorities; women; and some members of the LGBTQIA+ community are portrayed in the media we consume on a daily basis. When an identity group is consistently perceived as the "other" and denigrated, especially if they are also excluded from having any status or power in the social infrastructure, vast inequities, and even in some cases condoned violence, occur against that nondominant group. And nondominant groups are not only those in the numeric minority. For instance, the population of Black people in South Africa was largely in the numeric majority, but the White population of South Africans maintained political, economic, and social power for generations under apartheid.

Training Implications

Although there may be some cases in which the defense orientation shows up in more explicit ways (xenophobia, racism, sexism), it is typically much more subtle or even unconscious to the individuals operating from that orientation. The training should primarily focus on building bridges and common ground among the different identity groups and using the power of storytelling to humanize those who are perceived as the "other." The training should provide skills for empathy and perspective taking of the "other."

Moving past the defense/polarization orientation requires a focus on normalizing and humanizing those who are seen as the "other." The saying "not good or bad, just different" is an important one for people in this orientation to accept to move forward.

Another important aspect to the training is giving space for individuals who are in the defense orientation to share their story, to feel heard for their experiences. Quite often, people in this orientation become defensive in DEI training if they are part of the dominant cultural group, especially if the training focuses on calling out their privilege, biases, and power. Many participants who are in the defense orientation will react to such conversations with anger or withdrawal, wanting to argue that they are being mischaracterized as the villain in DEI training. If you want to help move people beyond defense, you have to break down their defenses. Create opportunities for partner and small group story sharing and dialogues. Help those in the defense orientation become more curious to explore commonalities and differences with people who represent different identity groups.

Reversal is another way in which polarization occurs, where an individual actually distances themselves from their own identity group. They often idealize other cultural identity groups, and may even try to appropriate the other culture's norms or behaviors. This can sometimes take the shape of picking up the cause of a marginalized group, but with limited or superficial understanding of the experiences or needs of that oppressed group. They may genuinely want to become more sensitive or inclusive but attempt to do so by disavowing or trying to shed their identity, which can be perceived by those in their own identity group as disloyal and to those outside their identity group as disingenuous.

This can sometimes lead to cultural appropriation, which is defined as "the unacknowledged or inappropriate adoption of the customs, practices, ideas, etc. of one people or society by members of another and typically more dominant people or society" (PBS 2020).

Some examples of cultural appropriation may be White women wearing dreadlocks or cornrows in their hair or people attending music festivals wearing Native American headdresses. The line between cultural appropriation and cultural appreciation may be hard to determine for some. While some argue that almost everything in our lives has been appropriated from some other culture, from blue jeans to tacos, it is important to consider the history of members of the dominant identity group co-opting traditions, symbols, or practices of a nondominant group for financial gain. Many members of nondominant groups whose cultural practices are often appropriated are accused of being overly sensitive if they share their frustrations, but more often than not their frustration is centered on feeling that their culture is being misappropriated, or that the members of the dominant group care little about understanding or building connection with them.

Singer and rap artist Nicki Minaj, in calling out White female singers for cultural appropriation, aptly said:

> *If you want to enjoy our culture and our lifestyle, bond with us, dance with us, have fun with us, twerk with us, rap with us, then you should also want to know what affects us, what is bothering us, what we feel is unfair to us. You shouldn't not want to know that.*
> (Ceron 2015)

Training Implications

Training can be an important space for people who are in a reversal mindset to experience the discomfort of learning more about the skeletons in the closet of their identity group without falling into a "blame and shame" stance. The training should help people process how the identity group to which they belong may contribute to systemic inequalities.

For trainers, notice and gently call attention to reversal. Encourage people to take ownership of that identity component rather than try to distance themselves from it. Invite them to consider how they can leverage and learn from that aspect of their identity rather than renounce their membership from that identity group.

Minimization

Minimization is the transitional stage between monocultural and intercultural mindsets. In minimization, people no longer experience differences from an "us vs. them" orientation. The focus is primarily on commonalities instead of differences. Minimization emphasizes what people perceive as core human needs and universal values. For example, a person in the minimization stage would downplay any perceived differences and instead reinforce that everyone is really the same underneath.

About 65 percent of people who have taken the Intercultural Development Inventory have minimization as their primary orientation (Hammer 2020). It is often seen in organizations where people are intent on focusing on commonalities or eager to prove that they treat everyone the same. We often hear minimization in phrases such as "I don't see color," or "I treat all my employees the same." We also hear minimization in the belief of meritocracy. For example, "I don't care where you come from, all I focus on is whether you can do the job right." This comes from a well-intentioned place, in that people consciously do believe themselves to be fair-minded. Yet, implicit biases abound, and by ignoring or discounting the different lived experiences, needs, and challenges of individuals in our teams or organizations, the message we send is that we are unwilling to address the realities they face. By saying, "I don't see color," the message you send to a person of color is "I do not wish to see or acknowledge your experiences as a person of color."

In dominant or majority identity groups, minimization often reflects a superficial understanding of identity (their own and others'). Those who have privilege and societal ranking due to some dimension of identity (race, ethnicity, gender identity, religion, age) may not have to pay attention to differences because society is largely set up in their favor.

For those in nondominant groups, minimization is often more of a coping mechanism to survive in a world where the cultural norms are set up to support the dominant group and the needs, cultural values, and behavioral norms of the nondominant group are ignored, discounted, or prohibited. For people living day to day as the cultural "other," it can be exhausting and even dangerous in some situations to practice one's cultural norms or live authentically. So they go along to get along by assimilating to the dominant cultural norms.

For example, women in predominantly male organizations or industries have historically felt the need to assimilate to the existing culture that was created for and by men. Cultural norms pressure them to behave like "one of the boys" or go in the opposite direction and play into stereotypes of extreme femininity.

Training Implications

Since it is likely that a large portion of people participating in training will be in a minimization space, this is an important component to keep in mind in the design process.

To help people move past minimization, we need to invite them to appreciate and explore their differences. Methods like storytelling can be powerful for inviting divergent life experiences and perspectives to unfold.

Elevate the voices of nondominant groups by inviting their perspectives or offering up their stories as told by others if the nondominant voices in the room are absent or unwilling to speak up.

Acceptance

In the acceptance stage, the first stage that is part of the intercultural/ global mindset, people appreciate and understand identity differences. They are able to recognize and differentiate patterns between their own and others' cultural identities. They are open to learning more about cultural differences, and willing to reflect on their own cultural identities. However, they may not have the skills or willingness to adapt their behaviors to other cultural identity norms. Some behavior changes may be seen as too uncomfortable or challenging to master.

For example, many White people in the US saw the viral video of George Floyd's murder by a police officer and were activated. A question that echoed throughout social media platforms and conversations with others was, "What can I do?" People in the acceptance stage are often eager to learn more and to act in inclusive and equitable ways, but don't yet have the skills.

Another way in which the acceptance stage occurs is when individuals face a moral or ethical dilemma in adapting to other cultural norms.

For example, a US-born employee working with counterparts in Egypt who is responsible for making hiring or promotional decisions may face a struggle when their Egyptian colleagues encourage the employee to select their family members for jobs rather than selecting unknown candidates. US cultural norms tend to prioritize a more transactional approach of selecting the "best" candidate in terms of qualifications, and nepotism (or at least explicit nepotism) is often frowned upon. However, in many Middle Eastern cultures it is important to prioritize one's family or community, and therefore nepotism is widely accepted. If the US employee chooses to hire the non-family-member candidate, they may preserve their sense of morality of making a "fair" decision by their cultural standards, but they risk their relationship with their Egyptian colleagues.

Training Implications

Focus on skill building and application. People at the acceptance stage have an open mindset and are willing to engage in self-reflection of their identities. They do not need to be convinced that DEI is important, or that biases exist. What they need most is a safe space to learn and practice critical skills for equity and inclusion. This includes managing one's own communication, responding to others' exclusive behaviors, and navigating identity-based conflicts. Scenarios, role plays, and peer coaching can be powerful methods for helping people practice skills that will prepare them for real-life interactions.

Adaptation

Adaptation is the most advanced stage on the continuum. People in the adaptation stage are not only able to shift their own perspectives to understand others' experiences, but they also have the skills to adapt their behaviors to best fit different situations.

People in adaptation have often been exposed to a variety of different cultural contexts, from living, studying, or working with different identity groups. Many are well practiced and therefore comfortable in new or unknown situations. However, one challenge for people in the adaptation stage is an impatience with those who are not as far along the continuum as they are. It can be challenging for people at this stage to engage with someone, especially a person of their own identity group, who is coming from a more monocultural mindset.

Training Implications

Participants with the adaptation orientation can be of particular value in the training, in that they can model the perspectives and skills of equity and inclusion for their peers.

You may also need to remind people in this stage to have patience and openness for those who are struggling with understanding, accepting, or adapting to identity differences.

Head–Heart–Hands Approach to DEI Training

DEI training requires more than just knowledge sharing or even skills training. People need to feel it. They need to be touched at the emotional level, to have an awakening to their own and others' unique perspectives and experiences.

The Head–Heart–Hands model has been attributed to different sources, from ancient Greek philosophers to the Dalai Lama. It can be applied in the context of learning and organizational change and transition as a tool for progress. Benjamin Bloom's research on learning identified three domains in learners (Bloom 1956):

- Cognitive (intellectual skills and new knowledge): Head
- Affective (emotional reactions, values, motivations): Heart
- Psychomotor (movement, practical application): Hands

This model will help you design and deliver a training that accounts for all the developmental stages, from denial to adaptation. It helps to build a training where people walk away from the training experience with new knowledge and practical skills, as well as an attitude of curiosity and compassion.

Head

It's important to provide learners with a baseline of knowledge upon which they can continue to build their understanding of DEI. Our brains like to be stimulated and make connections between existing knowledge and new ideas. It's also important to provide learners with a sense of purpose. Why is this content important and relevant to them?

Questions for the trainer:

- What concepts do learners need to know and to what extent?
- What level of knowledge do they need? Do they need to merely be exposed to a theory or concept or have deeper mastery?

- What relevant data will support the learning? Are there specific studies that will reinforce the knowledge and particularly resonate with this audience? For example:
  - Studies indicating how DEI is important for business growth and sustainability
  - Studies indicating how DEI leads to greater creativity and innovation
  - Studies showing how implicit biases impact hiring and promotions
  - Studies showing the impact of systemic inequalities on a particular population

Heart

In comparison with most other training content, DEI training is one of the most challenging because it requires a deep focus on connecting to emotions. In his book, *The War for Kindness: Building Empathy in a Fractured World*, Jamil Zaki (2019) says that when you empathize with someone, you "take on their emotions, decode their thoughts, and worry about their welfare."

Effective DEI training provides people with the opportunity to delve into deeper levels of perspective taking and empathy. It's not enough to intellectually understand why another person believes or behaves the way they do. We need to tap into the emotions that drive those beliefs and behaviors, and to have genuine compassion and concern for the well-being of people with whom we may fundamentally disagree.

The most effective DEI training I have been a part of, where we have seen the longest lasting impact, is when people have the space and safety to explore the origins of their own perceptions and experiences, to become vulnerable with people from vastly different walks of life, and to develop meaningful connections across their differences.

DEI training may awaken strong emotions, including pride, pain, grief, anger, or guilt. It's important to permit emotions to surface and to create a space to examine those emotions without letting them detract from the learning. (In chapter 5 we will focus on how to create space for emotions in dialogue.)

Effective DEI training also can and should elicit positive emotions, like hope, compassion, relief, joy, and a shared spirit of unity. Trust is solidified when people feel they have shared deeply with one another and their experiences and perspectives have been met with openness and care rather than ridicule.

Questions for the trainer:

- What emotions are likely to emerge and how should we prepare for them?
- What level of emotional risk might different training approaches or activities create?
- What emotions are acceptable to demonstrate in this organizational environment?
- Who might feel more or less safe sharing or demonstrating emotions and who might not?
- How do I want people to feel walking away from the learning experience?

Hands

People want practical. DEI training needs to equip learners with skills for effectively navigating cultural or identity differences, as well as tools for effectively responding to challenges. Learners not only need to be introduced to the tools, but they also need sufficient time and space to practice those tools to feel more comfortable and prepared to employ them in real-life settings.

Make sure to devote considerable time in the training for practice. Consider experiential and interactive exercises, with plenty of time to debrief and discuss application in the "real world." Encourage and reinforce a spirit of experimentation, reminding people that it is expected that they won't necessarily get it right all the time. Give people space to share feedback with one another about what practices worked or didn't.

With DEI, there is often not one sole right or wrong approach. For many learners who are looking for a quick fix or one-size-fits-all solution, this can be disconcerting. There's no perfect list of dos and don'ts, because so much of DEI training comes down to understanding the context of a given situation and responding in kind. There are general best practices and approaches that can be offered, but the real purpose is to equip people with skills to engage in continuous self- and other discovery.

Questions for the trainer:
- What specific skills do learners need to practice?
- What level of ability do they need to demonstrate (proficiency, mastery)?
- What are the best learning methods to support skill development?
- How might learners' skills development be measured or evaluated?

Core Training Concepts

Although the content you select for DEI training will depend on the audience and organizational needs, there are foundational concepts that support any DEI learning experience. Be sure to address and reinforce these concepts throughout the learning experience:
- Visible and invisible dimensions of identity
- Implicit associations and biases
- Stereotypes
- "Us vs. them" thinking
- Privilege and power
- Micro-messages and subtle acts of exclusion

Visible and Invisible Dimensions of Identity

The iceberg metaphor can be a powerful learning tool. Consider an iceberg, where only about 10 percent of the mass is visible above the water line, and the rest is hidden under the surface of the water. Our identities are like an iceberg. There is very little that is visible to others, yet those visible characteristics predominantly drive the way we are perceived and treated by others (Weaver 1986).

We all make meaning instantaneously out of what we can see about others. For example, we can immediately see skin color, hair, face shape, height, size, and clothing, and will often make inferences about a person based on these visible characteristics. This also goes for what we can hear and the inferences we make from a person's accent, language, and vocal tone.

The challenge with focusing on the surface is that sometimes those inferences are incorrect, and even if they are correct, they do not give us the full story of the person.

The dimensions that are often unseen reveal much more of the story. This may include dimensions like invisible disabilities, sexual orientation, gender identity, religion, relationship status, national origin, ancestry, professional or academic experiences, personal interests and hobbies, and so much more.

What is beneath the surface is often far more indicative of an individual's sense of self, and can illustrate the story of a person's lived experiences, core values, beliefs, expectations, and interpretations of others' behaviors (Figure 3-2).

Figure 3-2. The Iceberg Metaphor

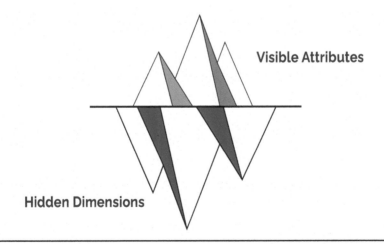

Questions for learners:

- What assumptions or inferences have you made about people based solely on what is above the surface?
- How do those inferences affect your perceptions, decisions, or actions?
- How might you assume similarities with a person who on the surface looks like you but in reality has had a different experience?
- When have you been misunderstood or misjudged because of some aspect of your identity that is above the surface? (This could be either a positive or negative experience.)
- What do we gain when we learn more about what's below the surface?

Implicit Associations and Unconscious Bias

Every human being's brain is constructed with certain blind spots. Implicit bias is a mental conditioning that occurs when individuals unconsciously rely on information about social groups that they have picked up from their environment. Once this information has been stored in a person's long-term memory, these "hidden" biases influence their perceptions, decisions, and behaviors, unbeknownst to them.

Implicit bias exists in all of us. It's a natural neural reaction to help us make quick decisions. However, these biases can cause individuals to make bad decisions based on faulty data, and can have adverse effects on their relationships with others. Regardless of our conscious beliefs, our brains function instinctively and automatically. As social animals, we humans have developed certain regions in our brain to observe and make meaning based on all the data (both correct and incorrect) that we gather about other humans.

We all carry automatic and intuitive associations about different dimensions of identity (gender, race, physical appearance, religion, and so on) that often oppose our consciously held beliefs and values. These assumptions are not based so much on factual evidence as they are on how right our assessment of the situation feels, and can even be constructed in part by biased media portrayals and other cultural artifacts that have contributed to our unconscious programming.

These social "mindbugs," as described by Mahzarin Banaji and Anthony Greenwald in their groundbreaking research, lead us to automatically experience a positive or negative reaction to individuals from certain social groups (Banaji and Greenwald 2011).

The Harvard University Implicit Association Test (IAT), created by Banaji and Greenwald, has been taken by more than 2.5 million people worldwide. The results are consistently astonishing. When faced with a timed test in which one has to associate positive or negative words with White faces versus faces of color, individuals of all races have consistently shown an inherent bias toward White faces over faces of color. Similar tests have been done around gender, religion, sexual orientation, and even mental health. Again, the results show that people tend to harbor unconscious biases that are often at odds with their own consciously held beliefs.

- 75 percent of those who took the race IAT showed an automatic preference for White faces versus those of people of color.
- This automatic White preference is known to signal discriminatory behavior. According to Banaji and Greenwald, "It predicts discriminatory behavior even among research participants who earnestly . . . espouse egalitarian beliefs" (Banaji and Greenwald 2011).

We all think we're less biased than we actually are (and assume others are more biased than we are). We tend to see how others' views and perceptions are clouded by their biases (ideological beliefs, stereotypes, and so on). However, we tend to believe that we ourselves make more objective judgments. We detect little "evidence" of our own biases, and often lack the self-awareness to recognize our susceptibility to implicit biases. In other words, when we look internally, we see ourselves as well-intentioned, objective, rational individuals. We may acknowledge the research saying biases exist, but we have a hard time recognizing how those biases play a role in how we personally see and interact with the world.

Tips for Training on Bias:

- Be ready to share relevant research, but don't overwhelm people with too many studies.
- Consider an interactive activity that uncovers hidden biases, such as scenarios asking participants to rate the performance of different individuals.
- Engage participants in discussion around all the ways in which bias could influence decisions in their organization.
- Explore strategies for mitigating bias in participants' teams and organizations.
- Be prepared for resistance, as some may question either the existence of biases or the importance of managing them.

Stereotypes

Stereotypes are overgeneralized beliefs about an identity group, often rooted in bias and societal conditioning. By stereotyping, we make multiple assumptions about an individual based only on their membership in an identity group, or even our perception that they belong to an identity group.

For example, stereotypes that exist about Americans may include:

- Obese
- Loud
- Arrogant
- Workaholics

Although there are people who represent each of these characteristics, they are not representative of many people in US culture. Yet, Americans traveling overseas often hear and even find themselves on the receiving end of these stereotypes.

There may be certain patterns or shared history that explain a common characteristic of or behavior by people from an identity group, but the problem with stereotypes is that they are overgeneralizations and do not lead to a comprehensive understanding of an individual or group. Some stereotypes may even appear on the surface to be complimentary, but are not necessarily true, useful, or advantageous to the people on the receiving end.

For example, the myth of people of Asian descent as the "model minority" has led to a number of problematic outcomes for people in the Asian American community. US stereotypes that Asians excel at math and science, or are naturally gifted musicians, are problematic in multiple ways. First, it lumps anyone of Asian descent into a pan-ethnic identity group that is not representative of their individual cultural backgrounds. It also wrongly assumes that anyone of Asian descent has a natural propensity for these specific fields. Math or musical skills are not tied to any particular cultural group. The model minority myth also smothers the stark reality of oppression and racism against people of Asian descent.

We all internalize implicit stereotypes from a young age, based on sometimes subtle messages we receive from our external environment (family, community, school, media, popular culture, and so on). Even when we consciously reject cultural stereotypes, they are still filed away in our long-term memory and, when we are pressured to make decisions, our brains will automatically grab those items to determine a decision.

Additionally, stereotypes can actually negatively impact one's performance. Individuals who are primed to connect with a certain aspect of their social identity that gives them a leg up will often outperform their peers. Individuals who are primed to connect with a certain aspect of their social identity that has historically been a disadvantage or been connected with a negative stereotype will underperform. In his book, *Whistling Vivaldi: How Stereotypes Affect Us and What We Can Do*, Claude Steele shares several studies demonstrating this phenomenon.

For example, studies have shown that girls will underperform in math and science tests when reminded of their gender and the stereotypes that exist that boys are better at math and science than girls. Similar studies have shown the same results with students of color versus White students. Similarly, White males who are reminded that people of color outperform White people in athletics, like basketball, will underperform (Steele 2010).

Thus, across the board, when individuals are reminded of some aspect of their identity that puts them at a disadvantage, they internalize that messaging and may perform worse.

Tips for training on stereotypes:

- Use examples from your own life experiences to illustrate how stereotypes can be destructive.
- Be ready to respond to someone who asks, "But aren't stereotypes rooted in some truth?"
- Ask participants to list some of the stereotypes they have heard about one of the identity groups they are a part of (for example, gender, generation, country or region of origin). Consider starting with an identity group that feels more emotionally safe to explore. In many US workplaces, sharing stereotypes around different age groups can be a good starting place. Then you can move into some of the identity groups that may feel a bit more emotionally risky, like race, ethnicity, or religion.

Us vs. Them

Different parts of the brain are triggered when we hear a story about someone we assume is like us versus someone we assume is not like us.

Researchers at Harvard University used brain-imaging technology to track the various parts of the brain that were activated when individuals were shown photos of two different male faces and descriptions about each (Banaji and Greenwald 2013).

When the description of the person was similar to how the participants self-identified, the neurons in the ventral region of the medial prefrontal cortex (the part of the brain that is engaged when we think about ourselves) lit up. When they heard a description of the other person, who was very different in relation to how participants self-identified, the dorsal region of this sector (which is engaged when we think about the "other") was activated.

Simply put, when we see or hear about people we assume are like us in some way, our brains react through the lens of how we see ourselves.

When we see or hear about people we perceive as different from us, our brains react through the lens of the "other."

We make moral judgments based on our emotional and intuitive reactions, not on rational thought or objective data. According to Jonathan Haidt (2012) in his book *The Righteous Mind: Why Good People are Divided By Politics and Religion*, the manner in which humans make moral judgments meddles with our ability to accept new perspectives:

> *Morality binds and blinds. It binds us into ideological teams that fight each other as though the fate of the world depended on our side winning each battle. It blinds us to the fact that each team is composed of good people who have something important to say.*

When presented with questions of what is moral or immoral, we make immediate decisions based on our intuition. These gut reactions become hardwired; even if we're not able to explain why we believe something to be immoral, or if presented with new information that may challenge that belief, we often do not change our mind. In fact, we often double down on our initial posture, holding on tightly to the notion that our perceptions are absolute and discounting any challenges to those beliefs as dubious.

We are conditioned to feel a sense of righteousness, to believe ourselves to be moral and good. When we encounter people who do not share our beliefs, we often judge them to be immoral (or to be of questionable morality). This relates to the limbic system's desire to keep us feeling safe. The cognitive dissonance we may experience if we acknowledge an oppositional perspective as legitimate is so uncomfortable for us that we urgently seek out messages that feel right to us and shut out the messages that feel wrong.

In fact, memory loss patients still instinctively identify who is "good" or "bad" even when they don't remember the data they learned about each person. In research conducted with patients suffering from acute memory loss, they were shown images of two different individuals and told a story depicting one individual as a "good" person (gave to charity, cared for family members, and so forth) and one as "bad" (greedy, mean, thief, and so forth). The study found that the patients accurately assigned the faces to the labels of "good" or "bad" afterward, even though they didn't remember the stories at all. They intuitively felt who was good or bad, even though they couldn't recall why (Banaji and Greenwald 2013).

Tips for training on "us vs. them" dynamics:

- Ask participants to think about some of the "us vs. them" dynamics that occur in their own organizational culture, based on social identity characteristics (race, gender, age) as well as organizational dynamics (division, job function, tenure).
- Reinforce that this is a natural function of our primitive brains. It is set up to keep us safe, and we all do this without realizing it.
- Ask for examples of instances where people have broken out of the "us vs. them" thinking and the impact this had on them and others.

Privilege and Power

DEI training must also examine the existence and perpetuation of societal privilege and power structures. *Privilege* refers to the automatic, unearned advantages that an individual may receive based on some dimension of identity over which they have little or no control. For instance, historically in many societies, men have had unearned advantages over women in terms of their status and opportunities. They are more likely to be considered for leadership and high-status positions, earn higher incomes, and in some cases afforded more rights than women.

We all have automatic advantages and disadvantages based on different dimensions of our identity. Privilege can be based on a variety of dimensions of identity, and who has privilege and who does not may vary from one culture to another. The combination of dimensions of identity that one has may further increase or decrease the amount of privilege a person is given.

For instance, in the US, a White cisgender woman may have less privilege than a White cisgender man but more privilege than a Black LGBTQIA+ woman.

Privilege does not mean that a person has a charmed life, is economically well-off, or has had everything handed to them without trying. People can have plenty of privilege because of aspects of their identity and still have struggled. There is no single identity group that owns pain and suffering. It can be difficult for people to recognize their privilege, even though it is often quite clear to others.

Tips for training on power and privilege:

• Consider where in the sequence of the training this best fits, as it can be uncomfortable for participants to explore.

• Use various examples of different dimensions of identity that may afford one privilege (for example, physical or mental ability, socioeconomic status, skin color, gender identity).

• Reinforce that each person's stories of struggle, pain, or inequality do not preclude them from having privilege in some way.

• When selecting activities on privilege, be very conscious of how the activities will affect people from various identity groups differently.

• Have a "now what" conversation to encourage accountability by asking participants to make solid commitments to address inequities. Focus on actions individuals with power and privilege need to take to help even out the playing field.

Often, interactive exercises on privilege can leave people feeling emotionally raw, and can even be retraumatizing for people from marginalized groups. The Privilege Walk is an activity that has been used widely in DEI trainings for years. In this activity, participants are asked to form a line starting at the same place, and then asked to take a step forward or step back based on a series of questions that indicate where they have had unearned privilege. These questions include things like, "Take a step forward if you grew up in house with two parents," or "Take a step back if you were ever called names because of your race, ethnicity, gender, or sexual orientation." This exercise can lead to powerful dialogue around how systemic inequalities compound to form very different life experiences for people based on identity characteristics over which they have no control. But the activity can also be an emotional minefield and can leave the people at the back of the line feeling demoralized or shut down. The experience can be valuable for those who have previously been unaware of their own privilege, but often at the expense of those with far less privilege. If you decide to use the Privilege Walk, make sure to have an experienced DEI facilitator lead the exercise. Elevate the voices of the people who have experienced the least privilege.

Micro-Messages and Subtle Acts of Exclusion

Micro-messages are tiny, subtle actions that we communicate often without realizing it, and that can have a significant impact on our relationships with others. Micro-messages can convey either positive or negative meaning.

Micro-affirmations are subtle behaviors people engage in that give others opportunities or advantages. Individuals often engage in micro-affirmations, even unconsciously, when they feel an assumed similarity with the other person or people. Their categorization of a person as part of their in-group tends to incite them to judge the person's behaviors more positively than another's. Micro-affirmations may include behaviors such as the following:

- More friendly, open interaction (smiles, eye contact, proximity)
- Generosity, compassion
- Mentorship and advice
- Constructive feedback to help them succeed
- Benefit of the doubt when they engage in negative behaviors

In the context of DEI, people who belong to an identity group that has been oppressed or marginalized often experience negative micro-messages. These are often referred to as micro-inequities or microaggressions.

Micro-inequities or microaggressions are subtle, hidden, hard-to-prove exclusionary behaviors, often unconscious, that may occur when a person is perceived as "different" or the "other" (Rowe 1990). These may include:

- Interrupting a person midsentence
- Not acknowledging a person's contributions or only speaking to others in the room
- Answering more questions from people of one identity group
- Raising one's voice, even though the person has no difficulty hearing
- Making jokes or using terms derogatory to some groups
- Consistently mispronouncing someone's name
- Mentioning achievements of some people but not others from a particular identity group
- Inviting people to social events that may make them feel uncomfortable or alienated, such as activities often seen as highly gendered, or ones inaccessible to people with disabilities

Micro-inequities and microaggressions are often referred to as "death by a thousand cuts."

By themselves, none of these individual acts might seem on the surface like a concern. But consider the impact on an individual from a marginalized identity group if they frequently, consistently receive one or several of these messages, if it is a pattern of behavior that becomes a part of their life, and if those behaviors occur consistently and frequently to other people in their identity group.

In their book, *Subtle Acts of Exclusion: How to Understand, Identify, and Stop Microaggressions*, Tiffany Jana and Michael Baran write that microaggressions are problematic because they are so subtle and hard to define. They offer several messages that people from marginalized identity groups hear or internalize when they experience subtle acts of exclusion.

For instance, an Asian American woman is asked by a new colleague, "Where are you from?" When she replies "Chicago," the colleague presses, "Yes, but where are you really from?" The underlying message the woman receives is: "You don't belong."

A gender nonbinary person may experience subtle acts of exclusion when a cisgender colleague misgenders them and when corrected sighs and says, "Everyone wants to make things more complicated. All these new pronouns, I just can't keep up!" The underlying message is: "You are a burden."

Responding to acts of exclusion requires people to be willing to explore the impact of their actions on others, not get lost in explaining their positive intentions.

Tips for training on micro-messages:

- Invite people to share personal examples. Many people feel an immediate connection with this topic because they have personal experiences receiving negative messages.
- Assume good intent but focus on impact. It's easy for people to become defensive or eager to explain the good intentions behind their actions. Encourage them to focus on impact instead.
- Micro-messages are in the eye of the beholder. Remind people to believe others when they say that what they experienced hurt.
- Provide three sets of skills:
  - Managing our own micro-messages
  - Responding to others' micro-messages
  - Receiving and acting on feedback when we engage in micro-inequities

Summary

Designing an effective DEI learning experience is a complex undertaking. It requires a good deal of consideration for the audience, the organizational culture, and current and past events that may impact the training. Training should in some way incorporate foundational concepts, including identity dimensions, implicit bias and stereotypes, systemic privilege, "us vs. them" thinking, and micro-messages. However, the way in which these concepts are explored depends on the audience's needs. Effective DEI training goes beyond intellectual knowledge building and helps influence attitude and mindset changes, as well as giving people the opportunity to practice new skills and encouraging individual accountability.

Systemic change will not happen with one-off DEI training, no matter how relevant and well developed it is. DEI needs to be reinforced and reflected in every aspect of the organizational culture. You have an opportunity to ensure that all learning and development processes and activities incorporate DEI in a meaningful way. Next, chapter 4 provides strategies and tips for embedding DEI principles into the overall training and development experience.

Worksheet 3-1. Training Design Worksheet Example

This sample training design worksheet illustrates how to consider the components discussed in chapter 3 for planning and designing effective DEI training for a specific organization and audience.

Component (some of this may become apparent from needs assessment)	Implications for DEI Training	Considerations and Plan
Macroculture • Origin story • Symbols, artifacts, images • Espoused values • Lived/practiced values • Distribution of power • Common language • Norms around communication, verbal and nonverbal (e.g., how do people interact with one another?) • Approach to conflict	• Broadly communicated values around honesty, respect, quality • Prioritization of work quality and output; little focus on people or team building • "Don't bring your personal life into the workplace" often heard in conversations • Tension point: meritocracy vs. equity; do we hire and promote for diversity or do we hire solely based on professional experience and qualifications? • Conflict avoidant: Conflicts are not addressed by management and fester	• Explicitly link DEI content to organization's values • Separate training for managers linking DEI to employee engagement and high-functioning teams and high performance • Explore the additional mental and emotional labor when there is no sense of safety to be our authentic selves at work • Provide data showcasing how biases influence decision making in terms of hiring and promotions, and the subsequent consequences in terms of talent • Introduce conflict management tools
Subcultures	Sales department has historically been mostly male; hired several women in last year but there has already been turnover of women in the department	Include activity on micro-messages with specific examples of gender biases, focus on tips for men to be inclusion allies for female colleagues

Component (some of this may become apparent from needs assessment)	Implications for DEI Training	Considerations and Plan
External forces (cultural, economic, political, environmental)	Black Lives Matter movement has compelled a lot of employees to ask organization leadership to focus on racial equity and justice	• Define racial equity and incorporate dialogue on antiracism as a core component of fostering DEI • Share articles and videos that build awareness of the history of racial inequity and oppression as a pre-training assignment
Audience or participants	• Needs assessment results indicate that executive leaders have trouble holding themselves or others accountable for exclusive behaviors • Women in sales department reported experiencing gender bias by male colleagues	• Deliver customized training to leadership team focusing on practical strategies for modeling DEI behaviors and holding others accountable • Conduct training for sales department that focuses on addressing bias, invites dialogue to raise awareness to the challenges women face, and offers strategies for men to be allies for their female counterparts
Organization's learning and development structure	• Existing training includes EEO compliance and new employee onboarding • No existing formal management training for supervisors or managers	• Design ongoing learning experiences that focus on inclusive communication • Develop training for all supervisory employees with competencies that foster DEI on teams. Link to performance expectations.

Worksheet 3-1 (cont.)

Component (some of this may become apparent from needs assessment)	Implications for DEI Training	Considerations and Plan
Training environment and resources	Physical space for training is a large conference room that has a wall of glass facing the office space	Request funding for off-site location for training. If that's not possible, conduct smaller class sizes and cover the wall of glass with chart paper to ensure privacy.

Worksheet 3-2. Participant Analysis Worksheet

Use this worksheet to consider the learning needs of diverse participants and determine how to customize training for various groups. This will help you to determine whether you need group-specific or mixed-group training. Consider the unique knowledge, skills, and attitudes to address with participants, and the relevant examples, scenarios, or stories that will help engage a particular audience.

1. Create a participant map by first identifying all the participants who will be involved in training.

2. Now cluster participants into appropriate learning groups. (For example, does it make sense to cluster by management level, department, or knowledge/experience level?)

3. For each training group, determine the following for the participants who will be learning together:
   a. Existing level of knowledge and skills
   b. Specific characteristics or behavioral traits that impact training methods
   c. Expectations of or attitudes toward DEI
   d. Responsibilities and level of accountability related to fostering DEI in the organization
   e. Relevant demographics (such as race, ethnicity, gender, or age,)

Group 1

Knowledge/skills	
Characteristics	
Expectations/attitudes	
Responsibilities	
Demographics	

Group 2

Knowledge/skills	
Characteristics	
Expectations/attitudes	
Responsibilities	
Demographics	

Worksheet 3-2 (cont.)

Group 3

Knowledge/skills	
Characteristics	
Expectations/attitudes	
Responsibilities	
Demographics	

4. Create learning objectives for each training group's specific learning needs:
   a. Consider the knowledge and skills each group will need to develop in the training
   b. Identify potential learning methods that will work best with each group
   c. Identify learning outcomes (what is expected of each group following the training)

Group 1

Knowledge/skills	
Learning methods	
Learning outcomes	

Group 2

Knowledge/skills	
Learning methods	
Learning outcomes	

Group 3

Knowledge/skills	
Learning methods	
Learning outcomes	

Chapter 4
Make All Training Inclusive, From Design to Implementation

Imagine you are participating in a communication skills training at your organization along with a diverse cross-section of co-workers. The instructor posts the slides on the screen. The image on the first slide shows a White man with salt-and-pepper hair in a gray suit standing and smiling down at a young White woman sitting in front of a computer as he hands her papers. The next several slides show a series of images of people in Western business attire smiling, talking, shaking hands, or giving high fives.

The instructor reads several quotes from famous authors and thought leaders. You notice all the quotes are from White American or British men.

There is an exercise where participants are asked to read a scenario and talk about how best to address the communication challenges the characters experience. In the scenario you were assigned, the supervisor is a male named Jim whose employee, Patty, is engaging in problematic behaviors. Patty is not responding to his email requests for updates on a project and then breaking down in tears when Jim tries to give her feedback.

The skills for effective communication include a section on active listening, where the instructor stresses the importance of making direct eye contact and leaning in closer to show full attention.

As part of a module on honesty and trust, the instructor shows a video clip from the 1950s sitcom I Love Lucy, where the main character, a housewife named Lucy, engages in a hilarious series of mishaps because she is not open and honest with her husband, Ricky.

The resource list provided at the end of the training includes a number of authors, all of whom are White and male, with the exception of one White female author who is cited for research on the importance of empathy and vulnerability.

Can you name all the potential DEI issues with this training?

How do we embed DEI into every aspect of learning and development? Start by deconstructing every aspect of your design to identify blind spots and stereotypes. It's not enough to build well-designed DEI training from an instructional standpoint. For successful and sustainable progress to occur, we need to examine the underlying biases that exist at the very core of an organization's learning development infrastructure. Regardless of the type of training or the topics covered, all training should be grounded in inclusive and equitable practices. In this chapter we explore how to design and deliver training experiences that are representative of diversity and inclusive for all participants. At the end of the chapter, there are two worksheets to help you create a checklist for inclusive design and ask the right questions for inclusive training delivery.

Designing Inclusive Diversity Training

Typically, training is designed for those who are part of the dominant identity group. This is not often intentional. As we have discussed in previous chapters, implicit biases and blind spots influence everything we do.

Take, for example, that according to the US Bureau of Labor Statistics, as of 2020, training development specialists are majority female (57 percent) and White (82 percent), with 13 percent Black, 2.7 percent Asian, and 14 percent Latino/Hispanic. Training and development managers had similar statistics, with a majority female (55 percent) and over-whelmingly White (85 percent), and only 9 percent Black and 10 percent Latino/Hispanic. The majority of instructional design or training profes-sionals also have advanced degrees (60 percent hold a master's degree) (Bureau of Labor Statistics 2021).

Thus, the majority of people who are responsible for building out an organization's training infrastructure and for managing learning devel-opment experiences tend to fall within a narrow set of demographics.

The way in which training is designed, delivered, and evaluated is filtered through the identity lenses of a field that is dominated in the US mostly by White women with advanced degrees.

So where to begin?

First, let's break down the existing structure of the organization's training brick by brick. This doesn't necessarily mean gutting the system and rebuilding it. It's about using a DEI lens to explore where there are gaps, overreliances, and potential biases:

- Whose voices, perspectives, and needs are consulted when designing training?
- Who is responsible for the design itself? Who oversees the design process and has final approval?
- Whose voices, perspectives, and needs are absent?
- What implications does this have on how the training is designed and delivered?

Because we are inherently drawn to make unconscious connec-tions based on our individual beliefs and experiences, the training we design and deliver is likely to reflect some of our biases and blind spots. These include images we select, names and roles we use, multimedia we choose, and the experts and inspiration we seek.

Diversify Representation in Visuals

Search the internet for the following images:

- Leader
- Doctor
- Engineer

- Teacher
- Nurse
- CEO

Studies examining Google search results for 96 different occupations as late as 2019 show biases in terms of gender and skin color. Although there is more overall representation of gender diversity than in past studies, there was still a dearth of gender anti-stereotypical images, (e.g. male nurses, female construction workers). Further, although there has been an increase in representation of BIPOC people, the skin tone tends to be lighter, with less representation of darker skin tones (Celis and Keswani 2020).

In terms of gender nonbinary or transgender images, there are either very few images or the portrayal is limited or misrepresentative. In 2019, Shutterstock saw a 64 percent increase in the search term "transgender," and searches for the term "gender fluid" on Getty Images tripled in just one year (Schrupp 2019). Yet the number of images available are usually in the single digits. Trans people are rarely shown in day-to-day activities or public life. In 2015, media company Vice created the website Broadly to focus on gender identity. Broadly launched the Gender Spectrum Collection, a gallery of photos available online featuring images of transgender and nonbinary models in professional, academic, and personal settings. The website includes guidelines for usage that can be informative for designers:

> Images of trans and nonbinary people can be used to illustrate any topic, not just stories related directly to those communities. Consider accessing these photos for stories on topics like beauty, work, education, relationships, or wellness. Including transgender and nonbinary people in stories not explicitly about gender identity paints a more accurate depiction of the world we live in today.
> (Gender Spectrum Collection)

People with disabilities, although they make up approximately 15 percent of the population, make up only about 2 percent of characters in TV or film (Heumann 2019). What little representation there is usually reinforces stereotypes that people with disabilities are objects to be pitied or rescued, or are to be lauded as a symbol of inspiration for overcoming adversity.

Although the creators of internet search engines have become more aware of bias and intentional about representing diversity in their image searches, there is still a deep degree of mental conditioning that many of us need to overcome in terms of whom we picture in certain positions. Therefore, it's imperative that instructional designers and trainers bring a DEI lens to the development of all content.

All too often, PowerPoint slides and training materials are filled with images of light skin-toned, cisgender people without visible disabilities, generally males in positions of leadership or power. Moreover, many of the images that show racial diversity feature physically attractive, thin, or physically fit people in Western business attire smiling broadly. Think about who is represented in the images you choose and how accurately those images reflect the population of employees, customers, or communities served.

Be intentional about using images of people of color, people with disabilities, people of various ages, people of various sizes, and so forth. In addition to representation of diversity, look for equitable and culturally competent gestures, expressions, and interactions. Avoid using images that reinforce stereotypes, such as women or people of color in non-dominant positions or stereotypical roles. Consider the clothing that is featured and whether it is culturally appropriate for the audience.

If you are designing training for an international or globally diverse audience, consider cultural influences when selecting images. Select images of people who represent the unique diversity dimensions of the country or region for which you are designing the training. Avoid harmful stereotypes in images. Show images of individuals that evoke pride, confidence, and interactions in everyday life.

Check your images for cultural sensitivity in terms of interpersonal communication and interactions. For example, it may not be culturally appropriate to show an image of a woman shaking hands with a man in a majority Muslim audience, where women and men do not typically touch one another in public settings. Don't lump people from an entire region or continent together if training for a specific group. For example, when selecting images for a training in South Korea, make sure to find images of Korean people. When training in Kenya, find images of Kenyans. You may also want to share images that show appreciation of diverse subcultures, including regions, tribes, or religious groups. When in doubt, reach out to representatives of a particular culture to check your image selections to ensure they are representative of the diversity of the audience and sensitive to cultural norms. In chapter 6, we will further explore design considerations for globally diverse audiences.

Create a Checklist for Graphics

How diverse are the graphics in terms of visible diversity (gender, skin color, sexual orientation, religion, physical or mental disability, age, and physical size or weight)?

What hair styles and clothing do people wear in the images and what message might that send? (For example, are all the images of Black women with straightened hair? Do all the images of women show thin people wearing pencil skirts and heels?)

If there are multiple people in an image, how are they interacting? Who is shown having power? Who is showing deference?

I worked on a project with a religious organization to address gender and other social identity biases in congregations and religious leadership. Although the number of women and people of color has increased significantly in this religious group's leadership, women and people of color often face bias in their communities. We created a video to raise awareness of bias, asking people to look at a variety of images of religious leaders, including White women and women of color who are part of the faith community. We showed images of people engaging in anti-stereotypical behaviors, like fathers studying with their children, men cooking for their families, gay and lesbian couples and mixed religion families celebrating religious events together, and women leading prayers. We also provided information on how women of color, plus-size women, and people with disabilities are often perceived and treated by others in biased ways. The purpose of the video was to launch dialogues on how to mitigate biases in everyday interactions and decision making in the community. It created an avenue for people to heighten their consciousness of where these biases may live in their own minds and develop new neural pathways to associate leadership in the community with people who historically have not been included.

Counter Stereotypes in Names and Roles

Have you ever noticed that every trainer's name for hypothetical characters is "Jim" or "Bob" or "Mary"? As in, "Let's say you walk into the break room and Jim is talking to Mary when their boss Bob comes in."

I mean, who are these people? Did we learn these names in training school?

The names we select can also indicate subtle stereotypes, implicit biases, and preferences. Typically, the most common names used in scenarios or hypothetical situations sound Western and White. Considering the fact that the training field is overwhelmingly White, this is indicative of the inherent biases that we all bring to our work. People will tend to immediately think of names that are most familiar (Table 4-1). The Social Security Administration lists the following as the most popular names from 1920 to 2019 (Social Security Administration 2021).

Table 4-1. **Most Popular Names**

Male	Female
1. James	1. Mary
2. John	2. Patricia
3. Robert	3. Jennifer
4. Michael	4. Linda
5. William	5. Elizabeth

So, if 82 percent of training development specialists are White (especially if they are part of the Baby Boomer and Gen X populations) they likely have a lot of people in their lives named Jim, Bob, or Mary.

What stereotypes might you perpetuate in the job functions you assign people in scenarios? For instance, what gender, race, or ethnicity are the people in positions of power (supervisors, executives)? Often, the default is to make the supervisor a male, and quite often the senior executive a White male. Who is the executive assistant? Who is the engineer? Who is the accountant? Who is the general counsel?

Check yourself for blind spots or stereotype traps, and intentionally create personas that counter the stereotypes that persist in our society.

Additionally, be intentional about using names and personas that represent diversity in terms of gender, sexual orientation, race, ethnicity, age, and national origin in your examples and scenarios.

I was supporting a large tech company in designing a training on inclusive leadership, and we developed a series of scenarios presenting identity-related team conflicts. In the first round of designing the scenarios, we chose images that represented visible diversity in terms of gender and skin color. However, we realized that we had assigned each of the characters very American, Anglo-sounding names. For example, we showed an image of a Black manager named David, and an Asian woman named Amy.

We then hit the pause button.

Research shows that job candidates who "Whiten" their names on their resumes to more Western, Anglo-sounding names get more calls for interviews (Kang et al. 2016). For example, if Dashawn changes his name on the resume to David but alters nothing else, he gets significantly more calls for interviews. Similarly, José changes his name to Joe and gets more calls.

We realized we were falling into the same trap of Anglicizing the names, which reinforces the notion that people with Anglo-sounding names are preferred to non-Anglo-sounding names. Considering that this company was globally diverse, we knew we had to do a better job representing the diversity of the workforce in terms of names as well as faces. We thus changed the names to reflect that diversity.

Create a Checklist for Names and Roles

- What names are included in the training design in terms of scenarios, cases, or descriptions?
- What names do you (or whomever is training) typically use when sharing examples?
- Whom are you "casting" in different job descriptions and what stereotypes might you perpetuate in doing so?

Be Intentional With Videos and Multimedia

Video clips are a popular method for engaging learners. People love to be entertained, whether it's watching short video clips from a movie or TV show or a TED Talk featuring a provocative or inspiring thought leader.

Who is featured in the video clips you choose?

The TED website has a playlist of the 25 most-watched talks (TED Nd). Twenty-one out of the 25 speakers are White.

If you are using videos, be intentional about showcasing diverse actors, speakers, and academics. In additional to mere representation, it's important to look for video clips that are culturally appropriate and free of biases and stereotypes.

For instance, a few years ago I was part of a team delivering leadership training that included a module on listening skills. A colleague suggested a video called "It's Not About the Nail," a comical video short featuring a couple on a couch. The woman is trying to describe a painful experience she is having to the man, who is looking uncomfortable. At one point, she describes the pain by saying, "I don't know when it's going to stop," and turns to face the man so the viewer can see a nail sticking out of her forehead. When the man tries to point out that the problem is the nail, the woman becomes frustrated and chides her partner for never listening to her. I remember chuckling, but also having a small twinge in my stomach about the gender stereotypes that were present in this video. I pushed them aside, not wanting to be overly sensitive, and agreed to play the video in the classroom. It turned out I wasn't alone in my reaction to the video. Several female participants in the training complained to me they found the video problematic in its representation of women as being overly emotional, irrational, and stubborn, and painting the man in the video as the maligned hero having to play along to appease his partner.

It was a lesson for me to be more intentional with the videos I select to ensure they are not reinforcing stereotypes.

Craft Culturally Competent and Inclusive Text

In addition to ensuring your images are representative of diversity, equity, and inclusion, consider the words you use in training.

What phrases or words might carry a different connotation that is perceived as exclusionary? For example, the phrase "off the reservation" has been used in American slang to represent a person not complying with expectations. This phrase originated from the forced removal of Native Americans from their lands, and describes the failure to comply with new laws confining them to the reservations.

These are some other common English phrases that have exclusive historical connotations:

- "Sold down the river" refers to enslaved people in the US, who were often sold farther South if they were accused of disobeying.
- "Spirit animal" is often used to describe an animal, person, or object you strongly identity with. However, for Native peoples, spirit animals, also known as "totems," are a deeply sacred spiritual tradition, and the cultural appropriation of the word can be harmful.
- "Uppity" to describe someone who is arrogant or trying to rise above their designated station. This term was used mainly by White Southerners during Reconstruction to punish Black people who did not show deference to White people.
- "Gypped/Jipped" to describe someone being cheated or swindled. This derives from a derogatory term used to describe the Roma people, who migrated from northern India all over the world. They were persecuted for generations, accused of being thieves and child abductors.

- "The peanut gallery" is often used to describe someone who needlessly criticizes or mocks others, but its origins refer to the segregated seats in theaters for Black people. "Peanut" was used because peanuts were introduced to the US at the same time as the slave trade.
- "One of the guys" to refer to women who engage in what are considered more masculine activities or who "fit in" with a male group is potentially harmful in that it intimates that women have to act more like males in order to be accepted.
- "Man up" to tell someone to be tougher or more aggressive implies that men are superior in strength and that acting like a man will lead to greater success and power.
- "Drama queen" or "diva" are often used to describe women (and sometimes gay men) as being overly emotional or demanding with the intention of getting attention. It perpetuates the stereotype of women being irrational, and it also sends the message that it is not acceptable to express one's emotions.

Also, consider what words are used to describe people that may have stereotypes embedded in them (for example, "dramatic" to describe a woman or "fiery" to describe a Latinx person).

Research shows that women and men are often evaluated differently even when they perform the same tasks, and many of the words used to evaluate them include gender stereotypes. For example, a 2018 study analyzed peer evaluations of students at the US Naval Academy. Women were assigned more negative attributes than men, and the most frequent words used to describe them indicated gender biases. They were more frequently assigned positive words like "compassionate" and "enthusiastic" and negative words like "inept," "selfish," and "frivolous." Alternatively, men received fewer negative assessments, and the words to describe them included characteristics that were more likely to support their career advancement, including words like "analytical," "competent," and "dependable" (Smith, Rosenstein, and Nikolov 2018).

It's crucial to scan any training design for opportunities to not only scrub these stereotypes but to reverse them. Implicit biases are overcome when we are consistently exposed to different ways of seeing people until it becomes normalized in our unconscious.

There are countless other terms that may be insulting or offensive to historically marginalized groups. The intent is not necessarily to be paralyzed by the potential impact of any one word or phrase in your training. Rather, it is important to become more aware of the power and history of certain phrases and do your best to erase the stereotypical language or turns of phrase that can be harmful.

Recognize Diverse Expertise and Inspiration

All too often, authors and thought leaders cited in training programs are not representative of the diversity of our population. In a search for the 25 best leadership books of all time, *Soundview Magazine* (2020) listed all male authors, almost all of whom are American and White. Similarly, Amazon's bestsellers in leadership and motivation is filled with White, male authors. The few female authors represented include books related to warmth, empathy, and female empowerment. The vast majority of inspiring leadership quotes in online databases like brainy-quote.com are by White men.

This is just for leadership and management! Consider every other training program—from technical skills to compliance training. Where are there opportunities to represent a more diverse group of leaders and authors?

Similarly, consider the real-life case studies or examples that are included in the training to illustrate best practices or application. More often than not, case studies used in training programs include stories of White, middle-aged, male leaders successfully innovating, address-ing complex challenges, or advancing their company to successful new heights. The stories often center on the success of the one leader, as though that individual singlehandedly fixed the company's problems. A lot of the case studies that are shared are myths that have been told and retold, painting the individual leader as the hero, but do not fully repre-sent the collective effort of others in the organization. Sometimes, the White male leader was actually the biggest obstacle to success!

Take, for example, the narrative of Steve Jobs, late CEO and founder of Apple. Leadership trainers love to use Steve Jobs as an example of a paragon of innovative leadership. The stories of his temper and abusive behavior toward others are often dismissed because of his vision and inspiration, as he moved from computers to the iPod to iPhones and iPads. However, the truth behind the myth is that Steve Jobs was dead set against creating a phone. He did not think anyone would want it and was perfectly happy to continue making iPods. His team had to work tirelessly to convince him to let them create the iPhone (Grant 2021). This is not a denigration of Steve Jobs's genius or ability to inspire. Rather, it is a reminder to notice who is featured in stories of success, courage, innovation, and leadership and how they reinforce implicit associations that overrepresent White men.

Think about the examples you use in your case studies and the reputation the organization or its leaders may have around DEI. For instance, a number of very successful, large companies have been spotlighted in recent years for their poor performance on DEI. If you choose to use them as a case study in a training, consider how to be purposeful or explicit in acknowledging that part of the story.

Inviting guest speakers or panels of experts to speak to your organization can be a powerful learning opportunity. However, whom you choose to speak to the group is as important as what they say. Too many times I have seen panels or multiple guest speakers who all look and sound the same and are not representative of the diversity that exists in the organization. When there is someone from a marginalized group, like a woman or person of color, consider when they are asked to speak and what subjects they have been invited to discuss. If the training includes a panel, the moderator should ensure equal airtime and elevate the voices of panelists who are part of marginalized groups. For example, if you have a White man and a Black woman, start the panel with a question to the woman.

It's also important to consider who is invited to speak and their reputation in the organization. For instance, what are the potential consequences of inviting a speaker who is a subject matter expert in a technical area but is known in the organization for engaging in disrespectful behavior or making inappropriate jokes about women? The message you are sending is that such behaviors will be overlooked in favor of the person's technical expertise. Ask yourself:

- Which organizations or leaders are represented in your real-life case studies?
    - Are you extolling the best practices of a company that has a bad track record of DEI?
    - Are the leaders in your case studies representative of diversity?
- Whom are you quoting?
    - Are your quotes mostly coming from White people? From men? From Anglo or Western cultural backgrounds?
- Whose research are you citing?
    - Are the research authors mostly male? Mostly White? Mostly from Anglo or Western cultures?
- Whom are you inviting to speak?
    - What diversity is represented among the guest speakers?
    - If you have a panel of speakers, how much airtime will each person receive?

Use Clear, Simple Language

Language is everything in training. It sets the tone, establishes the flow and pace, and drives the learning. Language and identity are deeply intertwined. The way we interpret words and phrases is dependent on a variety of dimensions of our identity—our native language, geographic upbringing, academic experience, socioeconomic background, cognitive and learning abilities, and so much more.

When we design training content, our voice becomes a prominent part of the training. Naturally, without being conscious of it, we design training in the way that we would want to learn the content. The word choices, descriptions, examples, and instructions for activities are filtered through our language lens. We often may not realize how this impacts the development of the training and how it is interpreted and understood by diverse learners.

It's important to consider the level of language complexity you use in the training as well. Will non-native English speakers be able to comprehend the content? Will the metaphors or common phrases make sense to them? For example, in the United States, certain phrases such as "it's a piece of cake" or "working the graveyard shift" are immediately recognizable to American native English speakers but may not make any sense to non-native speakers.

In addition to maintaining clear language for non-native English speakers, consider the literacy level and academic experience of the audience. Typically, the simpler the language, the better for everyone. Use short sentences with simple structure. Avoid too much descriptive language if it's not necessary to the message. This will help to ensure all learners in the training have a clear understanding of the key concepts. This is especially true when you are presenting a lot of new, technical knowledge. People may withdraw, or become frustrated or distracted, if they are on the receiving end of a firehose of new language all at once.

Ensure Accessibility

I once had a participant reach out to me in advance to request the materials prior to the training. She had dyslexia and said that it is always challenging for her in a live classroom to keep up with reading the written material. We were easily able to accommodate her request, but it was a light bulb moment for me as a trainer to offer that option in advance to any participants who needed extra time for reading or reflection, be it due to a learning disability, language proficiency, or even introversion.

Make sure the training content you design is accessible to all. If the materials are difficult to read or see, or if the activities are not accessible for those with limited mobility, not only is the learning compromised but people may also become frustrated, embarrassed, or withdrawn. By designing training with diverse abilities in mind, you create an equitable learning experience for everyone. Additionally, individuals with different needs will be able to fully focus on the training content rather than struggle to participate.

When designing accessible content, there are regulations instructional designers must follow. Section 508 of the Rehabilitation Act requires all electronic and information technology developed or used by the federal government to be accessible to people with disabilities. These can serve as guidelines for any designers to ensure their training materials are accessible.

Consider these tips for inclusive design. This is by no means an exhaustive guide for accommodation or compliance with the ADA. I recommend doing further research or working with someone who is well versed in ADA compliance to ensure your designs are compliant.

Font Style

The Americans With Disabilities Act (ADA) does not have a specific font size requirement, but compliant fonts are generally clear, clean, and distinguishable. Steer clear of cursive or handwriting styles, as they are difficult to read for the visually impaired.

Although there is no one-size-fits-all for font, sans-serif fonts are typically preferred. PixelPlex hosts a list of fonts compliant with ADA recommendations; it includes sans-serif styles like Arial, Calibri, Century Gothic, Helvetica, Tahoma, and Verdana (PixelPlex n.d.).

Many people with nearsightedness or farsightedness may struggle to see small print or images. People with dyslexia may be able to read the font size but find it difficult to distinguish certain letters. For example, l (small L), 1, and I (capital i) may all look the same to a person with dyslexia. These letters are mirror images of one another and can be difficult for people with dyslexia to differentiate:

b and d

p and q

Specialist fonts, including Dyslexie and OpenDyslexic, have been designed for people with dyslexia, are free, and are widely available to designers.

Font Size

Although there is no specific requirement for text size, website developers usually recommend at least 16px font for web body text. With print materials, a minimum of 12- or 14-point font is best. For slides, 24-point font is a best practice for body text, with a minimum of 28-point for titles.

Text Volume

For everyone's sake, keep the sentences short and simple with as few words as possible to capture a concept or learning point. I typically recommend no more than six bulleted lines of text per slide and only one line per bullet. This makes it easier for all learners to follow and is especially important for people with visual impairments and learning disabilities.

Color

Eight percent of men and 0.5 percent of women have a color vision deficiency, which is commonly referred to as "color blindness" (Prevent Blindness n.d.). This can impede their ability to differentiate between shades or colors, especially red and green, which both end up looking the same. When choosing colors for graphics or slides, use high-contrast colors to make it as easy as possible for participants to see.

Images

Graphics are a powerful way to illustrate a concept, to focus learners' attention and interest, and to convey emotions. However, graphics can be problematic for those with visual impairments.

With both digital and print materials, make sure any images you use are high definition, with simple and powerful images that are easy to understand. Include only one image per slide or page. Too much detail or too many images at once can be confusing or distracting.

When using web-based images, include "alt text" for each image. Visually impaired learners may use a digital reader, which relies on alt text to describe the image to the learner. In print materials, include a caption underneath the image with a description for a digital reader to follow.

Video and Audio

When using video clips, provide an audio description for the visually impaired. Include closed captions and a transcript for people who are deaf and hearing impaired. If using audio clips, like podcasts, make sure to provide a text transcript.

Classroom Space

I once conducted a training for a group of 100 judges in a large conference space. Although we did a considerable amount of advance preparation, I failed to ask the coordinators if anyone had physical accommodation needs. We had built the training around a large-group experiential activity that required people to get up and walk around the room and stand for a considerable amount of time to debrief the activity. This led to a number of challenges when the training commenced. Two participants used wheelchairs, and several had less-visible physical challenges that made it very difficult for them to stand for prolonged periods of time. Although we made adjustments in the moment to accommodate the needs of these individuals, it took away time and also made the individuals who needed assistance feel like a burden to their colleagues. We turned it into a learning moment to discuss the importance of creating inclusive spaces for people with different needs, but I left as a trainer feeling guilty for not having preemptively created a more inclusive learning environment. It was a reminder to always prepare for such accommodations in advance.

If the training is taking place in-person, make sure every seat has a clear line of site to the front of the room and the projector screen. Consider the space between seats and ensure there are clear aisles or pathways that are large enough for people to easily walk or maneuver a wheelchair if needed.

Provide adequate space for learners to place their personal items on or underneath chairs or tables to minimize the possibility of tripping over bags or articles of clothing.

Make sure access to the training facility and classroom are ADA compliant and have ramps, spacious elevators, and wheelchair-accessible restroom facilities.

Activities

The choice of learning method is critical for ensuring all learners are equally able to participate. Consider the choice of activity to ensure it is accessible for every learner. When designing activities that require physical activity, identify alternative options for those who may not be able to participate as easily. For instance, in a classroom exercise, if the activity requires someone to stand for a considerable amount of time, place chairs nearby and invite those who need to sit to do so. If the activity includes multiple groups working on projects in the same enclosed space, people with hearing impairments will find it difficult to hear their groups amid the ambient noise. If possible, consider using breakout rooms or separating the groups by some distance to minimize background noise.

Breaks and Transitions

Build in plenty of time for physical and mental rest. Whether the training is in-person or virtual, it's helpful to give learners a break every hour or so. Give sufficient time for restroom breaks for those who may need a little extra time, especially if restrooms are some distance away. If you have learners who are nursing, make sure to build in breaks for them to get to a designated private space to pump if they need to.

Provide advance notice when you will be transitioning from one activity to another, or when you will expect people to move around. It will take some people longer to collect their items or to stand and walk to a different space, and a little extra time and warning will give them a chance to do so without attracting unwanted attention to themselves.

Accommodations for Hearing Disabilities

If someone needs sign language interpreters, you will need to know in advance to hire at least two interpreters for the class so they can take turns. Consider how to prepare classroom space and activities to create a clear line of sight for the sign language interpreters to be seen by the participant. When delivering content, the trainer should always look at the participant when speaking or listening to the participant's response, rather than looking at the interpreter. If the participant reads lips, try to make sure they have clear visibility to you. Encourage participants at the beginning of the class to face the rest of the class when they speak for the benefit of other participants. If you have soft-spoken participants in the class, you may need to repeat in a clear voice what was said so everyone can hear.

Accommodations for Visual Disabilities

Ask in advance of the training if participants need any visual accommodations. Some participants may bring digital readers or may require a reader. Others may just need to sit close to the screen and may need materials to be printed in larger font. Blind participants will need adequate space for a support animal or cane. Make sure to create open walkways free of obstacles. For participants with visual impairment, make sure to read or describe the text and images on the slides as you present.

Delivering Inclusive Diversity Training

In addition to planning training content that represents diversity, equity, and inclusion, consider how the training should be delivered in terms of your interactions with participants in a live learning setting. Regardless of the subject matter, you as the trainer play a significant role in the learners' experience. You set the tone for the learning experience from the first moment learners enter the space.

Plan in advance what sort of learning environment you wish to create and how you will engage with learners. This includes greeting learners upon entering the space. As learners enter, you should have a consistent protocol for greeting to ensure equity. If you greet some learners as they enter, try to greet everyone in a similar way. Trainers are human beings too, and you may unconsciously fall into the very human habit of gravitating toward individuals with whom you share commonalities. This can lead to dynamics of perceived inequality if the other learners see you talking and laughing with some learners but not offering the same attentiveness to others. For instance, if an older male trainer exchanges banter with several older male participants about their favorite sports teams, but doesn't engage with female participants with the same amount of warmth or attention, this can set up a dynamic where the women in the learning space feel less included. It's often a very subtle and possibly unconscious dynamic but can have an influence on who participates and remains engaged.

Notice how you respond to different learners. We are often not aware of the subtle cues we send that drive connection or disconnection with learners. These subtle acts of communication, like nodding the head or an enthusiastic response to a comment, may indicate interest and respect, while an exhalation of breath, pressed lips, or a furrowed brow may indicate dismissiveness, disagreement, or irritation. Trainers have the power to either encourage or discourage participation and engagement, and it is often in the smallest micro-messages that these moments occur.

Consider Power Dynamics

The learning experience can be significantly affected by who is in the room and the level of comfort people have with one another. When possible, consider which learners to put together in the training program. For example, if the training is intended to provide an opportunity for honest conversations about challenging workplace issues, it may be more effective to separate managers from employees if there are low levels of trust or safety.

In addition to considering management status or position, there are less formal power dynamics that often show up in a learning environment—whether based on tenure, age, gender, academic experience, or job function. For example, if administrative and operational support staff are in the same learning environment as technical experts like engineers, there may be an unspoken power dynamic where the technical experts are automatically given more status and end up taking more "space" in the learning setting. Be intentional about inviting the perspectives of people who are in the nondominant groups to equalize the dynamic.

Mix People Up

To the extent you are able, try to ensure the training includes a diverse group of individuals. This may not be possible in open-enrollment programs, but if you are bringing a cohort of participants together for a collective learning experience, try to maximize the diversity of the group in terms of dimensions like gender, racial or ethnic background if known, age or years of experience at the organization, and so forth.

To maximize diversity in the class, consider pre-planning breakout groups or creating the seating arrangement in a physical space to mix up the participants. People tend to sit with people they know or with whom they share something in common, whether that be their racial or gender identity, or their job function or level in the organization. You can intentionally encourage diversity by assigning seats or assigning small groups to participants in advance.

Invite Learner Participation

Design and deliver the program in a way that encourages maximum participation by all learners.

Setting group learning norms at the beginning of the program is a great way to encourage active participation and set expectations for respectful, inclusive behaviors. Regardless of the content of the training, consider taking a few minutes early in the program to post behavioral norms or guidelines.

You can reinforce an inclusive learning environment in small, subtle ways, such as requesting that breakout groups nominate a representative who has not spoken up as much. Repeat back or affirm the contributions of participants in nondominant positions. For example, if a younger employee or an administrative support employee shares a story or contributes a helpful comment, you can not only affirm their contribution in the moment but also refer back to it later in the training to further reinforce the value of their contribution. This might sound like, "This next method we'll explore is similar to the best practice Asad shared earlier today."

Summary

Fostering a culture of DEI goes beyond conducting DEI training. There are a multitude of things training professionals can do to embed diversity, equity, and inclusion into any learning experience.

Whether you are creating new training content or revising existing content, bring a DEI lens to the process. Consider how diversity is represented in your content, including faces, names, text, case studies, cited resources, and guest speakers.

Make sure the training is accessible to people with different physical and cognitive needs, including making your content ADA compliant and ensuring the physical learning space accommodates diverse needs.

Finally, consider your role as a trainer in fostering an inclusive and equitable learning environment by managing learners' own implicit biases, maximizing the diversity of interactions among participants, and encouraging participation among diverse learners.

In the next chapter, we take a deeper dive into the process of delivering effective DEI training, exploring best practices to facilitate DEI dialogues and manage the intricacies of the learning environment.

Chapter 5
Delivering Transformational DEI Training

A few years ago, a colleague and I were facilitating a leadership training and decided to conduct a somewhat risky experiment. We put a line of masking tape on the floor and told participants to read two statements on the projector screen and then move to one side of the line or the other depending on the statement with which they most agreed.

The first slide was coffee versus tea, and they gamely went to their preferred side and playfully argued about the merits of their choices with the folks across the line.

In the second slide, cats versus dogs, the volume in the room rose. People on each side of the line shouted out not only what made their choice good but also what made the other side's choice bad. The cat people said things like "Cats are independent" and "Dogs are needy and require way more maintenance." The dog people argued, "Dogs love you unconditionally" and "Cats are obstinate and mean. You can't trust them."

Notice how within the space of just a few moments, the line of masking tape became a psychological as well as physical divide. Although the arguments were still playful because the emotional stakes were fairly low, participants started to build a sense of "us" with the people on their side of the tape. They heartily agreed and defended their colleagues' viewpoints. Participants looked at the people on the other side of the line as the adversary. They were far less interested in hearing what the other side's point was except to prepare their counterargument.

Then we really turned up the heat. On the slide, we showed the following two statements:

- "Athletes should have the right to kneel during the national anthem."
- "Athletes should stand and salute the flag during the national anthem."

This was at the height of the controversy over San Francisco 49ers quarterback Colin Kaepernick and other NFL players kneeling during the national anthem to protest police brutality and systemic injustice against African Americans.

The room went quiet. People hesitantly chose their sides without talking much. There were some awkward smiles exchanged but there was no laughter or joking this time. Participants didn't seem to want to look at one another.

This time, we asked the group to engage a little differently. We invited them to come forward and share their reason for choosing that side of the tape. We asked them to speak from their own experience and to share what emotions they were feeling as well. We asked everyone to be open, to listen deeply to the stories of other participants, particularly the stories of people on the other side of the line. We told them the intention was not to debate, judge, or convince anyone. The purpose was to learn and share.

A White man in his 60s stepped forward and said, "I'm a war veteran and I lost friends in combat. To me standing to salute the flag is an act of patriotism to honor those who gave the ultimate sacrifice. When I see the players kneel, I feel angry and hurt. It's like it dishonors those service members who gave their lives for our country."

There was thoughtful silence. After a moment, a Black woman in her 40s responded, "I can understand how that is painful to you, and as a veteran myself I share your pain of losing friends in combat. I stand on this side because as a Black mother I have had to give my young son the talk to tell him how to behave if he's stopped by law enforcement. I live in fear every day that he might be punished or killed because of the color of his skin. So for me, I believe that those players kneeling is an act of patriotism."

The White man listened and then said, "Thank you for giving me a different perspective. I have a son, too. That gives me a whole lot to think about."

Neither of these two participants tried to one-up each other or argue why they were right. They merely shared their personal stories and views, while also honoring the other person's experience. Not only did the two participants gain insight from their exchange, but the entire class left that dialogue changed as well.

How do we deliver transformational learning experiences?

DEI training is probably the most challenging subject to facilitate. It can be intense, emotional, and uncomfortable. It can be exhausting for both participants and trainers. It can also be the most rewarding and meaningful work a trainer does.

When done well, DEI training can be powerful, eye opening, and healing for the learners. However, there are many cases of training gone wrong, where participants and sometimes trainers leave the experience feeling wounded, angry, and even traumatized.

This chapter will explore ways to leverage experiential practices for effective learning, define the unique role of a DEI trainer, discuss best practices for facilitating DEI dialogues, provide tips for handling difficult situations, and examine ways to develop your ability to facilitate challenging or uncomfortable DEI conversations.

Experiential Learning and DEI

David Kolb's experiential learning cycle has long been an industry standard for training designers and instructors. Kolb's model of experiential learning outlines four stages (1984). Let's look at each stage in the context of DEI:

- **Concrete experience.** In this phase of the cycle, participants encounter a new situation or experience or reinterpret an existing experience. In DEI training, it is crucial to engage participants as active players in their learning. Concrete experiences invite participants to explore new ways of thinking about identity, become aware of potential identity blind spots or biases, and expose themselves to new behaviors to promote inclusion. The concrete experience is essential to re-create human interactions in the classroom that represent the kinds of diversity-related challenges people experience in the real world, as well as to provide a platform for participants to discuss how those experiences in the real-world impact them.

- **Reflective observation.** In this phase, participants take time to reflect on their reaction to the concrete experience. They begin to make meaning of the experience and identify inconsistencies between the experience and their own understanding or knowledge. This is an important part of DEI training. Participants need time to process their emotions related to the new content or situation they just experienced. Reflective observation is often a place of self-discovery in DEI training, where participants come face-to-face with situations and perspectives that challenge their beliefs about themselves and others. They often experience some internal conflict, and even interpersonal conflict, when processing the experience. The reflective observation also helps demonstrate that diverse individuals process the concrete experience differently because of their identity.

- **Abstract conceptualization.** In this phase, participants begin to generalize the learning and draw new conclusions based on their reflection of the concrete experience. They make connections between the new learning and their real-life experiences. They form new ideas or modify existing ones. In DEI training, this is crucial to guide the process of answering the question, "So what?" Participants are more likely to retain the new awareness and knowledge if they see its relevance to their real world.

- **Active experimentation.** In this phase, participants apply the new learning to their surroundings or make modifications in the next experience. This phase helps participants explore how they can use what they have learned in future scenarios. It also encourages commitment to action and behavioral change by allowing participants to practice new skills in a safe learning environment.

ACTIVITY: UNCOVERING HIDDEN ASSUMPTIONS AND GROUP DYNAMICS

The objective of this activity is to explore how quickly people classify themselves and others by groups and unconsciously engage in exclusionary behaviors.

Concrete Experience

In this part, the facilitator asks participants to close their eyes. The facilitator places different-colored dot stickers on each participant's back so they cannot see what sticker they have but others can. In advance of the exercise the facilitator will have identified how many of each colored dot sticker to use, to ensure that some groups are far larger, some are smaller, and one person has a color that nobody else has.

The facilitator then tells the group the only rules of the exercise are that nobody is allowed to talk, and they can't remove the stickers from their own or anyone else's back. Then the facilitator says, "Find your group." Participants then have to silently move around the room and decide how to group themselves. Once the group has settled and nobody else is still debating where to go, the facilitator calls time and begins the debrief.

Reflective Observation

The facilitator asks participants questions to reflect on the experience.

- How were you able to find your group?
- How did you know what group you belonged to?
- What did you observe others doing in this exercise?
- Who had a different experience? For the person with the singular colored dot, what was that like for you?
- What assumptions did you make? What was the impact of making those assumptions?

Abstract Conceptualization

The facilitator asks questions to help participants add meaning and connect the experience to real world examples.

- When do we make similar assumptions in our work or personal lives?
- What groups do you see in your organizations? How do similar behaviors show up in your organization, with certain people being invited into a group while others are pushed out?
- How might minority groups or solo status individuals experience your organizational environment?
- What behaviors (inclusive or exclusive) that you witnessed in this activity show up in your organization, and what is the impact?

Active Experimentation

The facilitator asks questions and participants discuss actions they will take based on this exercise.

- If we conducted this exercise again, knowing what you do now, how would you approach it differently?
- What can you do to challenge unhealthy group dynamics in your organization?
- What specific practices will you engage in to ensure people from other identity groups feel included and valued in your organization?

Connect Head, Heart, and Hands

As we covered in chapter 3, experiential learning requires a combination of intellectual, emotional, and practical learning. Participants need to be exposed to new information and knowledge that is not only of interest but clearly relevant to their lives, their needs, and their goals. Participants also need to feel an emotional connection to the new knowledge or experience. In DEI training, this is a crucial component for attitude and behavior change. The learning has to strike a deep emotional chord in the participants. DEI training will unquestionably bring forth strong emotional reactions. The training has to be designed with the intention to harness those powerful emotions in a constructive way. That's where the hands come into play. The learning must be practical. Participants need to be able to answer the question, "Now what?" They need to be exposed to concrete tools, and have space to apply new skills.

Let the Learners Drive

Individuals learn best when they feel a sense of autonomy. Self-directed learning places the power in the hands of the learners to manage their own journey, rather than being told what to think and what to do.

In DEI training, participants are bringing so many dimensions of their identity with them into the learning space. They experience the learning activities through their unique individual lenses, and their reactions to each learning activity will be colored by that unique identity lens. Their learning needs will also be different based on their lived experiences and their identities. It's important for instructors to balance the structure of the curriculum with the flexibility to accommodate the unique group dynamics of each class. In DEI training, it is often in the less fettered exercises and group discussions where participants learn the most from one another.

Explore Learning Edges

Individuals learn when they are stretched outside of their comfort zones. Experiential learning encourages participants to expand beyond their current knowledge and skills, providing a safe space for experimentation and error.

In DEI training this is inevitable and essential. Effective DEI training invites people to engage in self-discovery, to explore ideas and beliefs that may be drastically different from their own, and to lean into conversations on topics that are fraught. Instructors need to create a safe environment for people to have uncomfortable moments, to ask questions, to make mistakes, and to learn from their mistakes.

The Paradoxes of DEI Training

In DEI training, trainers must play a unique role. DEI training requires a high level of agility in their ability to change course, switch up methods, and respond to the shifting dynamics in the classroom. There needs to be structure and an adherence to the agenda, but also an ability to recognize when the conversation that spontaneously emerges from an activity needs to go longer even if it takes up more time.

There are often multiple emotional arcs occurring simultaneously in a DEI class. While some participants may be engaged and enthusiastic, others may be resistant, defensive, even angry. While some may feel like their stories of oppression and injustice are finally free to be given voice, others may struggle with shock, guilt, and even shame when encountering new awareness of how they may have been contributing to the problem. And yet others may be skeptical or suspicious of the program and the content, but for very different reasons.

In DEI training, you have to be able to balance seeming paradoxes:

Be an Objective Observer and Be Immersed in the Shared Experience of the Class

It is critical that the facilitator be fully present in every moment of the class, observing individuals' verbal and nonverbal reactions, facial expressions, gestures, and interactions with other participants to monitor the emotional climate in the classroom. Due to the sensitivity of the content and the deep degree of self-exploration these learning experiences create, the trainer has to be very aware of how people are feeling. Simultaneously, the facilitator is co-creating the learning environment with the participants. The facilitator should never become an active participant, but does need to be fully aware of how their relationship with the participants is symbiotic. They are influencing the group dynamic through their emotions and behaviors, and at the same time the emotions and behaviors of the group are influencing them.

Be Neutral and Emotionally Vulnerable

Facilitators must maintain neutrality. They should avoid taking sides in a conflict or debate or pressuring others to share their political or cultural ideologies. Yet they cannot be robots either. The facilitator has to bring compassion and warmth to the learning environment. The facilitator can encourage others to be vulnerable by sharing their own stories and experiences. It can be especially valuable to share stories of mistakes made to demonstrate that nobody is perfect when it comes to DEI. Everyone makes mistakes and sometimes unintentionally steps on some toes, and everyone has the capacity to learn and grow.

Practice Deep Empathy and Hold People Accountable for Exclusive or Insensitive Behaviors

Facilitators must encourage others to practice deep levels of empathy, to ensure that each participant has the opportunity to share their experiences and emotions without judgment or dismissal. At the same time, if a participant shares an opinion or ideology that contributes to oppression or disparity against an identity group, or if a participant engages in behaviors or speech that are hurtful to others, the facilitator has the responsibility to stop the behavior from continuing. It can be a powerful learning moment for the individual engaging in the behavior, as well as for everyone else who observes the behavior.

Open up the Space for Conflict, Emotion, and Discomfort and Know When to Close the Conversation

DEI facilitators must create a learning environment that encourages people to enter uncomfortable conversations on issues that may have historically been off limits in the workplace. DEI training requires people to get uncomfortable, to explore identity-based biases, stereotypes, privileges, oppression, and even trauma. Simultaneously, the facilitator must properly determine when and how to resolve conflict, move forward, and draw the discussion to a close. Otherwise, participants may leave feeling frustrated or angry.

Have a Structure and Detailed Agenda and Improvise in the Moment to Capture Important Learning

DEI training is a dance that requires well-rehearsed choreography, leaving space for improvisation based on the environment and the reaction and energy of the audience. Facilitators need to have a solid structure in place to cover the learning objectives, especially when time is constrained. DEI training always requires a significant amount of time up front to set the stage and get people comfortable enough to open themselves up to explore the subject matter, be vulnerable, and be open to the cognitive dissonance that accompanies DEI work. Yet, the true magic of DEI training often happens in the unrehearsed moments, in the spontaneous conversations that participants create. Often, facilitators will find themselves having to adjust the agenda to allow for the rich and necessary dialogues to take place among participants.

Your Role in DEI Training

Those who conduct DEI training may find themselves playing several distinct roles throughout the training, depending on the topic, the learning methods, and the audience. They are:

- **Instructor.** You are acting as the subject matter expert, providing new knowledge and skills to the audience.
- **Facilitator.** You are acting as a guide to an open-ended dialogue that is driven by the participants.
- **Mediator.** You are mediating a conflict or debate between individuals or groups who have opposing views of an issue.

One of the critical skills for leading effective DEI training is to engage participants in dialogue. What is dialogue?

The word *dialogue* is derived from the Greek word *dialogos*. Let's break down the origin of this word to seek the true meaning of dialogue:

Dia = "*through*"

Logos = "*the word.*"

Therefore, think of dialogue as a flow of conversation that runs through a group of people, where the group collectively creates new meaning and understanding from each individual's thoughts and ideas. In his book *On Dialogue* David Bohm (1996) describes the purpose of dialogue as a way of "sharing a common content, even if we don't agree entirely."

How is dialogue different than discussion or debate?

In a discussion, the purpose may be to exchange, break down, and analyze individuals' ideas and opinions. Although this may create opportunities for different perspectives to be heard, it is more focused on breaking down the differences between ideas.

In debate, the purpose of the exchange is to present one's ideas or opinions as the right way to think. The intent is to win and to showcase the faults or inaccuracies of others' perspectives. There is no acceptance of multiple realities in a debate.

In DEI training, dialogue provides a space for exploring individual ideas and experiences with equal amounts of curiosity and the intent to co-create a shared reality that comprises all the realities existing in the group. Although discussion and even debate may have some use at times in DEI training, these approaches should be employed with caution because they can easily ostracize individuals and work against the purpose of DEI training, which is to encourage collective understanding and create a sense of community.

Psychological Safety in DEI Training

The facilitator's most important responsibility is creating a learning environment where all participants feel free to share their views, experiences, and concerns.

What Is Psychological Safety?

Harvard Business School professor Amy Edmondson coined the term *psychological safety*, defining it as a "shared belief held by members of a team that the team is safe for interpersonal risk-taking."

Edmondson says that psychological safety is "a sense of confidence that the team will not embarrass, reject or punish someone for speaking up" (Edmondson 2019).

In the context of the DEI classroom, the "team" Edmondson refers to is the group comprising both the participants and the facilitators. The facilitator plays a critical role in setting up the environment for psychological safety, but the responsibility to maintain psychological safety lies with everyone participating in the learning.

The DEI classroom must be a shared space that is held together by interpersonal trust and mutual respect. Experiential learning by its nature must encourage people to push themselves beyond their comfort zones, to take risks, to experiment and make mistakes. DEI training is most effective when people feel free not only to express themselves and their opinions and past experiences without fear of being ridiculed, but also to be motivated to challenge their beliefs, explore their hidden biases, and acknowledge how their actions or inactions may adversely impact others.

Edmondson says there are three key activities needed to build and sustain psychological safety:

1. Set the stage. Make sure everyone is clear and committed to the mission, goals, and purpose. In DEI training, this means:

- Clearly define the learning objectives and expectations of the group at the beginning of the training.
- Collectively set communication norms for facilitators and participants. Norms may include:
   - Everyone gets equal airtime to speak
   - Listen to understand others
   - Speak your honest opinion (use "I" statements)
   - Validate others' emotions even if you disagree
   - Leave perfection at the door
   - Give feedback to help others learn

2. Invite engagement. Encourage everyone to share their ideas, concerns, and thoughts, even if they're not sure they will be 100 percent right. This goes against our human instinct to avoid acknowledging inaccuracies or mistakes because we fear we will be judged or punished. Remind people of the complexity of the issue to build confidence among participants to take chances:

- Remind participants often of the importance of hearing all voices and opinions
- Share your own experiences of when you have made mistakes or offended others
- Pay attention to nonverbal cues and check in with, "I noticed you raised an eyebrow just now; what are you thinking about?"

3. **Respond productively.** Listen with intent to understand and appreciate others' contributions. Allow people to make mistakes without punishment or judgment. Offer constructive feedback:

- Respond in a neutral tone when someone makes a mistake or says something inflammatory.
- Encourage discourse rather than punishment or shaming. "Let's unpack this because I think it's a learning moment for us all."
- Be open to feedback from others. Invite and accept participant feedback on how you are doing as an instructor or facilitator.

Dialogue and Mindset

What is the growth mindset?

Not only do we hold biases about others, but we also hold them about ourselves. When we believe that personal characteristics are immutable, we can't create a path for expansion and change.

In her many years of research, psychologist and scholar Carol Dweck found that human beings have two mindsets they can adopt. Like two pathways that diverge, each mindset will lead to radically different beliefs, behaviors, and results. When we are explorers on this great journey of existence together, the opportunities are limitless. The Buddhist saying "For the learner there are endless possibilities; for the expert there are none" is a perfect example of this dichotomy. People who bring a growth mindset are endlessly curious, eager to stretch and challenge themselves, and accept making mistakes. They still may feel pain when they fail, but their failures don't define them.

Fixed mindset people become nonlearners. They literally turn off the learning receptors in their brains. When they receive feedback, they only tune in to messages that focus on their performance. Fixed mindset people want to be praised and rewarded for being superior, special, perfect. They get defensive when they receive feedback; they beat themselves up and lose not only confidence but also interest in activities where they don't succeed. If something feels challenging, they give up and look for what is stable, easy, and comfortable. If they fail, they never accept blame; it's never their fault. They scapegoat.

Dweck's work reinforces the importance of encouraging participants to open themselves up to divergent perspectives and ideas: "True self-confidence is "the courage to be open—to welcome change and new ideas regardless of their source" (Dweck 2006).

Can we be a little bit of both? Yes, we all have both mindsets. It's not an either/or. And one mindset or the other may become more prominent in different situations. We have choice. When we are intentional about adopting a growth mindset, we reap the benefits for ourselves, our teams, our organizations.

How do you tap into the growth mindset in the DEI classroom?

Your role as a DEI trainer is to cultivate an environment that encourages the growth mindset for your participants, and you need to model it yourself. Not only is it conducive to the experiential learning process, but this mindset is also linked to overcoming biases and the impact of stereotypes.

This may show up differently for members of dominant and nondominant identity groups. Members of a dominant identity group often fall into fixed mindset traps such as:

- "I'm not a (racist, sexist, homophobe)" or "I treat everyone the same."
- "I'm worried to say or do the wrong thing and be ridiculed so I'll stay silent or avoid the issue."
- "I don't see any of these issues in my team, organization, or community. This is a waste of time."
- "I'm already an ally. It's all those other people who need to change."

The fixed mindset can be triggered when people who belong to marginalized identity groups are reminded of stereotypes about them. As we discussed in chapter 3, Claude Steele found in his research that people often internalize negative stereotypes about themselves that can impede their performance. His research also indicates that when people adopt a growth mindset, they are are able to ignore the distracting self-talk that tells them they are inferior (Steele 2011).

Dweck found a similar pattern in her work. Among college women studying math and science, those with a growth mindset actually reported feeling a sense of belonging in their math classes. "They were able to maintain this even when they thought there was a lot of negative stereotyping going around . . . the stereotyping was disturbing to them (as it should be), but they could still feel comfortable with themselves and confident about themselves in a math setting. They could fight back" (Dweck 2006). On the other hand, those stuck in a fixed mindset found their confidence and sense of belonging withering. Dweck said, "the stereotype of low ability was able to invade them."

To encourage the growth mindset and overcome the fixed mindset in DEI training:

- Reinforce the importance of experimentation and openness. Remind participants that we are all humans on this journey, and none of us is an expert.
- Acknowledge when someone asks a question or shares an experience that felt risky for them.
- Ask for and receive feedback openly to demonstrate that you don't know it all either and appreciate new perspectives and ways of thinking.
- Gently challenge anyone who seems to have all the answers.
- Actively seek out and encourage input from members of non-dominant groups.

Preparing for Dialogue

Think of improvisational artists, including improv actors, jazz musicians, and freestyle dancers or rap artists. Improvisation is the act of making something that was not planned or rehearsed. It is completely new and built through a collaboration among the artists performing together.

Dialogue is like a form of improvisational art. Every dialogue is unique, built upon the individual contributions of the people brought together in that moment. Although it is by nature dynamic and fluid, built upon the unique collection of individuals involved and the moment in time in which it takes place, there is still an underlying foundation and structure upon which dialogue facilitators need to anchor themselves. Dialogue requires planning, practice, and preparation. Just as improvisational artists study and practice basic skills exhaustively prior to the performance, dialogue facilitators need to have a foundational skill set to apply to every dialogue. They also need to equip participants with the basic tools and behavioral norms to navigate the dialogue:

- Use these tips to prepare yourself for dialogue:
  - Set an intention. This doesn't mean you establish predictive outcomes. Dialogue is open-ended and will go where it needs to go, but have an intention for how you will show up, and how you will hold the space for others. Again, think of the improv artists who have a general sense of what they want even though much of the fun lies in the mystery of what will come about.
  - Name your own assumptions. Examine them, question them, and maybe see if you can let some of them go.
  - Get centered. Do some deep-breathing exercises. Imagine success. Engage in a mindfulness practice.
  - Consider the context—what is happening in the world, the news, the organization, your life, your participants' lives.
- Preparing participants for dialogue:
  - Consider pre-work or reading about dialogue
  - Share learning objectives
  - Create group norms
- Preparing space for dialogue and logistics (time, place, size of group):
  - Consider diverse team of facilitators
  - Set aside about two hours
  - Eight to 12 people is ideal for intimacy and equal participation; if you have more, definitely have two facilitators
- Location considerations:
  - In person: consider a large enough space for people to sit in different setups; consider a circle without tables or small

table groups for a larger class; make sure the space is hospitable (think about images on walls, lighting)

- ○ Virtual: use webcams and audio if possible so participants can see each other; limit distractions; consider breakout rooms if it's a larger group or for partner exercises

Practice Areas for DEI Training Delivery

In this section I describe five core practice areas for effective DEI training and facilitation. These are applicable to most interpersonal or human-centered topics and are particularly important to build psychological safety and engage all participants in inclusive dialogue:

- Cultivate curiosity
- Build community
- Acknowledge complexity
- Welcome healthy heat
- Build a constructive experience

Cultivate Curiosity

Ask questions and listen deeply. Override the instinct to tell, advise, or argue. Suspend judgment. Bring a truly open mindset to learn and understand and invite participants to do the same.

In his book *Humble Inquiry: The Gentle Art of Asking Instead of Telling*, Edgar Schein (2013) describes the importance of bringing an attitude of interest and curiosity to our interactions with others to build a relationship and more open communication.

Ask Questions

Although the word "question" automatically implies a mindset of curiosity, that's not always the case in practice. We are conditioned to tell rather than ask, and even when we do ask questions our intent is not always one of openness. We ask rhetorical or even accusatory questions, to prove our own points of view or win an argument. This is especially common when the conversation brings forth divergent or dissonant perspectives or beliefs. If individuals feel their beliefs or values are being challenged, they are likely to react defensively ("Yes, but don't you agree that . . . ?"). If they are given feedback that their behaviors are negatively impacting others, they are often prone to justify, excuse, or deflect ("That wasn't my intention. Don't you think you're reading too much into this?"). The cognitive dissonance participants inevitably face in DEI conversations can make it difficult to come from a mindset of curiosity.

Asking curious questions is a key practice for facilitators to leverage to help the participants stay in dialogue, to remain curious and focused on learning from one another. The intent is to understand others' experiences and perspectives, to challenge existing paradigms, and to collectively explore new insights.

Curious questions build psychological safety for the participants because they demonstrate openness, interdependence, and vulnerability. They empower the participants to drive the conversation, to fill the learning vessel themselves rather than have the facilitator tell them what to think or do.

Curious questions can be used to open up the dialogue, explore, assess, challenge, discover, and resolve.

Tips for asking curious questions:

- Start with "what" or "how." These types of questions imply that the questioner believes they have something to learn from others and demonstrates care.
- Keep it short and simple. Focus on one simple question at a time. Don't compound the question, add too many details, or create multiple sub-questions. The best questions are the simple ones. For example, "What does that word mean for you?" or "How does this occur in your workplace?"
- Ask questions you don't know the answer to. In dialogue, nobody is a trial lawyer. Curious questions imply that you as the question asker are open to hearing any number of responses. Curious questions are never rhetorical or leading. The give the power to the responder to share their perspectives, ideas, and beliefs. Curious questions are asked with the intent to empathize and learn.

Listen Deeply

Stephen Covey said, "Most people do not listen with the intent to understand; they listen with the intent to reply" (1989). Listening with the intent to understand is crucial to effective dialogue, and it goes well beyond merely hearing the words people say. Facilitators must listen with their ears, eyes, and intuition. It is often what is unspoken that reveals a great deal about participants' emotions or reactions to what is occurring in the conversation. In DEI dialogues, this is especially the case. Individuals may have differing levels of comfort expressing their honest feelings or experiences related to privilege, unconscious bias, stereotypes, oppression, discrimination, or harassment, to name a few. Each person participating in the dialogue is bringing a lifetime of experiences that have shaped their beliefs and behaviors.

Because dialogue is a fluid, dynamic process that is built moment by moment by the people participating, there is no way of predicting how individuals may respond or react to what is said. Therefore, the facilitator has to be fully focused on the energy and emotional state of the group, and simultaneously conscious of how each individual reacts to what is happening in the dialogue.

Facilitators must listen at the contextual level and encourage those participating in the dialogue to do the same. When we listen at that deeper level, we offer people a rare gift—the gift of being seen and heard and understood. Consider these levels:

- **Level 1: internal listening.** You may "hear" a person's words, but you're listening only for what you already think you know or what you want to hear and focusing on your response. You pay little attention to the person's nonverbal cues, and do not attempt to understand the meaning of the person's message more fully. Internal listening sometimes occurs at an even more extreme level, where you literally don't hear or notice what a person said. You may mentally "wander off," get lost in your own thoughts, and completely miss what was said in the dialogue.
- **Level 2: surface-level listening.** You pay attention to the person's words and emotions to understand them insofar as you can

make a connection to your own experiences, needs, and ideas. At this level, you are paying attention to the other individual's words and body language to gather information about their emotions. Yet your inner monologue is still activated, and it takes over. Typical responses that indicate you are doing surface-level listening include things like "That reminds me of a time when I . . ." or "What I would do in that situation is . . ." or "Something like that happened to me once . . ."

- **Level 3: contextual listening.** *Context* refers to the circumstances or conditions that contribute to an idea, statement, or situation, and can help it be processed and understood more fully. Contextual listening is holistic. It takes into account all the factors, past and present, that may affect the moment that is occurring in the dialogue. In contextual listening, you activate your intuition and are tuned in to the information about the other person's emotions, beliefs, and opinions that accompany the message. It's like listening to their head and their heart at the same time. You listen and notice changes in expression, energy, and group dynamics in yourself and others. You can make sense of what is happening in a space, even if no one tells you in words.

Build Community

 Embrace multiple realities, practice empathy, and use storytelling to develop trust and encourage vulnerability. Building community helps participants establish a common purpose from which to build their collective experience.

Embrace Multiple Realities

Acknowledge that one's perception of the "truth" is just that: a perception, based on that person's lived experiences. Facilitators must not only accept but actively encourage divergent perspectives to be voiced. Participants in the dialogue very likely have differing and even opposing views on issues related to diversity, equity, and inclusion. If they do not feel comfortable sharing their honest opinions and experiences for fear of being judged or ridiculed, they may stay silent and the opportunity for learning is lost.

In September 2019, the America in One Room experiment brought together more than 500 American citizens representing the geographic, cultural, and economic diversity that exists in the US for a four-day event where they were asked to talk about complex and divisive issues concerning the nation: immigration, climate change, taxes and the economy, foreign policy, and healthcare. It was the first time many of the participants were asked to share their views in close quarters with someone who belonged to the "other" side.

What happened amazed both the researchers and the participants. People came together, and just talked. They disagreed without dehumanizing one another. They discussed sensitive issues by sharing their personal stories. They were vulnerable with each other. In doing so, people softened their views of one another. Many promised to stay in touch after the event.

By the end of the four days, almost every participant agreed they learned a lot about people very different from themselves. They saw what others' lives were like and could appreciate their stories even if they didn't agree with their views.

Facilitators can embrace multiple realities by inviting discord but encouraging outside opinions. Sometimes the facilitator may need to play devil's advocate by offering opposing viewpoints as an opportunity to learn rather than an opportunity to criticize.

Embracing multiple realities can also be used as a mechanism for responding to exclusive or stereotypical comments. Rather than shutting down the person who said it, the facilitator can ask the group what other experiences or opinions may be in the room. For example, if a participant says, "I don't want to end up prioritizing diversity instead of hiring the most qualified people," the facilitator may respond with, "Thanks for sharing that opinion. I'm curious what other opinions people may have." This ensures the facilitator can remain neutral but does not permit potentially offensive statements to go unchallenged.

To embrace multiple realities consider asking questions such as:

- What life experiences led you to believe what you do?
- What if someone from that identity group was with us now? What might their perspective be?
- What other perspectives haven't we explored yet?

Practice Empathy

When facilitating dialogues on DEI, facilitators have to practice empathy at this depth, and to encourage participants to empathize as well. Let's break it down into two key practices: perspective taking and compassion:

- **Perspective taking.** Research has shown that perspective taking is a key indicator of effective DEI training. People are more likely to change attitudes and behaviors when they can take on the perspective of others, especially individuals who have lived a very different life experience.
- **Compassion.** Compassion requires us to practice empathic concern, where we genuinely care about others' well-being. Practicing compassion for those with whom we deeply disagree is a core practice for effective DEI dialogue.

This is easier said than done. We are the narrators of our own stories of hardship. And we often find ourselves wanting to "one up" each other when we have stories of being oppressed. It takes real effort to practice curiosity and compassion when we so naturally feel compelled to judge, to blame, to ask "What about . . . ?" The truth is, we all have facets of our identity that automatically give us advantages and disadvantages. Our stories of pain do not preclude any of us from having privilege in certain situations.

Storytelling

Storytelling has been a part of human life since the beginning. Telling stories provides valuable data about the experiences that contributed to individuals' beliefs and perspectives. It also creates emotional connection between the storyteller and their audience. Facilitators can use stories to:

- Build credibility and trust
- Connect with different participants
- Make content come to life
- Show vulnerability
- Demonstrate skills in action

For example, I was facilitating a diversity training and wanted to highlight the importance of becoming aware of unconscious biases and preferences. Rather than share the mountain of research I had accumulated on bias and preference, I told the following story:

Early in my career I was asked to manage two college interns for a couple of months. The first intern and I developed a great relationship. She had studied in the same program at the same university I had attended. She was a White American woman from the Midwest, just like me. She came in every day to talk with me, to ask questions, and to volunteer for more work. I was impressed with her and gave her extra encouragement and support. The other intern was also from the same university program. She was South Korean. She came in every day and went to her desk. Whereas the American intern asked for more projects sometimes even before her current assigned work was complete, the South Korean intern did what was assigned to her, and then waited until I checked her progress. She never volunteered or asked to do more. She didn't share her aspirations or ask me career questions like the American intern. I increasingly paid less attention to her, confused and somewhat irritated by what I deemed her "lack of interest." It was only after the internships ended that I realized how my own blind spots, my preference for the person who looked and talked and acted like me, had influenced my own decisions and behaviors with these two individuals. It was a huge wake-up call to me about how easily we can fall into the trap of bias. I keep the story of the two interns in the forefront of my mind every time I am recruiting, interviewing, hiring, and managing others. I want to be conscious and intentional about how I communicate with and lead others so I don't make the same mistake.

As a facilitator, it's a good idea to decide in advance what content or subject matter would be best represented by a personal story, and then take the time to write the story out and practice it in advance. This is especially important if the story brings forth strong emotions for you. Many personal stories of identity, especially those that highlight experiences or observations of prejudice, bias, discrimination, harassment, or bullying, can be retraumatizing for participants who have experienced something similar, as well as for the storyteller. You want to be vulnerable in your storytelling, but also be able to tell the story without getting emotionally hijacked. If you are still harboring intense feelings, be they anger, fear, guilt, or shame, it is best to wait until you can share the story in a way that best serves the learning of the group.

Acknowledge Complexity

 Exploring issues related to DEI can be messy and overwhelming. People may feel misunderstood, marginalized, or attacked. Assume noble intent, and focus on the impact of actions. Use "Yes, and . . . " thinking to validate different experiences and perspectives.

Assume Noble Intent, and Focus on Impact

It is going to happen: Someone will say something that causes a negative reaction in someone else. In DEI dialogues, we are opening up the doors to dissenting opinions and authentic perspectives and beliefs. Inevitably, a comment or behavior will be an emotional trigger. It's important to balance empathy, compassion, and curiosity with accountability for behaviors that are exclusive in nature, have a negative impact on other participants, or generally derail the dialogue.

When that occurs, the facilitator has to be ready to name the harmful comment and respond to it in a constructive way. Often, when people are given feedback that their actions were offensive, they respond defensively. When the response is "That wasn't my intent," or "You're taking this the wrong way," it can have a chilling effect on the dialogue. The underlying message in that response is, "Because I didn't have bad intentions, you don't have a right to feel the way you do."

The facilitator in that moment needs to do two things: Acknowledge positive intent (or at least lack of malicious intent) and, more importantly, lead the group in a conversation where the person or people who are offended can explain the impact of the statement or action on them.

Maya Angelou said, "When we know better, we do better." But we often can't learn how to be better if we feel accused, judged, or criticized. So start with stating an assumption of good intent. As civilized human beings in professional environments, most people do not mean harm and are trying to do right by others. Yet, we all have our blind spots when it comes to identity. We are often unaware of the impact of our words or deeds on others until they give us feedback. Facilitators can help people become more open to feedback from their peers if they first acknowledge good intentions. For example, if a participant makes a statement that is potentially offensive, or if you notice another participant seems upset by a statement, pause the dialogue and engage in an intent versus impact moment.

Then move to discussing the impact. It's important to reinforce to the person who made the offensive statement that having good intentions is not enough, and trying to explain or justify your actions by saying you meant well can actually be detrimental. Request that the person lean in to the power of listening, to being curious about the impact of their actions on others. If nobody in the group expressed offense, but you as the facilitator heard a statement that is potentially offensive, you may need to name it yourself and explain its potential impact on others.

For example, in the middle of a dialogue, a participant makes a statement about gender identity and pronouns and jokingly says, "I guess we have to all walk around naming our pronouns . . . he/they/it? What's the latest?" Some participants chuckle; others say nothing. There is no one in the dialogue who presents as genderqueer, but the facilitator knows this is an opportunity to align intent and impact.

Check intent: "Let's pause for a moment here. It sounds as though you have some confusion and maybe frustration with the request others make to refer to them by nonbinary pronouns. Is that right? It can be confusing and even uncomfortable for people who don't have the same experience or haven't met many folks in the trans or queer community."

Describe impact: "There are a lot of individuals who do not wish to conform to socially defined behaviors or characteristics typically associated with being either masculine or feminine. There are people whose identity is different from the expectations of the sex that was assigned to them at birth. It's likely that they have suffered a lot because of this aspect of their identity. By calling them by the pronoun they request, we can honor them and the courage it has probably taken for them to be their authentic selves."

As a facilitator, you can also explain intent versus impact using the following analogy:

If we accidentally step on someone's toe, do we say, "I'm sorry," or do we respond with the following:

"Well, I didn't mean to step on your toe," "I don't care when people step on my toes. I don't understand why it's such a big deal," "Everyone gets their toes stepped on sometimes. You need to just toughen up," or "It's not my problem that you are in pain."

When we acknowledge the impact of our actions, we not only show we care but we also learn how to do better the next time.

"Yes, and . . ."

Coming from the world of improvisational theater, "Yes, and . . ." requires actors to build a scene together on the stage by constantly adding to what another person says or does. In improv theater, actors are told to "bring a brick, not a cathedral" (Leonard and Yorton 2015). This requires collaboration and attention.

This technique implies that whatever is shared by one person has value and can be built upon to construct a fruitful dialogue. When people come with their own personal agendas or add statements that are not in service of building the scene together, improv actors call this "badprov" because the scene doesn't have the openness to go anywhere.

DEI dialogue invites dissent, which automatically can become divisive; for example, many feel compelled to say, "yes, but . . ." or "what about . . ." or "that is wrong and here's why." When we fall into "yes, but . . ." thinking, the scene cannot build. The dialogue goes nowhere.

"Yes, and" is the embodiment of embracing multiple realities. We validate another person's contribution, even when we disagree, in order to add our own perspective, story, or belief.

Welcome Healthy "Heat"

 Effective DEI training provides various degrees of intensity, where participants take ownership of their emotions and invite good controversy to thoughtfully address the divergent experiences.

Emotional Ownership

Our conflicts around identity carry emotions—of pride, anger, fear, even grief. Emotional ownership means recognizing how our emotions influence our stories while also managing those emotions so they don't cloud our ability to take the perspective of others.

Many of us are taught to leave emotions out of our conversations, and we may fear that expressing emotions can have repercussions. It is true that when our emotional triggers are pressed it activates our amygdala, which can incite us to tune out other perspectives or experiences that challenge our beliefs. However, not expressing emotions can be problematic, especially for those individuals from marginalized identity groups who have consistently been punished for trying to bring attention to their experiences. Women—and women of color in particular—often face additional scrutiny for expressing their genuine emotions.

In her book *Good and Mad: The Revolutionary Power of Women's Anger*, Rebecca Traister (2018) says,

> We must come to recognize—those of us who feel anger, who
> have in our lives taken pains to disguise it, who worry about
> its ill effects, who rear back from it and try to tamp it down

in ourselves for fear that letting it out will hurt our goals—that anger is often an exuberant expression. It is the force that injects energy, intensity, and urgency into battles that must be intense and urgent if they are to be won.

The key is to create a space where people can name their emotions and simultaneously create space for others to do the same.

Invite "Good Controversy"

In *The Art of Gathering*, Priya Parker (2018) defines good controversy as "the kind of contention that helps people look more closely at what they care about, when there is danger but also real benefit in doing so."

A dialogue where everyone's intent is to preserve decorum and harmony is not only boring but also can do more damage than good. It demonstrates a lack of psychological safety if people are not willing to disagree, to let the conversation become contentious.

Good controversy invites participants to have honest conversations about their core values and beliefs, their lived experiences, and their concerns.

Parker explores ways to intentionally bring "heat" to our conversations without burning the house down. She suggests plotting out a "heat map" to identify the most contentious or taboo subjects and determining the best way to discuss them (Parker 2018).

You need to give participants the proper equipment to withstand the hotter topic areas, and that's where group norms are crucial. In DEI training, it's also important to structure the learning experience to ease people in with less risky activities to get them warmed up for the hotter conversations. This helps to establish a baseline of comfort and trust before tackling the more contentious issues.

Build a Constructive Experience

 DEI training and dialogues provide a space for exploring the past, present, and future. Create space for honoring silence to deepen the learning. Make sure to leave time in the training to bring closure and a sense of resolution to the experience.

Exploring Past, Present, and Future

Create a flow to the training that provides participants with opportunities to learn and share how the past has influenced their current experiences. This may be done at a macro level by examining DEI in a historical perspective. It can also be done at a ground level by discussing the individual or shared experiences of participants in their personal or professional lives. Explore the current landscape to gauge existing strengths and pain points by discussing how participants experience the current organizational culture, as well as discussing current events. Finally, ensure that there is a focus on the future by asking participants what they would like to see change and what they can and will do to help achieve that future vision.

Honoring Silence

Facilitating DEI dialogues means more than knowing the right thing to say or the right questions to ask. It also means giving space for silence.

Silence adds weight to what was just said or shared with the group. When a participant shares a story or experience that is particularly emotional, it can be powerful to give a few seconds of silence to acknowledge and honor the importance of what the person said. Silence can help to reinforce the sense of community in the group.

Silence gives people time to reflect and process what they're hearing or experiencing. In a DEI training, there is a great deal of new knowledge and awareness that often brings cognitive dissonance, especially when a person's deeply held beliefs are called into question or behavioral norms are challenged. People may feel overwhelmed trying to process this. If they don't have the space to do so, the opportunity for learning is lost.

Silence also is important to give those who need more time a chance to speak. Natural introverts often struggle to find opportunities to voice their opinions in training sessions and dialogues, as they are steamrolled by extroverts who are more at ease sharing their ideas and opinions with little reflection time. This also goes for people who are from cultures that are accustomed to silence. When a question is asked, it may take a few minutes for some participants to feel ready to share. In typical

American classrooms, we ask a question, get a few immediate responses, and then move on. Meanwhile, some individuals miss the opportunity to share valuable insights.

Silence can give you, the facilitator, time to determine where to guide the conversation. Sometimes the facilitator needs a moment to consider the group dynamic, energy level, and emotional state to figure out where to go next with the dialogue.

Think about your own relationship with silence. How comfortable are you letting the group just be silent?

Some tips for allowing for silence:

- **Silence yourself.** Practice the acronym WAIT. Ask yourself, "Why am I talking?" We often are so unaccustomed to allowing silence that we fill the space with words. What value are you adding with your words? By speaking you are drawing attention to you. When does the attention need to be guided elsewhere?

- **Ask for others to practice silence.** Some participants are uncomfortable with silence, or perhaps more accustomed to talking. As a facilitator, sometimes you have to stop the conversation and ask the group to give a moment of silence. For instance, "What Ellen just shared was powerful. Let's give that a moment to sink in." Or "There is a lot of emotion coming up in the space right now. Let's honor that and just be quiet and present with it for a moment."

Bringing Closure

One of the hardest parts of facilitating a dialogue is knowing how and when to bring it to a close. Dialogue is by nature about opening up conversation, building an experience together, and exploring different experiences and opinions. DEI dialogues can be especially tricky to close because they open the doors to a lot of different emotions and can leave people feeling raw.

Think of the dialogue process in terms of both divergent and convergent practice: We first open up the space to explore different experiences, opinions, ideas. The group has a collective experience that brings about a shift in the way everyone sees the world and one another. When emotions are unblocked and released, it creates a shift in the energy of the group. People are changed by the experience. When that occurs, the process can turn to one of purpose-setting, action, and closure.

Bringing closure to a DEI training requires you to use contextual listening to recognize when the shift has occurred in the group, when they are ready to move forward. You may notice more relaxed body language, softer language and vocal tones, even laughter. All of these might be indicators that the group is moving toward resolution.

When closing the dialogue, consider the following:

- Name what you are feeling now.
- Where do you feel the group is in terms of its work around DEI?
- What can we celebrate or feel proud of in terms of what we have accomplished today?
- What further work needs to be done?
- What needs to be said that hasn't already been said for us to feel complete?
- What is the call to action for you as a group?
- What will each of you commit to doing as a result of this dialogue?

Bring closure by asking for participants to commit to action. Effective DEI training experiences give participants substantial time to reflect and consider what they will commit to changing in their own behaviors. You can really lock this commitment in by asking participants to pair up with someone else in the class to be an accountability partner and schedule regular check-ins for peer coaching.

Handling Difficult Situations

DEI dialogues are sure to bring out strong emotions, which can be healthy and lead to wonderful learning moments. However, there are times when emotional reactions induce destructive conflict or derail the dialogue process. The facilitator's job is to recognize potentially disruptive behaviors and respond accordingly.

When Someone Cries

Tears are one of the embodiments of a combination of emotions. People may shed tears of anger, grief, shame, or joy. Our workplace cultures are not particularly welcoming to the act of crying. Individuals may feel afraid to show such a strong emotional reaction out of fear of being judged as weak, oversensitive, or dramatic. Likewise, people are not comfortable witnessing tears. We're not sure whether to console, ignore, or ridicule. Regardless, we are conditioned to try to make the crying stop as quickly as possible. Saying "Please don't cry," "It's not that bad," "It's OK," or "Look on the bright side" are all well-intentioned, but the underlying message is "It is not OK for you to display this emotion."

When someone cries in a dialogue session, it can be a moment that signifies a breakthrough. It can be the first step toward healing an invisible wound. Tears are often involuntary. If a participant in a DEI training begins to cry, they are in the grip of a powerful emotion, and it's the facilitator's job to allow the individual to fully experience that emotion and to guide the rest of the group through their own reactions to the person's tears.

What to do:

- Always have tissues nearby and hand the person the whole box.
- Do not give hugs or consolation, and ask participants to refrain from doing so. This isn't meant to be cruel, but to instead invite people to let the person have the space to feel what they are feeling without interruption.
- Ask for silence, and be silent and still yourself. Take some deep breaths.
- You may even after a moment say, "This is a good time for us to take a deep breath together." Ask the group to take a few deep breaths together.
- Reinforce the courage the person has for allowing themselves to have the emotion. Remind the group that this work gives us permission to experience our emotions, and tears are natural.

- Give people the freedom to take a beat by leaving the room to work through the emotions in private if they prefer. Some folks need to process intense feelings in private.
- Once the person is ready, give them the space to say what needs to be said.
- Gently remind the rest of the group that their role is to be witnesses to one another's emotions, but not to try to fix anyone or solve other people's problems. Ask them to give the participant the opportunity to choose how they want to talk about their story, and not to bombard that person during a break.

When Someone Displays Anger

Anger is an equally natural reaction in DEI dialogues. People may become angry when reminded of a painful memory, or because of something that is said or done in the class itself. Anger may show up as defensiveness, frustration, cynicism, or rage. Often, anger is combined with or masking other emotions, like fear or shame. It may be a by-product of feeling invisible or unheard.

In DEI dialogues, people may walk into the space already angry. Anger may show up at a simmering level, with someone making sarcastic comments or remaining silent and sullen. Or it can boil over into raised voices, arguments, and even physical threats or behaviors.

What to do:

- Acknowledge the anger. Don't ignore it. Say, "I can sense something is coming up for you," or "I am sensing some tension; let's talk about it."
- Hit pause and process what's happening. "What's causing you to feel this?" or "What's this conversation bringing up for you right now?"
- Ask the group to stay in a place of curiosity. This is especially important if the individual displaying anger is the lone voice expressing an opinion or reaction.

- Empower the group to respond constructively if needed. "Where do we want to go from here?"
- If the behavior becomes disruptive or threatening, shut it down. "We cannot move forward in this conversation until everyone agrees to commit to the process of civil dialogue."
- Ask the person to leave. If the behavior isn't changing, let the individual know this is not the appropriate time or place for them to participate. They are welcome to rejoin later when they're able to participate in a constructive way.

I once co-facilitated a mandated diversity and inclusion training for an educational institution. One participant came in and refused to even introduce himself to us. He sat at a table alone and proceeded to read the paper. We invited him to participate and he ignored us, then loudly stated that he was forced to attend and had no intention of doing anything but sitting there until the training ended. Even though he didn't speak after that, his silence and lack of participation was enough of a disruption to the sense of safety in the classroom that we took an early break with the group and gave him the choice to either participate or leave, explaining why his participation was important. He chose to leave. We took time after the break to recalibrate as a learning community and asked the participants what they needed to be able to move forward together. We later found out that the individual who had left was on probation and had exhibited similar outbursts of anger in other workplace interactions.

When Someone Doesn't Talk or Participate

There may be a lot of reasons for a participant to remain quiet in a dialogue. Some people are by nature introverted or just quieter. Some people prefer to observe and listen before offering their perspectives. Some may not feel comfortable to share their honest opinions in the space, either because of their previous experiences or because of the makeup of the group. Then there are people who may not talk or participate because they do not believe the training is relevant to them, or they just plain don't want to be there.

What to do:

- Set norms up front encouraging everyone to actively participate in their own way
- Consider round-robin sharing to ensure everyone has the chance (and responsibility) to speak
- Do small group or partner activities
- Check in during a break
- Use culturally appropriate nonverbals (eye contact, smile, welcoming hand gestures) to encourage participation
- Conduct activities where participants anonymously write their responses or opinions on sticky notes or index cards that the facilitator reads out loud

When a Participant Says Something That Triggers You

As a DEI facilitator, you are not an automaton. You are bringing your own human emotions and experiences into the space. This means inevitably something a person says or does will trigger an emotional reaction for you.

What to do:

- Know in advance what words or actions tend to trigger adverse emotions for you
- Practice curiosity and compassion for the other person
- Ask if the person is willing to have a dialogue with you
- Take a break
- Call in your co-facilitator

When a Participant Attacks Another Participant's Character

If conflict arises in the dialogue, it's possible that a participant will accuse or attack another person. This may come out as stereotypes: "All [insert identity dimension] people" or "Your kind." Or it can be universalistic language about an individual, such as "You always" or "You never . . ."

What to do:

- Remind participants of the importance of remaining curious with one another

- Encourage a conversation around behaviors rather than judgment of character
- If it persists and is causing harm to a particular individual or group, ask the person engaging in the accusatory language to leave

When Someone Says Something Insensitive or Inflammatory

This is a common issue in DEI training. People may be unaware that what they say is potentially hurtful to others. It's a great opportunity to model behaviors that you want to encourage participants to use in their day-to-day lives.

What to do:
- Ask, "Can you explain what you mean by that?" or "When you said [this], what does that mean to you?"
- Ask for others in the group to offer their perspectives
- Explain the impact of the statement
- Make a request for behavior change
- Thank the person for being vulnerable and courageous enough to learn from their mistake
- Thank the group for being vulnerable and courageous enough to share feedback with their colleague

When Someone Withdraws, Shuts Down, or Leaves the Room

There are several ways a participant may withdraw. They may mentally or emotionally shut down, and stop actively participating. They may go silent, disengaging from any meaningful conversation with you or others. They may physically withdraw from the learning space by walking out of the room. This often indicates an intense emotional reaction to what is happening. Some individuals may withdraw because they are overwhelmed or unsure how to process the conversation. Some may feel defensive or resistant, especially if they are experiencing a great deal of cognitive dissonance. Others may be offended by or frustrated with a comment. Still others may be retraumatized by the discussion or activity.

What to do:

- **Check in.** Ask the class to talk among themselves and give them a question to discuss. Then go to the participant and ask them how they are doing.
- **Listen.** This is a good place for silence. Let them talk if they want to, or just sit with them for a moment in silence. When they are ready to talk, they will.
- **Ask what they need to re-engage.** Empower them to decide what they need to do for themselves or what they need to ask of you or the group.
- **Let them go.** Sometimes it's best to give the person the space they need. They will either choose to return on their own or not. This may not be the right time for them to participate in the DEI training, and sometimes you need to be OK with that.
- If they remain physically in the class but are not participating, and it's becoming disruptive to the group dynamic, you may want to **give them the option to leave or come back at a later time** when they are ready to be fully invested in the dialogue. This is not meant to be punitive, but to ensure a healthy dialogue for the group.

Power Dynamics (Abuse of Power)

People in authority positions may (intentionally or unintentionally) take advantage of their power to hijack the conversation. This may happen when a person in a position of formal authority (boss, senior leader) takes over or insinuates their opinion is the only right one. It may also occur when a person from the dominant culture in the organization or society (White, male, cisgender) dismisses or delegitimizes the experiences of people from the nondominant culture. This might sound like the following:

- That (ism) doesn't happen anymore . . . and certainly not here
- I'm not . . . therefore it's not an issue
- What we really should be talking about is . . .
- It wouldn't be a problem if people didn't keep bringing it up

What to do:
- If possible, prior to the training have the talk with people in positions of power about their role. If managers and leaders are participating in a course alongside employees, make sure to set expectations early about how they should cede power to others.
- Have the conversation offline. You may need to wait for a break and then call the person's attention to how their actions are potentially making it harder for others to express themselves honestly. Invite the person in the power position to practice silence and listen deeply to others' experiences.
- Shift your eye contact and body language to direct attention to others. Often, the most vocal participants or the participants in power positions naturally get more attention directed to them so they feel encouraged to keep talking. Intentionally direct questions toward people from nondominant groups to encourage their participation.
- Explicitly state that what is being shared is the perspective of a person in a powerful or privileged position. Sometimes you need to call it like you see it. Ask if there are other opinions that people would be willing to share. This isn't to shut down the person in power, but to even the playing field and encourage other voices that are often silenced.
- Consider doing an anonymous poll of issues if that leader is open to hearing feedback. If there is fear of speaking out publicly, consider this a way to spark honest dialogue. Hand out index cards for people to respond and then pass to you as facilitator to read.

Getting Comfortable With Uncomfortable Topics

DEI training requires a deeper level of comfort having conversations about hot-button issues that may elicit diverse perspectives and strong emotions. Many expert trainers who are highly skilled in facilitation may still find themselves feeling uncomfortable or unsure of how to handle topics that have long been considered taboo to discuss in professional environments. DEI training requires us to explore issues like discrimination and harassment, systematized racism and oppression, sexism, bias, prejudice, and privilege. Polarization in our society and the fraying of relationships across political ideologies have added extra heat to the fire. Sometimes these topics feel too hot to touch, yet they are integral to successful DEI training.

As a facilitator, how can you become more prepared to facilitate the most challenging conversations?

Study History

It's important to do your homework on the history of various identity groups and acquire an understanding of the roots of historic prejudice and inequity. You don't need to be an expert on the detailed history of oppression for everyone who's ever been marginalized, but the participants in the class will expect you, as the facilitator, to come with a solid knowledge of the subject matter you are discussing. You may have more in-depth knowledge of some aspects of history that have adversely affected you or your loved ones. It's important to also know the history of people who do not share your identity.

For instance, a White woman without a disability may be familiar with the history of women's rights issues and gender bias, but less knowledgeable about the experience of people of color or people with disabilities. A cisgender Black man may have deep knowledge about racism and colorism, but less familiarity with the experience of women or gender diverse people. A White Christian man who grew up in a low-income household is very familiar with the struggle of people in lower socioeconomic brackets but may be less familiar with the experience of people from marginalized or persecuted religious groups. Regardless of your identity, you have pockets of knowledge and blind spots. The more you study and learn, the more prepared you are to empathize with the experiences different people bring into the training room.

What to do:

- **Consider your power and privilege.** We all have stories of pain and disadvantage. Nobody owns suffering. And we all have aspects of our identity that give us certain unearned advantages in this world. The more unearned advantages you have, the more privilege and power you amass in society. Take some time to reflect on where you have unearned advantages because of the various dimensions of who you are—be it your gender, skin color, economic background, academic experience, religion, sexual orientation, physical and mental ability, and so on. Recognizing where you have privilege is not intended to cause guilt or shame. However, we need to acknowledge where we have an advantage over others because of something we can't control.

- **Embrace imperfection.** You are going to mess up. It's OK. In the work of DEI, nobody is perfect. There is no way to be perfect because this is about diverse human beings bringing their individual identity stories and conflicts and beliefs, and every situation will be unique. When you make a mistake because you said the wrong thing, or didn't say anything, or missed an opportunity to go deeper, first and foremost own the mistake. Then forgive yourself and ask others to forgive you. Show that you understand the pain you caused and commit to doing it differently next time. Ask for others to help you learn and grow and be accountable. This is hard work. We have to make ourselves vulnerable. We have to let go of the need to be perfect and focus on the need to be in community with those around us.

- **Acknowledge your blind spots.** We all have hidden biases and blind spots because of our identities. How you interpret what is happening in the DEI training space is going to be influenced by your own identity lens. Ask yourself the following questions:
  - What am I seeing and hearing in this moment?
  - How might my own identity impact what I'm seeing and hearing right now?
  - What might I be missing?
  - What can I do to check my assumptions?

I was leading a DEI course that included a site visit to the National Museum of African American History and Culture in Washington, DC. In preparation for the program, my colleagues and I went to the museum together to experience it and prepare for how we wanted the participants to experience it. As we made our way through the first floor of the museum, which focuses on the history of slavery in the early days of America, I was in instructional designer mode. I was singularly focused on the plan for structuring the learning experience. My colleague, who is Black, stopped me and said, "Give me a few minutes. I need to sit down." She went to a bench and just sat quietly, looking ahead. I realized she wasn't sitting down because her feet hurt. She was experiencing a deep emotional reaction. I realized that I had not considered how the experience of the museum would emotionally impact her. It was her first time. I had visited the museum several times on my own. I suddenly recalled the first time I had entered the museum, and how I was stunned into silence for hours afterward. Not only was this her first time at the museum, but as a Black woman, this was her heritage. I felt like a callous oaf. I apologized. Then I realized it was not about me being forgiven for my transgression. It was a moment to focus on my colleague and what she needed. So we sat together and talked a bit about what the experience was bringing up for her. I realized how easily we all can fall into our blind spots, especially when our experience or interpretation of an event or situation does not have the same physical, mental, emotional, or even spiritual effect as it does on others.

Summary

Delivering DEI training is a complex undertaking. As a DEI trainer, prepare to facilitate dialogue on challenging and personal issues by creating psychological safety and a sense of trust and openness. Share from your own experience and invite others to do the same. Encourage people to learn from one another and override their natural inclination to argue or defend. Prepare yourself for heightened emotions and challenges that may occur so that if and when they do happen you have sound strategies for managing them. Be realistic with what you can accomplish in a training experience.

Although a solid DEI training program that engages people at the intellectual, emotional, and practical level can lead to significant behavior change for participants, training alone does not lead to sustainable change. In chapter 6, we will explore strategies for continuity and collaboration across the organization to embed DEI principles and practices at the systemic level.

Chapter 6
Strategies for Continuity and Collaboration

When my daughter turned six she got a bicycle for her birthday. It was her first big kid bike without training wheels. She was excited to learn how to ride it. She hopped on and promptly lost her balance. We worked with her for an hour, holding the bike and giving guidance, but she couldn't get the balance right and became so frustrated that she began to cry. We assured her it would take time and practice, but she no longer seemed eager.

We tried to practice with her for the next couple of weekends, but when she didn't master it right away she got frustrated and lost interest. The bike sat in the garage for another year and became a home for spiders. We tried at times to pull the bike out and invite her to try again, but she went back to riding her scooter, which she had already mastered and felt comfortable on. We didn't want to push her too hard and make her resent us or the bike, so we gave up and assumed one day she would be interested.

Then we learned that her elementary school had a policy in which every student in second grade is expected to learn to ride a bicycle. The policy is actually part of a greater initiative launched in 2017 by Washington, DC, Public Schools, in partnership with the District's

Department of Transportation, to ensure that all second graders learn to ride a bike.

At first, we were concerned that this would lead to performance anxiety and embarrassment for our daughter. However, we found out that the school district embedded the bike-riding unit into the second-grade curriculum. The program was put in place to support students in learning to ride a bike, regardless of their incoming skill level.

What impressed me most about the school district's approach was not only had the administration created a policy around a core skill it believed was important for children at that age to learn, but it had also integrated learning and support into the entire semester. The students learn about independence, perseverance, and supporting others who are struggling. Some of the teachers even integrate learning about bicycles into history and science studies. The approach is to instill a collaborative spirit and a collective goal for all second graders to achieve together.

To support this goal, the school district provides bikes and helmets for all children, so students are free to bring their own but there are plenty for those who do not have a helmet or bike at home. The physical education teachers spend class practicing with the students, giving tips and pointers and providing extra support depending on where a student is in their abilities. The culminating event is a bike ride for all second graders on the nearby bike path. Students are encouraged to work together and help one another to prepare for the big event, and they cheer for each other when their peers are able to ride around the school track without tipping over.

During the semester when she was learning to ride, my daughter never seemed anxious or afraid. It still took her a while to get the hang of riding, but she was eager to share what she had learned about the history of the bicycle, how bicycles transfer our energy to kinetic energy to power the bike, and pointed out how the chain connected to the gears. By learning all about the bike, she had developed a curiosity that waylaid her fear of the physical process of riding.

She glowed with happiness when they returned from that final class bike ride. If the school had merely mandated that all children learn to ride bikes in second grade, but left the responsibility solely to families to teach their children, it would have created a disparate and fractured process in which a number of children would not be able to achieve the goal. If the school had only relegated learning to ride a bike to PE class, the students might have learned but would not have been as invested collectively. They would have seen the practice of bike riding in PE as a means to an end. However, the school staff recognized that if they wanted children to not only learn to ride a bike but also appreciate the process of persevering in the face of new challenges, they needed to design the process differently. The fact that bike riding had become a part of my daughter's daily life and a core component of her interactions with classmates and teachers took the fear out of bike riding and made it a collective journey where everyone supported one another in achieving the communal goal.

How do we make training a part of something sustainable?

Fostering a Holistic, Organizational Approach

Organizations that foster DEI take a holistic and sustained approach to embedding DEI into every thread of the institutional fabric. Standalone, one-off training will not lead to long-lasting change. In fact, in some cases, research indicates it can backfire.

Three big challenges we find are:

- Although DEI training may increase awareness of issues like implicit bias, stereotypes, and racial inequality, a generic diversity training class offered once will not likely lead to lasting behavior change if it's not part of a broader organizational strategy.
- Training individuals does not by itself address systemic barriers and inequities that continue to perpetuate advantages for those with societal privilege and disadvantages for those without. Individuals need to experience DEI as a part of the everyday fabric of their organizational life and need to feel a

sense of commitment to one another and to the organization to contribute to DEI.

- Good intentions do not transform into sustainable change unless there are clearly defined DEI goals with measurable success indicators.

Take heart. This does not mean DEI training is ineffective! What it indicates is that DEI knowledge and skills must be reinforced across the learning landscape, systems and policies in the organization need to be DEI focused, and accountability measures must be put in place. This chapter explores ways training professionals can collaborate with diversity, equity, and inclusion leadership in their organization to ensure long-term success. Three worksheets at the end of the chapter focus on integrating DEI into an organizational strategy, conducting a curriculum review, and evaluating learning outcomes.

The three overarching pillars for DEI to lead to successful, sustainable change are:

- **Strategy.** DEI has to be a strategic imperative and part of goal setting and decision making.
- **Continuity.** DEI efforts must be owned by everyone in the organization and embedded into all aspects of the organizational life.
- **Accountability.** The organization needs to identify clear metrics for progress and frequently evaluate programs, policies, and people to ensure the organization is achieving DEI goals.

Regardless of whether your organization has a dedicated DEI leader or office, it is important to team up with the individuals responsible for and committed to DEI. In some organizations, that might be an entire team of people whose full-time jobs are focused on DEI. In others, it might be an informal structure, which requires more commitment from key individuals to build and maintain momentum.

Integrating DEI Into the Organizational Strategy

Even if your role is not primarily linked to DEI, it is important to understand the constellation of organizational components that must be linked for DEI to be sustainable and successful.

Global Diversity, Equity, and Inclusion Benchmarks: Standards for Organizations Around the World (GDEIB), published in March 2021, is a report based on the expert guidance of almost 100 DEI practitioners from across the globe. The GDEIB offers best practices for organizations to engage in successful systemic change. The GDEIB includes 15 categories broken into four main groups: foundational, internal, bridging, and external.

Foundational Group: "Drive the Strategy"

The three categories in the foundation group—vision, leadership, and structure—represent the critical building blocks upon which any DEI initiative must be developed:

- **Vision, strategy, and business impact.** The organization has a clearly articulated vision for DEI, and has developed a strategic plan with measurable goals that are aligned with the corporate strategy. There is a detailed business case outlining the importance of DEI for the organization that is aligned with the organizational values, mission, and vision.
- **Leadership and accountability.** Leaders across the organization are visibly and actively committed to DEI and have the skills to model inclusive and equitable behaviors. They are held accountable for their actions and hold others accountable for fostering DEI.
- **Structure and implementation.** The organization has an internal structure to implement DEI goals. The ideal is to have a dedicated DEI team, led by a chief diversity, equity, and inclusion officer. However, DEI efforts may also be housed in Human Resources or an EEO office. Regardless of where DEI is housed, it should be run by people with expertise in the field.

As a training and development professional, you may not be directly involved with every component of the strategic planning and implementation of DEI in your organization, but you must play a critical role in it. This likely will include some sort of professional learning. It's helpful to have a seat at the table early in the planning process to bring a training and development lens and share best practices for effective learning. It's also important to determine early in the strategy process how training will be integrated into the organization, who is to be trained, and how success will be measured.

Training and development professionals should also play a key role in determining the specific competencies leaders will need to learn and practice in order to role-model DEI across the organization. Having a coherent plan that clearly outlines leadership competencies and behaviors will help ensure that the training design is successful.

Training and development professionals will need to work directly with members of the DEI leadership and their team to align all learning development activities with DEI organizational goals.

Internal Group: "Attract and Retain People"

The four categories in the internal group are centered around strengthening the effectiveness of leaders and employees. Often, this is the group under which training professionals reside, as it is most closely aligned with human resources, training, and professional development. However, it is still important for training professionals to understand the connection between their roles and other categories and to collaborate appropriately.

- **Recruitment.** Organizations are intentional and active about the terms of recruiting a workforce that is equitably representative across all levels and job functions. Diversity on interviewing panels is standard, and those involved in the recruitment, interviewing, and hiring process are well trained in the impact of biases.
- **Advancement and retention.** DEI is integrated into talent development, performance management, career advancement, and retention strategies. Individuals from underrepresented groups receive coaching, mentoring, and sponsorship opportunities, and promotion of underrepresented groups is proportional to the representation of those groups in the organization.

- **Job design, classification, and compensation.** The organization regularly reviews job classifications, requirements, and compensation to eradicate any potential biases.
- **Work-life integration, flexibility, and benefits.** Organizations need policies and practices that meet the needs and wants of diverse employees, including services like subsidized dependent care, remote work and flex schedules, accommodations for disabilities, lactation rooms for nursing parents, and fitness and nutrition services. These services allow employees with different needs to be productive, engaged contributors regardless of their situations.

Training and development professionals should be knowledgeable about organizational policies and practices that foster DEI and should make sure all training related to employment (such as employee onboarding, HR, supervisory skills, anti-discrimination and anti-harassment training) is up to date and provides an accurate and consistent message to employees.

Bridging: "Align and Connect"

The four categories in the bridging group help connect the foundational work with the internal and external focus of DEI.

- **Assessment, measurement, and research.** Ensure that DEI metrics are part of the information gathering and reporting process and there is a consistent mechanism for evaluating how DEI efforts contribute to organizational success.
- **Communications.** Internal and external communications provide consistent, accessible, and up-to-date messaging around DEI that is aligned with the organization's DEI vision, mission, and strategy.
- **DEI learning and development.** The organization has integrated DEI learning practices to ensure that all leaders and employees have competencies to foster an inclusive and equitable workplace.

- **Connecting DEI and sustainability.** DEI is integrated into the organization's long-term sustainability efforts, with a focus on issues like social equity, economic prosperity, environmental health, and ethical decision making.

As a training and development professional, your role in the assessment of DEI will vary depending on what mechanisms are already in place, but generally you will want to be part of or at least privy to assessment data and performance metrics for leaders and employees. To hold people accountable for their performance related to DEI goals, you must provide training to build knowledge and skills.

You can play a key role in terms of ensuring that communications related to training and development (for example, training advertisements, internal or external training and development webpages, and training materials) reflect diversity and are inclusive and equitable.

You also will play a critical role in the development and implementation of all learning activities related to DEI. This is where training professionals can play a role not only in making sure that DEI-specific training is relevant and effective but also ensuring that DEI competencies and practices are integrated into all forms of training in the organization. The most effective approach goes beyond check-the-box, one-off training to provide ongoing opportunities that promote the principles related to DEI as well as learning and practicing skills to foster DEI.

Working toward sustainability, training and development professionals can also equip employees and leaders with the foresight and tools to consider the long-term implications of decisions. A major challenge in many organizations is overcoming inertia when profits and productivity are high. Leaders needs to be constantly mindful of how their decisions today will influence the industry, workforce, and organization of tomorrow.

External Group: "Listen to and Serve Society"

The four categories in this group represent the organization's commitment to serving and interacting effectively with diverse communities, customers, and vendors.

- **Community, government relations, and philanthropy.** The organization advocates for members of diverse communities locally, regionally, and in broader society in a way that aligns with corporate vision and mission.
- **Services and product development.** DEI is embedded into the design and development of the organization's products and services, with input and collaboration among diverse customers, community members, and other external stakeholders.
- **Marketing and customer service.** The organization conducts frequent market analyses to understand the needs of diverse customers, and marketing and customer service efforts are representative of diverse populations and free of stereotypes. Customer service professionals are trained to provide culturally competent responses to diverse customers.
- **Responsible sourcing.** The organization is committed to purchasing a significant percentage of goods and services from organizations committed to high standards in DEI, sustainability, ethical behavior, and fair trade. Additionally, the organization supports current and potential suppliers in efforts to maintain high standards and to compete equitably with other suppliers to promote global prosperity and sustainability.

The role of training and development professionals in this area may be a bit more limited, but they can definitely be integral to ensuring that external-facing employees have the skills they need to promote DEI in their work, whether it's customer service, marketing, budgeting and acquisitions, or product development.

Ensuring Continuity

In addition to being a core part of the organizational strategy, DEI must become deeply interconnected across the organizational landscape, woven into the very fabric of the way things are done. This means that regardless of department or job function, everyone sees themselves as a key player in DEI efforts. When DEI is relegated to only one division, whether that is Human Resources, EEO, or a dedicated DEI office, its power and reach can be diminished.

All too often, DEI efforts lose momentum because of a lack of ongoing exposure to or reinforcement of DEI concepts. If most employees are only exposed to DEI in one-off training events, it is much less likely they will retain that knowledge or apply the skills learned.

Five Steps for Embedding DEI Knowledge and Skills in Your Training Curriculum

Training professionals have a unique and critical role to play in providing continuity of DEI efforts, because they typically interface with many departments and functions across the organization. Training and development professionals have the opportunity to regularly connect with everyone in the organization, and they can leverage that connection to develop shared language around DEI, reinforce critical knowledge and skills, and foster behaviors and practices that align with DEI.

In chapter 4 we discussed ways to make any training representative of diversity, and equitable and inclusive in the way it is designed and delivered. Training professionals also have the opportunity and responsibility to embed content that reinforces DEI knowledge and skills into the overall training curriculum for the organization. The five-step process toward that end is detailed here.

Step 1: Conduct a Curriculum Review

Conduct a thorough review of all formal and informal training content in the organization. Identify where and how DEI concepts appear. Consider opportunities to add or revise learning objectives to embed DEI concepts into the training curriculum. Identify ways to weave DEI concepts into the curriculum even if it doesn't require changing learning objectives. For example, a training on project management may not need a new set of objectives specifically related to DEI, but the content may need to be refreshed or enhanced to present the impact of identity lenses and implicit biases on how we set timelines, assign tasks, and measure success.

Step 2: Consider the Specific DEI Concepts and Skills Different Learners Need

When determining ways to embed DEI into all aspects of training and development, assess the existing level of knowledge different learners may bring. Determine the relevant skills needed for that learner group and design the training in a way that will fit their learning needs.

For example, managers and supervisors will most likely need more focused training to prepare them to effectively lead diverse teams, in comparison with budget and acquisition employees who may need to learn practices to promote DEI in terms of vendors and ethical sourcing.

Step 3: Integrate DEI Language and Skills Into All Other Interpersonal Skills

Reinforce the content and skills taught in DEI-specific training. Generally, DEI can and should be woven into all people-focused training. Identity lenses, core values, beliefs, and personal experiences related to one's societal identity and conditioning all play a powerful role in how we understand and communicate with one another.

For example:

- **Communication.** Our identity significantly influences how we communicate with others and how we interpret others' communication.
- **Managing up and influencing without authority.** By understanding the different identities our leaders and managers bring with them, we can engage in perspective taking, build trust, and influence their decisions.
- **Conflict management.** The most challenging (and destructive) form of conflict is often not due to a technical problem, but to an identity problem. Understanding how our brains react in times of identity-based conflict, learning about diverse conflict styles, and developing practices for dialogue are important skills for effective conflict management.
- **Feedback.** How individuals are culturally conditioned to give and receive feedback has a significant impact on workplace

productivity and relationships. Knowing our own and others' perspectives, emotional triggers, and feedback communication preferences all lead to better results when giving and receiving feedback.

- **Innovation and creativity.** DEI is integral to fostering innovation and creativity. Inviting and exploring divergent perspectives and ideas and creating psychological safety for people to disagree and debate processes are pillars of innovative cultures.
- **Change management.** People have different ways of reacting to change and dealing with the emotional process of organizational transitions. Learning about and responding effectively to different individuals' needs in times of change and turmoil lead to more streamlined solutions and sustainable transformation.
- **Team building.** Teams are made up of people, all of whom bring their individual identities, motivations, and needs. Fostering trust and rapport on the team requires exploring the different personalities and experiences of team members and building an environment where everyone on the team can thrive.
- **Customer service.** Customers bring their own unique experiences, perspectives, communication styles, and needs. To best serve them, it is important to recognize how our own identity lenses and implicit biases may impact the way we communicate with our customers.
- **Leadership and management.** Leadership, management, and supervisory skills training all play a prominent role in fostering DEI. Leadership or management training programs for any level, from aspiring leaders to senior executives, must incorporate and reinforce knowledge and skills around DEI.

Step 4: Embed DEI Into Technical Training

DEI doesn't just have to live in "people skills" training. In fact, it can play a valuable role in enhancing myriad technical skills.

For example:

- **Human resources.** HR training should absolutely provide comprehensive knowledge and skills for managing biases, engaging in equitable and inclusive practices with all employees, and promoting DEI across the organization. Although this seems obvious, all too often HR professionals are not given the degree of learning needed to champion DEI in their organizations.
- **Analytics and data-driven decision making.** Even when preparing and analyzing data to make decisions, implicit biases can potentially impact results. Analytics training should include content that prepares learners to recognize and mitigate potential biases, to ensure that the data collected is representative of diverse populations, and to present findings that consider the organization's DEI goals.
- **Project management.** Project management training has various opportunities to embed DEI principles and skills. Project managers need to be able to acknowledge and manage their own assumptions and implicit biases when prioritizing tasks, delegating responsibilities, and collaborating on project teams. They also need to be familiar with the organization's DEI goals and know how to align project management goals and objectives with the organization's broader DEI strategy.
- **Contracting and acquisitions.** Whether it is managing contract teams, performance monitoring and quality control, or managing challenging contractor situations, contracting and acquisitions professionals must recognize how their own biases and assumptions may influence their interactions with contractors. They also need to know how to hold contractors accountable for fostering DEI in their practices.
- **Performance management.** Performance management training requires a DEI lens. Anyone involved in the performance management process should learn how to intentionally manage their own assumptions and biases, and to foster DEI at every stage of employee performance management, from goal setting and delegating to monitoring and evaluation.

Step 5: Embed DEI Into All Learning and Development Activities

Organizations often have significant opportunities for publicizing and reinforcing DEI learning goals. By leveraging these events and resources, you further weave DEI into the organizational language and culture:

- **Conferences.** If your organization leads annual events like conferences or symposiums, make DEI a regularly scheduled theme. Bring in guest speakers or host workshops that are relevant to the audience. Additionally, plan these events with DEI in mind. Make sure the speakers represent various dimensions of diversity, schedule the events in locations that are accessible, and provide materials that represent diversity and accommodate different needs.

- **Offsites and strategic planning retreats.** Make DEI a standing agenda item. Ensure that diverse individuals are fully able to participate in the event in terms of time and location. Encourage contributions from underrepresented groups.

- **Commemorating history and heritage events.** I will offer the caveat that superficial celebratory events can feel performative, especially if they're the only visible effort the organization is making around DEI. If you choose to host events to commemorate historically underrepresented groups (including heritage months and holidays) make sure the approach is culturally appropriate and has a deeper purpose than mere celebration. When planning these events, ask for input and participation from representatives of the identity group. Consider appropriate messaging and content to educate others and elevate the voices and experiences of those groups. For example, one of my clients has a DEI Council that puts out a newsletter commemorating heritage months and invites guest speakers to present untold or overlooked stories. The organization also hosts monthly dialogue sessions where employees view a relevant documentary and discuss what they've learned and how they might apply those learnings in their own workplace as advocates for DEI. This is only one component of a long-term DEI strategy, which includes company-wide DEI training and learning, DEI performance goals, and ongoing assessment and evaluation.

- **Learning management systems and online resources.** Many organizations offer ongoing learning for employees through a dedicated learning management system or an internal library of content or resources. Review these resources to ensure they reflect your organization's DEI goals, and be intentional about offering ongoing content and learning nudges to employees beyond formal training. LinkedIn Learning provides a collection of short video courses on a wealth of topics, including diversity, equity, and inclusion. Google has created a free guide for organizations to develop "whisper" courses, which are easy-to-create templates for emails to send to managers and employees to reinforce practice of particular skills. For example, a DEI "whisper" may be an email sent to managers to remind them to encourage diverse perspectives and ideas in their group and one-on-one meetings (Stillman 2017).
- **Newsletters, blogs, podcasts.** Many organizations now host a variety of content that is shared internally with the workforce and sometimes externally with the public or select stakeholders. Be intentional about reinforcing DEI in these communications by not only spotlighting diverse individuals and groups but also speaking about the relevance of DEI for the organization, the industry, and the populations you serve.

Accountability for Achieving DEI Goals

In addition to a sound, systemic DEI strategy and continuity of DEI efforts across the organization, there needs to be accountability for achieving DEI goals and contributing to the organization's DEI vision and mission.

Many organizations wait until their DEI efforts are in motion to address accountability. This can be problematic when there are no clear indicators of success put into place. Not only does this often deter leadership from providing resources for further DEI work; it also can lead to frustration and demoralization if employees do not see progress. Even when progress is made, if it is not measured, documented, and communicated to the organization, it can get lost or diminished.

Accountability should be a part of the DEI work from the beginning. The organization needs to identify and measure progress related to DEI goals. It also needs to determine a plan for holding leaders, employees, and even external stakeholders (such as vendors, contractors, and consumers) accountable for fostering DEI. These steps include determining appropriate metrics to track, creating an evaluation process, and providing regular reporting.

Determine Metrics

Although there may be common foundational metrics for organizational progress in DEI (for example, recruitment and retention metrics and employee engagement scores), every organization must determine the metrics for success based on its own corporate strategic goals.

- Employment metrics
  - Recruitment of underrepresented groups (race, ethnicity, gender, disability)
  - Promotion of underrepresented groups
  - Hiring from within versus outside the organization
  - Representation of underrepresented groups in all job functions and levels
  - Representation on executive board
  - Retention of underrepresented groups
- Organizational climate
  - Employee engagement or satisfaction surveys
  - Exit interviews of outgoing employees
- HR metrics
  - EEO complaints and investigations
  - Non-EEO grievances (bullying, conflict, hostile work environment)
  - Disciplinary actions for misconduct or unethical behaviors

- Employee absences
  - Employee requests for transfers or new management
- Employee performance measurement
  - Performance evaluations
  - 360-degree feedback
- Customer satisfaction
  - Customer feedback surveys
  - Customer reviews
  - Customer service complaints
- Quality
  - Quality of products or services increases
  - Fewer errors, less waste of resources
- Profit and loss
  - Increases in revenue
  - New business lines
  - New consumer populations
  - Expenses related to recruitment and talent development
  - Expenses related to lawsuits or employee turnover
- Innovation
  - New or refined products or services created
  - Complex problems solved more quickly
- Reputation and public opinion
  - Increase in positive responses from customers on social media
  - Positive news media coverage
  - Recognition and awards

Create Evaluation Mechanisms

Determine the appropriate measures by which you will benchmark progress. This may include both short-term and long-term metrics.

For example, if a key challenge that was identified in the assessment phase is that the organization does not have adequate representation of racial and ethnic diversity, especially in leadership and management positions, then a DEI strategic goal for the organization should be to increase diversity in the employee population across all levels. The organization will need to determine the appropriate metrics for achieving this goal.

Possible metrics may be quantifiable and directly related to the goal:

- Increase number of candidates from underrepresented groups who are invited to interview by 25 percent in all positions
- Increase number of POC hires and promotions by 25 percent

Metrics may also be supportive of the goal even if they are not directly correlated:

- Develop a formal mentoring and coaching program for aspiring employees and include at least 30 percent POC employees in the program
- Provide implicit bias training to all selection panels and hiring managers

You may not be directly involved in determining all the DEI strategic goals and metrics. However, you can play a critical role in developing measurements related to training and development.

Following Kirkpatrick's model of training evaluation, let's examine the four levels of evaluation that you may use to gauge the effectiveness of DEI-related training:

- **Level 1: Reaction.** This is the degree to which participants found the training favorable, engaging, and relevant.
- **Level 2: Learning.** This is the degree to which participants developed new knowledge, awareness, skills, and attitudes. It identifies both competence and confidence to apply new knowledge and skills learned in the training.
- **Level 3: Behavior.** This is the degree to which participants apply their new learning on the job.
- **Level 4: Results.** This is the degree to which targeted outcomes occur as a result of the training. This level indicates the return on expectations for the training (Kirkpatrick 2016).

When designing training that includes DEI, always begin by considering the desired learning outcomes and how you will measure success.

Make the learning objectives and competencies specific and measurable and consider the mechanisms you will use to evaluate the training.

Level 1, Reaction: Post-Training Feedback Survey

The most common evaluation tools for Level 1 are surveys provided to participants immediately upon completion of the training. Typically, these surveys measure Level 1 (reaction) and to some extent Level 2 (learning). The surveys give valuable data on what participants liked or disliked about the training, and how effective and relevant they believe it was.

Level 2, Learning: Pre- and Post-Tests

Administering a knowledge test prior to and immediately following training can measure participants' learning directly related to the training program. The knowledge test should be directly tied to the training program's learning objectives. The knowledge test can directly measure existing competencies by quizzing the participants on the content that will be covered.

Example:
What percentage of Fortune 500 CEOs are White males?
a. 80%
b. 75%
c. 90%
d. 50%

The knowledge test can also be more of a self-reporting assessment to gauge how well learners believe they understand the content. These can take the form of Likert scales measuring agreement, satisfaction with existing knowledge, or frequency of practice.

Example:
I am aware of how my implicit biases impact my decisions and behaviors at work.
1 = Never 2 = Rarely 3 = Sometimes 4 = Frequently 5 = Always

You can also measure participants' confidence or attitudes toward DEI content.

Example:

I am comfortable engaging in dialogues with colleagues about diversity issues.
1 = Very uncomfortable 2 = Slightly uncomfortable 3 = Comfortable 4 = Very comfortable

Level 3: Behavior

Evaluating individual behavior changes can be a little trickier, but it's important to ensure the effectiveness of the training program in bringing about positive change. There are a few methods to consider, ranging from high touch to low touch. All these have the potential for bias. To mitigate biased evaluations (by yourself or others), be as specific as possible with the behavioral indicators to be observed and reported.

- **Observation.** Directly observing participants' behaviors in their day-to-day work environment can provide valuable data on how they are able to apply the training. This may include observation in staff meetings or shadowing a person for a period of time. This approach can be useful but also time consuming, logistically challenging, and biased based on the observer's identity lens and interpretations of the individual.

- **360-degree feedback.** Consider sending a 360-degree feedback survey to the participants' peers, direct reports, and managers asking them to provide input on what they have observed and experienced. What behaviors have they witnessed the individual exhibit that help or hinder an environment of DEI? This approach can itself be limiting on its own because every team member will interpret their colleague's actions through their own biases and filters.

- **Self-reflection or assessment.** Self-assessment tools can be helpful, asking participants after the training how they have been able to apply their new knowledge and skills. This may take the form of a post-training survey that is administered several months out to provide people adequate time to engage in behavior changes and see results. There is potential for bias in this approach as well, depending on the identity lenses and biases of the person assessing themselves.

Level 4: Results

It is challenging to directly link training outcomes with organizational results, especially with DEI. However, it is not impossible. When designing training, clarify the organization's expectations of the training. Map the training objectives to the organization's DEI strategic goals. Think about how the training outcomes can be represented as business outcomes.

When measuring results, look for patterns and organizational results that correlate to the training content. For example, if a DEI training program for HR professionals and hiring managers focused on examining and mitigating bias in the hiring and promotion process, then look at changes in the number of underrepresented populations who are interviewed, hired, or promoted in the six to 12 months following the training.

Provide Regular Reporting on Progress Toward DEI Strategic Goals

Provide frequent updates to leadership on the progress toward DEI strategic goals and the contributions of training and development. Regularly report to the organization and your own department or team on the priority of DEI strategic goals and how training supports those goals. Reporting can also pinpoint barriers or challenges and provide insight to determine when the solutions you have in place need to be adapted or discontinued.

For example, if a DEI training program for leaders and managers has been in place for a year, but there has not been an increase in positive ratings on performance evaluations for DEI-related competencies, then it may be time to review and revise the training content or approach.

Summary

Although training and development professionals are not necessarily driving DEI strategy for their organization, they play a crucial role in supporting overall organizational change. It is important to understand how your work fits within the larger constellation of DEI work, so that you can design, implement, and evaluate training programs in a meaningful way.

Training and development professionals play an important role in both supporting strategic change and providing continuity of content across the organization to embed DEI into the organizational culture.

It is also important to foster accountability by establishing observable metrics to gauge process. Focus not only on individual behavior change but also on overall organizational results.

In the next chapter, we will explore DEI training and development from a global perspective and identify how to adapt training to globally diverse audiences.

Worksheet 6-1. Integrating DEI Into the Organizational Strategy

Drive the Strategy	Y/N and Explanation	Needed Action (what might you need to consider or what steps do you need to take?)
Does the organization have a DEI vision statement? If so, what and where is it?		
Does the organization have a DEI strategy? If so, what and where is it?		
Does the organization detail the business case for DEI? If so, what is it?		
Are leaders actively committed to DEI? If so, how do they demonstrate it?		
Are people held accountable for their actions that help or hinder DEI efforts? If so, how are they held accountable?		
Is there an internal structure focused on DEI, like a DEI committee or council, or a chief diversity officer? If so, what is that structure and who leads it?		
Attract and Retain People		
Does the organization actively recruit for equitable representation at all levels? Please describe what processes are in place.		

Attract and Retain People	Y/N and Explanation	Needed Action (what might you need to consider or what steps do you need to take?)
Is DEI integrated into talent development, performance management, career advancement, and retention strategies?		
Are jobs designed and classified to intentionally mitigate biases?		
Is compensation equitable?		
Align and Connect		
Has the organization collected data on the state of DEI?		
Does the organization have set metrics to manage progress on DEI goals?		
Are there communication mechanisms in place to inform and encourage DEI efforts in the organization?		
Are there regular learning practices or training programs that focus on DEI-related competencies?		
Is DEI seen as a part of the organization's sustainability efforts?		
Listen to and Serve Society		
Does the organization advocate for diverse communities in a way that is aligned with its mission and vision?		

Worksheet 6-1 (cont.)

Listen to and Serve Society	Y/N and Explanation	Needed Action (what might you need to consider or what steps do you need to take?)
Is DEI embedded into the design and development of the organization's products and services?		
Does the organization understand the needs of diverse customers?		
Does the organization provide culturally competent customer service to diverse populations?		
Does the organization engage in responsible sourcing in terms of where and from whom it purchases goods and services?		

Worksheet 6-2. Curriculum Review Matrix to Ensure Continuity of DEI Content

DEI Concepts/ Skills: What competencies need to be developed and reinforced?	Behavioral Indicators: What specific behaviors do people need to practice to demonstrate this competency?	Current Training: What existing learning content includes this DEI competency?	Additional Opportunities: What other learning events or content should include this DEI competency?
Example: Inclusive communication	Example: Manage micro-messages Value diverse opinions Encourage feedback from others	Example: Module on "Inclusive Communication" in Leadership Skills for New Supervisors training Module on "Micro-messages" in Managing Unconscious Biases training for all managers	Example: Add module to Influencing Skills training Add module to Project Management training Write a blog post or add a checklist for inclusive communications to online resource page on internal website

Worksheet 6-3. Accountability: Evaluating Learning Outcomes Tracking Sheet

Training Program	Kirkpatrick Level			
Example: Managing Unconscious Biases	**1: Reaction**	**2: Learning**	**3: Behavior**	**4: Results**
Pre- and Post-Training Knowledge Assessment				
Training Evaluation Questionnaire				
Semiannual and Annual Performance Evaluations • Question 11: Treats all team members with equal respect • Question 12: Actively seeks to recruit, reward, and retain the most diverse and qualified team • Question 13: Regularly participates in diversity, equity, and inclusion events Annual employee engagement survey shows an increase in positive responses from women and people of color				

Chapter 7

US and Beyond: Diversity and Inclusion in a Global Setting

A few years ago, I traveled to Kazakhstan to deliver a leadership program for a group of high-ranking government leaders. My colleague and I spent a week with 20 of the country's top ministry officials as well as local and regional leaders. The majority of these individuals did not speak English, and we had two translators, one speaking Russian and the other Kazakh. All but one of the participants were men, and most of them were older.

Although the training program was focused on general leadership topics, my colleague and I decided to also integrate content that would promote learning around diversity, equity, and inclusion. We knew that the way DEI is addressed in US classrooms would not resonate with this group, and we had to be very conscious of how we addressed cultural issues related to gender, sexual orientation, religion, and ancestral origins. Islam is the primary religion in Kazakhstan, followed by Russian Orthodox Christianity. Kazakhstan's culture and history are heavily based on the Turkic nomadic lifestyle, but also have been influenced by Russia and China. Kazakh culture therefore combines multiple cultures to create its unique identity.

There were a number of challenges we had to maneuver. We had to figure out how to manage the time and pace of the program using interpreters. We had to structure the program to be culturally appropriate in terms of meals, breaks, and socializing. We wanted to make sure the content was accommodating of Kazakh societal values. We wanted to ensure the activities were culturally appropriate and translated well to this audience, knowing that they would have different expectations for how to interact with us and one another in a learning environment. We had to be conscious of their status in their country and ways to show proper respect. We also wanted to ensure we were both considered equally credible as subject matter experts.

We sent the written materials and our instructor notes to the interpreters in advance so they could become familiar with the subject matter and more easily translate topics in the learning environment. We also met with them prior to the training to answer their questions and describe some of the more intricate topics or instructions for activities. We also wore translation devices, as did the participants. We had to slow down our speaking cadence and allow for longer pauses to give the interpreters time to translate. The first day was the most awkward but it became easier as we went.

We built in longer breaks for meals and social time. The Kazakh culture is very oriented toward hospitality toward guests, and the participants were eager to make us feel comfortable and honored. They also wanted to have time to socialize with one another, and the breaks would inevitably extend far beyond even what we had set aside, which meant we had to adjust our expectations for what content could be covered each day. We found that the social time was crucial for the participants to be engaged.

We assumed that my colleague, a middle-aged White American man and a former military officer, would be received very differently than I would. We developed a strategy in advance to have my colleague take the lead the first day of the training, but regularly defer to me as the subject matter expert in certain areas of particular interest to the participants. As the week went on, I took more time leading topics and activities once the participants had settled in and perceived me as a credible expert.

Our hosts invited us to dine with them and the participants one evening about halfway through the program for a traditional Kazakh meal. It was the first (and quite possibly the only) time I have eaten horsemeat, which is a common dish. They told stories and asked us questions about America. There was live music and entertainment, which went late into the night. The next day I needed more coffee than usual, but I noticed that the participants were energized and jovial, and engaged with my colleague and me with greater warmth. Our evening together had created a bond that hadn't existed before, and they were more engaged in the training with us from that point on.

The first two days we engaged in more lectures, interspersed with small group discussions or question-and-answer periods with us. As the week progressed, we decided to take more of a risk, conducting experiential activities, including a simulation, scenarios and role plays, and even drawing pictures. We weren't sure how they would be received. To our astonishment, most of the participants loved the interaction and were very willing to engage in playful activities. They bantered with one another and with us. Although we did not specifically bring up diversity and equity in terms of what might be hot-button issues like religion, sexual orientation, or gender, we did explore issues of implicit bias, in-group and out-group dynamics, and micro-messages. We invited the participants to share the dimensions of identity or diversity that were most important to them in their daily work lives and determine ways to build more respectful and culturally sensitive teams. This afforded them the opportunity to own the conversation.

My colleague and I found ways to invite the one female participant to share her opinions, knowing that it would potentially be more difficult for her to speak up. We did this by orchestrating private conversations with her outside of the class, listening to her experiences and opinions, and then encouraging her to share those thoughts with the larger group.

At the end of the program, we conducted an elaborate ceremony, in which each participant received a certificate of completion and was invited to share their final thoughts. We spent more time than we normally would in an American setting for this finale, knowing it would be important for each participant to be able to speak at length to their colleagues.

I learned a great deal from that program, both in designing for a globally diverse audience and managing my own assumptions and biases. Although I have traveled extensively and studied intercultural communication, I still bring my implicit US-centric cultural norms and expectations with me. I walked into the program automatically prepared as an American woman to defend myself against what I assumed would be a fairly hostile audience. Instead, I found a warm, inviting group of participants who showed me respect and hospitality that I will never forget.

How do we make training relevant in a globally diverse setting?

How Intercultural Differences Influence DEI Content and Delivery

My career started in intercultural communication. My graduate studies focused on intercultural training and the impact of culture on how we perceive ourselves, how we interact with and understand others, and how we communicate in the workplace.

Intercultural communication is the study of cultural differences that influence the way we send messages, the way we interpret others' messages, and the way we build relationships with others. Although every individual brings their own unique identity characteristics into their communication, there are deeply seated cultural patterns that influence our communication with and understanding of others. These cultural patterns can become more pronounced in globally diverse teams and multinational audiences.

This chapter presents a global perspective to DEI work, including intercultural communication concepts, examples of DEI approaches in other countries, and considerations when doing DEI training abroad or with multinational audiences. A worksheet at the end of the chapter presents questions for global training preparation.

One of the main challenges we often face in conducting DEI training with a multinational audience is when the training is designed only with a US audience in mind and does not take into account the differences and expectations of globally diverse audiences. There are two main areas where DEI training must consider intercultural differences: content and delivery.

- The content of the program needs to be relevant and appropriate to the audience, and the dimensions of identity that are spotlighted need to resonate with its societal and cultural norms.
- The delivery of the program needs to consider intercultural differences in communication styles, relationships between instructors and participants and among participants, and cultural expectations around classroom dynamics.

Selecting Appropriate DEI Content

The way DEI is addressed in the US is a product of our collective history and societal norms. Compared to other cultures, in the US most dimensions of identity are typically fairly open for discussion DEI training. Racial identity and inequality have always been a crucial theme, and now there is an even greater demand to address racism and White supremacy head on. It is not atypical to explore issues of gender bias and discrimination, as well as sexual orientation and identity, socioeconomic disparities, disability, and religion.

Some dimensions of identity that are commonly discussed in DEI training in the US may be irrelevant in other cultures. Talking about race and ethnicity may be important in a variety of cultural contexts but may look different depending on where you are. For example, although China has more than 50 different ethnic minority groups across the country, for both demographic and political reasons ethnic diversity is not a topic that is often discussed. Regional background, socioeconomic status, education, generational differences, and language are more prominent in terms of indicating diversity of perspectives and behaviors (Gundling and Zanchettin 2007).

DEI training is meant to be provocative, to challenge the status quo that may impede on human or civil rights. However, there may be identity dimensions that are considered inappropriate to discuss in a professional or classroom setting. For instance, sexual orientation and identity can be a challenging topic in some multinational settings if the host country or culture outlaws homosexuality. As of 2021, the Human Rights Campaign reported that 69 countries worldwide have laws criminalizing private, consensual same-sex activities. In nine of those countries the so-called crime is punishable with the death penalty, and in three countries even LGBTQIA+ advocacy is considered propaganda and outlawed (HRC 2021). Most countries do not have comprehensive policies to properly address human rights violations against LGBTQ+ people, and even when such policies are in place there is little data collected to evaluate how effective they are (United Nations 2016). Thus, it is possible that including content on LGBTQIA+ issues in a country where those identities are outlawed can make the trainer seem out of touch with cultural norms or could even potentially create an unsafe environment for the trainer or some participants.

In contrast, not every country that does have legal protections of some kind for LGBTQIA+ people has universal support or inclusion. For example, DEI trainers may find themselves working in a region of the US that has relatively low support for LGBTQIA+ inclusion. Yet in that context, it may be important to intentionally engage in conversations around LGBTQIA+ inclusion to clearly demonstrate expectations around inclusiveness and equity.

In any DEI training, it is important to recognize and acknowledge how dominant cultural systems and norms impact everyday life, and the divergent experiences that people from nondominant identity groups may encounter. How much are people expected to assimilate to the dominant cultural norms in a given society or community? Does the dominant culture perpetuate inequities or have societal advantages over nondominant groups?

In the US, DEI training often explores dominant and nondominant identities in terms of dimensions like race, ethnicity, gender, and socioeconomic class (to just name a few). In a globally diverse setting, there may be locally unique differentiators between dominant and non-dominant cultural groups.

In India, for example, there are numerous parallels to US social inequities, but the nuances matter. The history of the caste system in India, which has been in existence for thousands of years, continues to influence the social standing and opportunities available for different groups of people based on their ancestry and what section of Hindu society they are descended from. Although discrimination based on caste has been outlawed for decades and affirmative action quotas have been put into place, many communities still experience segregation, and those who belong to what has historically been referred to as the "Scheduled Caste" or Dalit (which translates as "broken or scattered") are often still perceived as "backward" and experience disparate treatment in society. In terms of intersectionality, the women who are part of "Scheduled Caste" identities, who face additional discrimination and harassment for their perceived status in the social order, are often excluded or invisible in terms of advocacy for women's rights and transgender individuals (Baudh 2021).

It is important as a trainer conducting DEI work in a global setting to be aware of your own implicit cultural values, beliefs, and expectations. All too often DEI work conducted by US-based individuals or organizations is narrowly focused on American societal issues and definitions of DEI. These do not necessarily translate to other cultures and can alienate or frustrate participants. Moreover, as a DEI trainer, even when you are aware of the cultural nuances, you may find yourself in a setting where your personal values or beliefs clash with those of the host culture. As we have discussed elsewhere, simply knowing that different ways of seeing the world exist does not preclude us from having emotional reactions to behaviors that we're conditioned to perceive as antithetical to our core values. Our cultural conditioning is so deeply buried in how we make sense of our surroundings that we can easily find ourselves triggered in cross-cultural exchanges. It is incumbent as a DEI trainer to prepare yourself by considering how you will potentially respond to ideologies or behaviors that are not in alignment with your beliefs.

Tips for Managing Content in a Globally Diverse Setting

- Find some local culture guides—a few trusted local resources, preferably individuals who represent diverse subgroups or minority groups in the region, to provide you with cultural considerations and to help you navigate the nuances so the content appeals to the audience and is relevant and appropriate.
- Adapt your training design to the audience. Use culturally relevant names and images for scenarios or case studies. Check for language that may not translate culturally, like slang or US-centric expressions.
- Provoke new insights and awareness in a culturally appropriate way. You don't necessarily have to avoid issues that are important to address; however, fine-tune the approach so people are more willing and open.
- In culturally mixed audiences, try to find common ground and universal experiences to engage everyone.
- Prepare how you will respond to situations where the cultural norms espoused by participants or the host organization are in conflict with your values or beliefs.

Creating a Culturally Competent Learning Setting

Two important considerations when preparing the setting for a global training experience are language and location. In international environments, it is likely you will have to consider the appropriate languages to use in training. Is there a common language spoken by all participants? What is the level of proficiency in that language? What language do the trainers speak? If you are using multimedia, such as video clips, what language is featured?

Tips for accommodating different linguistic needs:

- Determine whether interpreters are needed, and if so, between which languages.
- Determine what language materials should be printed in.
- If you are using videos or other multimedia, make sure you have a translated transcript or closed captioning.

- If the training includes non-native speakers of the language the training is taking place in, speak clearly and a bit more slowly to ensure people can follow along.
- Consider a facilitation team that includes a native speaker of the home language who can translate more challenging concepts or respond to questions.

In a multinational training setting, consider where and when the training will take place. Think about how accessible the training facility is for participants, as well as the ease of commuting back and forth to the training location (especially if people are traveling from far distances). Consider the safety of the area, and accessibility for people with special accommodation needs. Think about the best time of year for training in that location in terms of climate and convenience. Consider the time zone, and if people are traveling from far away, how much time to give them to recover from jet lag. Consider time zone differences for virtual participants.

Tips for considering location and timing:
- Is the training location easily accessible by air, train, or car?
- What audiovisual or technological restrictions might there be?
- What time of year will the training take place and how does that factor into the ease with which people can attend the training?
- How much time might people need to get to and from the training facility?
- Will people be jet lagged?
- In what time zone is the training taking place, and if people are attending from other regions, what time of day is it for them?
- How safe and accessible is the facility?
- Will people with different dietary restrictions have access to the food they need?

Adapting Training to Different Cultures: Five Factors

Let's explore five common cultural factors that may influence individual and group values, norms, and beliefs in a globally diverse learning environment: context, collectivism, expressiveness, power distance, and orientation to the environment.

A few elements to consider:

Intercultural research has its own potential biases. In the field of intercultural communication, there are numerous studies that have identified differences in terms of cultural values and behaviors. For the purpose of this book, we will examine five cultural factors that may influence the way participants from different cultural groups communicate in the learning space. It is important to note that the most frequently cited scholars who have written about cultural dimensions or values (for example, Geert Hofstede, Fons Trompenaars, Edward Hall) were White men of European descent. When considering these cultural factors in your training design, examine potential biases or false universalities that may be a consequence of a Western framework.

Cultural identity is relative. Although we will explore each of these five factors along a scale, this does not intend to describe culture as an "either/or" delineation of identity. Rather, it's a spectrum. Where one individual or identity group falls on the spectrum is typically in comparison to other identity groups. This is commonly referred to in anthropology as cultural relativity. The way we perceive the patterns of another culture is relative to our own (Meyer 2014).

Culture inherently includes "us and them" thinking. In her book *The Claims of Culture: Equality and Diversity in the Global Era*, Seyla Benhabib argues, "We should view human cultures as constant creations, recreations, and negotiations of imaginary boundaries between 'we' and the 'other(s).'" She posits that struggles around "otherness" stem from all of us fighting to avoid being the other, the outcast. According to Benhabib, "It is very difficult to accept the 'other' as deeply different while recognizing his/her fundamental human equality and dignity" (Benhabib 2002). Thus, even nations with culturally heterogeneous populations and communities are not a panacea. In fact, often there is constant tension and unrest related to groups that are castigated or marginalized for being different.

There are cultures within cultures. Consider subcultures that exist within any national or regional culture, which may have significantly different cultural values, norms, and shared experiences from the dominant culture. We will explore this later in the chapter.

It is also important to account for how an individual's values and perspectives "fit" within the larger cultural norms in which they exist. People may not necessarily always align with the dimensions that are valued or practiced by a shared cultural group, depending on their personality, upbringing, and life experiences.

Cultural Factor 1: High vs. Low Context Communication
What are you really saying?

The way we communicate and where we place the meaning of our messages depend on our culture. In low context cultures, the meaning of the message is explicit in the words we use. The old American adage, "Say what you mean and mean what you say" is a clear representation of this form of communication. Many low context cultures have a shorter history or mixture of many cultures. For example, in comparison to other countries, the US is a very low context culture. This is not surprising considering we are a nation of immigrants. To build a society, our country's inhabitants had to create simple, easy-to-follow communication norms where the meaning of one's message was easy to interpret across culture and language divides.

Many higher context cultures have a longer shared history. In high context cultures, the meaning of one's message does not need to be explicitly stated in their words. In fact, quite often one's words may not represent their meaning at all. The subtext of the message is buried in subtle nonverbals, or in what words are omitted. In high context cultures, the message sender believes they are showing respect and honoring the message receiver's intelligence and ability to read the message by sharing in this nuanced way.

One common example I have often encountered in my intercultural experiences is that of how people express disagreement. Take a look at the following responses:

- "No."
- "Yeah . . . no." (If you grew up in the Midwest, like I did!)

- "I would love to, but I just can't right now."
- "*In sha' Allah*" ("If Allah wills it").
- "That will be difficult."
- "I will do my best."
- ". . ." (Hesitation followed by a sharp intake of breath.)

All these responses roughly translate to the same message: *No, I will not or cannot do that task*. However, the delivery of the message may be quite different based on one's culture. In cultures like the US, Israel, and Germany, which are comparatively lower context cultures, the message is typically explicit with little room for misinterpretation. In cultures like Japan, India, and Brazil, which are comparatively high context, the message is embedded not necessarily in the words but in subtle cues, including vocal tones, pauses, facial expressions, and body language.

Sometimes the meaning of the message is found in what is not said. A person from a relatively high context culture may offer their disagreement by stating only what they agree with. For example, imagine you are in the classroom and discuss a concept that has three supporting points, and when asked for their opinion a participant nods and smiles, responding with, "Oh yes, I agree with points one and two." The fact that they omitted point three may indicate they do not agree with that statement.

There are significant considerations for DEI trainers when designing an experience that will accommodate these diverse dimensions of context. Whereas some training participants may be willing to explicitly state their opinions in a direct way, others will be much more subtle and rely on implicit messages to share their opinions. A trainer coming from a low context culture may very well miss cultural cues from high context participants.

Erin Meyer, the author of *The Culture Map: Breaking Through the Invisible Boundaries of Global Business*, refers to this as "reading the air." She describes an experience where she was asked to present to a group in China. At the close of her presentation she asked if there were any questions. When no one raised a hand or said anything, she assumed there were no questions and sat back down. Her Chinese colleague stood up and asked the question of the audience again. This time, he waited several minutes, and then called on an audience member who had not moved or spoken. "Yes, do you have a question?" Much to Meyer's surprise, the audience member said yes and asked a question. When she inquired of her colleague after the presentation how he knew the participant wanted to say something, the Chinese colleague responded that it was important to look at who had shining eyes.

Context differs within any country's culture, and often even within organizational cultures. I have found that certain audiences even within departments of organizations I consult with differ in terms of context.

For trainers working with a higher context audience, consider the following:

- Leave more time than usual for silence after you ask if people have questions.
- Carefully observe the room for changes in posture, eye contact, and facial expressions.
- Pay attention to what is not spoken. Silence can sometimes indicate agreement, disagreement, or distaste.
- A smile or nod is not always an indication of agreement; in fact, it may indicate disagreement or embarrassment.
- Pay attention to the stories or metaphors participants use. Often, the message is buried in the subtext of these stories. When in doubt, ask clarifying questions rather than assuming you understood the message.
- In terms of content delivery, consider using stories, metaphors, or images to convey a point rather than explicitly stating it.
- Listen more, speak less.

For trainers working with a lower context audience, consider the following:

- Provide clear, detailed instructions for activities.
- Share stories or examples that are explicitly connected to a concept.
- Suspend judgment when people respond bluntly—it's not their intention to be rude.

- If people argue or challenge what you say, do not assume it is meant to attack your credibility, but perhaps to actively engage with you and other audience members.
- Don't be ambiguous when discussing more delicate topics. Be transparent and explicit. People may read that as a lack of authenticity or fear on your part to "name" the issue openly.

Cultural Dimension 2: Individualism vs. Collectivism

Me vs. we.

This cultural dimension scale has a deep influence on the shared values and priorities of people in a particular culture. The individualism scale is the degree to which a culture places value on the needs of the many versus prioritizing the needs of an individual. In individualist cultures, the ties between people is looser, with a focus on caring for oneself and one's immediate family. Individualistic cultures tend to value personal time and individual freedom. Originality, self-reliance, and independence are considered important character traits. In collectivist cultures, people prioritize the needs of the community.

Collectivist cultures prioritize being part of a group and contributing to the greater goals and needs of the group even if it requires sacrificing one's individual needs or wants. Generosity, dependability, and attentiveness are considered important character traits (Hofstede, Hofstede, and Minkov 2010).

This can shape a person's self-perception as well as their relationships with and expectations of others. In a more individualistic culture, people tend to describe themselves based on their unique characteristics, likes, or interests ("I am athletic and I love to read and cook"). Although people in individualistic cultures enjoy and need group membership, their reliance on that group membership as a core part of their identity is lower than with collectivist cultures. People from individualistic cultures are less inclined to ask for or offer help in comparison with those from collectivist cultures. This is not an indication of selfishness or inhumanity. It is simply their cultural conditioning to believe that independence and self-sufficiency are character strengths. On the other hand, they may see asking for assistance as a sign of weakness or a character flaw.

People from collectivist cultures tend to see their identities as inextricably connected with the group. Their self-concept is often based on the role they play in their identity group rather than their personal interests or characteristics ("I am a caring daughter" or "I am a loyal friend").

There is a word in Zulu, *ubuntu*, which is part of a longer phrase, "*Umuntu ngumuntu ngabantu,*" which roughly translates to "I am, because you are." This is at the heart of a collectivist mindset, that we each exist as people because of others. This does not necessarily mean that individuals cannot be celebrated or held accountable for their actions. People are awarded or disciplined based not on personal achievements or mistakes, but on the degree of impact their actions have on the community.

When training people from more individualistic cultures, consider the following:

- Connect DEI to individual needs and success. You can do this by sharing information on how leaders who foster DEI are more successful.
- To a lesser degree, consider instilling a sense of urgency by warning how individuals may be judged or even disciplined for not fostering DEI.
- Provide participants with ample opportunities to share their own personal stories.
- Start by defining individual goals and expectations, then work toward common needs.
- Ask participants to consider times when they have experienced being "othered" and the impact it had on them. One way to promote empathy and compassion for individualists is to connect it with their own experiences of pain.
- Translate concepts to practical and specific tools and techniques participants can practice on their own to foster DEI.
- Provide ample opportunities for individuals to share personal perspectives in an open forum.

When training people from more collectivist cultures, consider the following:

- Connect DEI to the greater good of the team, the organization, the community, or the overall society.
- To a lesser degree, instill a sense of urgency by warning people of the impact on the group if individuals do not engage in inclusive and equitable behaviors. (For example, rather than "You will suffer consequences" focus on "The organization or the group will suffer.")
- Start by defining common goals and expectations, then work toward focusing on the unique needs of individuals.
- Encourage the group to identify and practice behaviors that will serve the collective.

Cultural Dimension 3: Emotional Expressiveness vs. Restraint
Tell us how you really feel.

Regardless of high or low context communicators, the degree to which people openly express their emotions is an important cultural communication dimension that can influence the learning environment.

Expressive cultures find it appropriate and favorable to express one's emotions publicly. Doing so is seen as a means of engagement, interest, and trust. For example, in many Middle Eastern and Latin American countries, people are comfortable expressing a full range of emotions heartily, from joy to grief to anger.

In restrained cultures, it is considered inappropriate to express emotions publicly. It may be seen as a loss of control, weakness, or immaturity. Conveying emotion is not necessarily taboo, but it is expected to be done in a dispassionate way. People may engage in open disagreement or confrontation but do so with a great deal of regulation of vocal tones, body language, and voice volume. They argue the "facts" and steer clear of mentioning feelings.

Growing up in a multicultural family, I saw these dimensions on display regularly. My father's Armenian-Cuban side of the family was highly emotionally expressive. At meals, people would vociferously argue their points, raising their voices, waving their arms, and laughing loudly. My aunties would tell us stories of their childhood experiences as refugees with expressive body language and tears. To be sure, the tales they told us were incredibly painful and full of grief. It was a part of their identity to share their pride, pain, and joy openly. My mother's Polish side of the family could also be boisterous at times, but only when the emotions were positive. Humor and happiness were acceptable emotions, but openly expressing anger or grief were silently discouraged. They would most assuredly argue and engage in conflict, but often in an emotionally controlled way, debating points and details rather than articulating their feelings. My mother's family had plenty of stories of trauma, grief, and hardship. However, they told those stories in an almost clinical way in comparison to my father's family. I came to appreciate that neither side of the family was right or wrong in the way they communicated or expressed themselves. They were operating from their own cultural paradigms.

Emotions play a critical role in DEI work. However they express them, people will likely experience heightened states of emotion as they reflect on and share experiences related to identity, equity, and inclusion. The training needs to create a space for people to experience and channel their emotions in a culturally appropriate way.

When training people from more emotionally restrained cultures, consider the following:

- Provide people with time for quiet reflection, journaling, or visual arts (images, drawing, or painting) to describe the emotions they experience.
- Manage your own interpretations of participants' behaviors—just because they're not showing emotion in a way that makes sense to you does not mean they are not feeling emotions, perhaps even very strongly.
- Name and validate the possible range of emotions people may be experiencing so they do not have to express it themselves (for example, "I can imagine this conversation creates a sense of frustration or irritation for some in the room").

- Ask questions that omit "feeling" words (rather than "How did that make you feel?" ask "What is that like for you?" or "What was the impact on the team?").

When training people from more emotionally expressive cultures, consider the following:

- Provide people with open space to share their feelings freely.
- Manage your own interpretations of participants' behaviors—heightened expressiveness may seem to you like a loss of control but it may simply be them indicating engagement.
- Engage the group in mindful moments or deep breathing exercises if the emotional temperature climbs to an uncomfortable degree. Acknowledge that the emotions are powerful and natural, and invite the group to bring themselves to a mental state where they can have more constructive conversations.
- Remind participants (especially if you are in a mixed group) to give space and time for those who have not shared yet.

Cultural Dimension 4: High vs. Low Power Distance
Who's in charge?

Cultural values around hierarchy and power may play one of the most influential roles in a global DEI setting. Geert Hofstede, a social psychologist who specialized in intercultural differences, described power distance as "the extent to which the less powerful members of institutions or organizations accept that power is distributed unequally" (Hofstede, Hofstede, and Minkov 2010).

Low power distance cultures tend to be more egalitarian than hierarchical ones, where people expect to have an equal say, be involved in decision making, and have more autonomy, regardless of their role in a society or organization. In lower power distance cultures you may often see less formality in terms of interactions between people in power positions (supervisors, executives, community leaders) and lower status positions (employees or younger community members). People in lower status positions feel free to jump the chain of command and voice their honest opinions to people several levels senior to them. Younger members of the organization or society are not as likely to show deference to their elders, and they adopt a fairly informal attitude in their relationships. There are more decentralized structures, with delegation and more power given to the team or community.

High power distance cultures are more hierarchical, where people expect those in power (leaders, elders) to speak first, make decisions, and distribute assignments. High power distance cultures tend to reward individuals who follow the rules of the social order, show deference to authority figures, and generally "know their place" in the systemic hierarchy. In higher power distance cultures there is a clear chain of command, where one must report only to the person directly above them. Younger people are expected to show deference to their elders and tend to be more formal when interacting with those in power in terms of greetings, expressions and gestures, and attire.

Training participants around the world has given me a front row seat to how power dynamics influence relationships and interactions in a learning environment.

For example, in the courses I teach at American University, my students represent cultures from all over the world. My first semester teaching (ironically teaching a class on intercultural communication!), I made the mistake of insisting that my students just call me by my first name. I was not that far removed from being a student myself, and even though I had lived abroad and studied cultural differences, my own cultural paradigm was based on the deep conditioning of growing up in a relatively low power distance society. I noticed immediately how many of my American students obliged and called me Maria. However, my students from other countries, particularly students from East Asia, continued to call me Professor Morukian.

I decided to use it as a collective learning moment, and I asked the students about their initial reaction to my request that they call me by my first name. One of the Asian students said, "I often find myself in this situation. When American professors ask me to call them by their first name, even though I understand it's cultural, I have a visceral reaction in my chest. It is so uncomfortable to me, based on how I was brought up. I just can't bring myself to do it."

Since that time, I have never insisted participants or students refer to me by my first name. I wait to see how they address me. I am also conscious of power dynamics in situations where I must show deference to others because of their position, their age, or their influence in an organization or society.

Power distance can be quite different depending on where one lives within a country or the industry or organization to which one belongs. For example, in the US, there tends to be a cultural pattern toward higher power distance in Southern states. Children are taught from a young age to refer to their elders as "ma'am" or "sir," which carries through into adulthood when addressing someone who is perceived as having more status due to age, seniority, or position. The military and many federal agencies I have worked within tend to have higher power distance cultures. There is a clear chain of command and an established hierarchy that people are expected to follow.

When I first started working at the Department of State's Foreign Service Institute as an internal leadership development trainer, I attended a meeting with a group of leaders. As I took my seat at the conference table, I smiled at people as they entered. They looked at me and smiled hesitantly, then averted their gaze. I was confused by their actions. Then the senior director, who was a career ambassador, entered the room. She looked at me and said brusquely, "You're in my seat." My cheeks flushed as I apologized, gathered my notebook, and stumbled to a chair along the back wall. I was equally embarrassed by my faux pas and enraged by my new colleagues, who did not alert me to the fact that I was in the boss's appointed seat. Yet I realized that there was such a deep and intrinsic cultural pattern around hierarchy that it didn't occur to people that I may not know the rules. Either that or they were trying to haze me. I guess I'll never know!

Power distance can be an interesting cultural dimension as it relates to conversations around diversity, equity, and inclusion, especially the concept of equity. Cultural norms around where people belong in the social hierarchy are so deeply entrenched that it can be difficult to address or challenge those norms, even when they impede DEI.

There is some argument about the definition of "power" in this case, and the actual level of acceptance of less powerful members versus an applied distribution of power that awards more to some and less to others, not by their own will. In both high and low power distance societies, there are usually identity groups that are marginalized, whose rights or power is either taken away or prohibited. For instance, Austria and Israel rank as two of the lowest power distance countries in Hofstede's cultural dimensions index. However, income inequality in Austria has risen in the last two decades, with an increasingly polarized social structure that disadvantages women, immigrants, and the poor. Israel is second only to the United States in having the highest income inequality in the developed world. Additionally, gender, religious, and ethnic inequalities leave many talented members of Israeli society out of the job market.

Income inequality is not necessarily the only factor that contributes to who has power in a society or institution, but it does play a crucial role in defining an individual's opportunities for employment, compensation, and career advancement, not to mention the power of social networks that are gained from access to good education, and safer and more prosperous communities.

Power distance dynamics will surely influence both the content you select in training with globally diverse groups as well as the delivery of the training.

When training participants from higher power distance cultures, consider the following:

- Do your research. Know who will be in the learning environment and proper ways to greet and interact with them.
- Be prepared to dress more formally, especially if there will be notable people (leaders, elders) participating.
- Consider where you will seat those individuals in the classroom. Quite often, they will expect to have a choice seating placement alongside others at the same level in the hierarchy.

- Be prepared to be greeted with more formality or deference from others if you are considered the senior.
- Be cautious when correcting or challenging a person who is in a place of power. You do not want to offend them or alienate the entire audience by appearing disrespectful.
- Participants will be more likely to share their honest opinions or challenge ideas in small groups than in the larger group. Break people up, trying to place participants in groups of fairly equal status, to encourage engagement. Ask each group to collectively write their ideas. You may even go so far as to read the responses yourself rather than calling on a participant to speak out, which could potentially be embarrassing.

When training participants from a lower power distance culture, consider the following:

- Adopt a less formal tone, and share personal stories about yourself.
- Reinforce the idea that you are all on equal footing, learning together.
- Take a more facilitative approach and encourage participants to take the lead in conversations.
- Use a process to ensure that everyone has an opportunity to speak up; manage the "over-sharers" (who may take up more airtime) to encourage diverse perspectives.
- Manage your assumptions—participants who challenge you or others, or who appear less formal in their attire or behaviors, are not trying to be disrespectful or rude. They are operating from a different cultural paradigm.

Cultural Dimension 5: Orientation to Relationships, Task, and Time

What do we prioritize?

Growing up, my family was referred to as the Mañana Morukians. My father was definitely the bigger proponent of this cultural practice, believing that anything that could be done today could also be put off until tomorrow if something else was more pleasing, interesting, or necessary. "*Lo hago mañana*" ("I'll do it tomorrow") was a common refrain of my father. However, even my mother, who came from a more scheduled and regimented cultural background, had a relatively lax perspective on punctuality when it came to social life. Both of my parents were notorious in their circle of friends for their flexible views on timeliness. One family friend joked that when hosting a party, they sent a special invitation to us that announced the start time of the event two hours earlier than what they told everyone else, so we would show up one hour late instead of three. We also were often the last people to leave the party. There were one or two occasions where I remember standing by the front door for up to an hour after we announced we were leaving, while my parents continued to talk to our hosts. It was not that my parents intended to be rude or didn't care about punctuality. Their general approach to time was that whatever was particularly of interest, or whoever needed them in that moment, took priority. If one of my aunties called my father five minutes before we were supposed to leave the house, he sat on the phone with them until the conversation was complete, even if it meant being a little (or a lot) late.

I have inherited the Mañana Morukian gene and catch flack for it often from some of my friends. I will, however, always be on time for events where my presence is really important, like when I'm teaching a class or one of my daughters has a piano recital or soccer game. But if something or someone needs my attention right now, I will focus on that even when it means being a little late to the next item on my calendar.

Research has been conducted on different cultural expectations around time, as well as prioritization in the workplace to personal relationships versus task achievement. I've rolled these up into one broader cultural orientation of relationships, task, and time.

In relationship-oriented cultures, people tend to place a greater value on building and maintaining long-lasting interpersonal relationships. They tend to be less transactional and emphasize well-being and community. In relationship-oriented cultures, time is more fluid. We refer to this as polychronic time. Tasks are often done simultaneously and out of sequence. The clock is a suggestion for start and end times, and there is typically an expectation that people will arrive after the formally written start time but will stay after the end time if the conversation needs to continue.

In task-oriented cultures, people tend to place a greater value on accomplishing set goals in an efficient manner. Relationships may be more transactional and short-term. Individuals prioritize goal setting, structured approaches for execution of tasks, and managing schedules. In task-oriented cultures, time is seen as sequential, and people prioritize following a certain order, sticking to schedules, and knowing that there is a time and place for everything. We refer to this as monochronic time. People who have a more monochronic mindset tend to believe that punctuality is crucial to show respect, that time is a commodity that must be valued by all, and that the clock should dictate when an event begins and when it ends.

This is not to say that task-oriented, monochronic time cultures do not value relationships. They absolutely do, and in fact would argue that it is because they value their relationships with others that they maintain punctuality. It is also not the case that relationship-oriented, polychronic cultures do not have a focus on the task and getting the work done. In fact, they would argue that it is because they want to get the highest quality product that they take time up front to build relationships.

One example that I have often come across when training in international settings is the communication disconnect around greetings. In the US, it is customary to greet one another by saying, "How are you?" However, that question is not necessarily an invitation for a real answer! The typical US response is "I'm fine." Other cultures find this confusing and sometimes insulting. I once had a Nigerian participant relay to me that he was taken aback when an American colleague asked, "How are you?" and then immediately began talking about work tasks without waiting for a response to the question. The Nigerian co-worker had assumed "How are you?" was an invitation to share, and he was about to tell his colleague some good news about his children's latest educational achievements when the American co-worker turned and started talking about deadlines. He described the conversation as making him "feel a chill inside my body."

In my work as a leadership development specialist with the US Department of State, I often found myself translating cultural expectations between US Foreign Service officers and their foreign national colleagues. Often, the source of conflict was based in this cultural dimension of task versus relationship orientation. Foreign nationals would perceive their US counterparts as aloof, uncaring, and overly anxious about deadlines. US employees would perceive their foreign counterparts as uncommitted, disengaged, and lax about deadlines. Neither approach is necessarily better or worse. Both can lead to efficiency and productivity as well as healthy work relationships, when people understand one another's priorities, practice patience with one another, and communicate openly about their needs. It's important to help multinational groups determine the right balance and identify mutually beneficial working norms that create adequate time for relationship building and accomplishing tasks.

When training participants from a more relationship-oriented, polychronic culture, consider the following:

- Build in more time for introductions and relationship building from the beginning of the program.
- Schedule more frequent and longer breaks for meals and refreshments.
- Plan group outings or activities after hours, especially if people are traveling to the training site.
- Take time to get to know participants, share personal stories, ask about their lives, and remember details. (Depending on the culture, find out in advance what is appropriate to ask people about their lives. Some cultures may expect you to ask about their families, personal interests, and so on. Others may be more reserved.)

When training participants from a more task-oriented, monochronic culture, consider the following:

- Be vigilant about starting and ending on time.
- Provide an agenda with clear time markers for various activities.

- Provide clear learning objectives and specify new knowledge and skills and how they will support participants' professional needs.
- Follow the agenda. If you believe it's important to veer from the schedule, articulate your plan and reasoning to participants. (For example, "I know the agenda says we are starting a new module after lunch, but I believe we need a bit more time to complete the content in this module, so we will make some adjustments to the delivery schedule.")

Summary

DEI training in a globally diverse setting requires a significant amount of research and refinement to align with the needs of a multicultural audience.

When designing training for a globally diverse audience, research the appropriate content and choose appropriate delivery mechanisms. Explore the multiple cultural identity groups, and the "us and them" divisions that may be present. Consider the cultural values and norms that may impact how you interact with the audience and how they interact with one another.

In the next chapter, we will explore the deep self-reflection work that DEI practitioners and training professionals must continuously do to be effective.

Worksheet 7-1. Preparing for Training in a Globally Diverse Setting

Managing Content	Action Needed
Who are your cultural guides and what dimensions of diversity do they represent in the culture (dominant and nondominant)?	
Is the current training design relevant to the audience in terms of names, scenarios, slang, and case studies?	
What topics may be more or less delicate, uncomfortable, or taboo? What do you need to lean into? What do you need to steer clear from?	
How will you establish connection and common ground with the audience?	
What personal cultural-value conflicts may exist for you? What emotional triggers do you need to prepare for? How will you handle any challenges?	
Accommodating Language Needs	
Will you need interpreters and, if so, how many and for what languages?	
What languages will materials be printed in?	
What videos or other media may require captioning, dubbing, or translated transcripts?	
Is it possible to co-present with a native speaker of the home language?	
How will you need to alter your presentation style and approach to communicate across any language or cultural differences?	

Worksheet 7-1 (cont.)

Location and Timing	Action Needed
How will participants access the training location? Does it accommodate the needs of diverse participants or leave anyone out?	
What AV and technological restrictions may you encounter and what contingency plans do you need to have in place?	
When will the training take place and does it accommodate the needs of participants in terms of environmental factors, religious or cultural observations and events, etc.?	
Where are people traveling from? Do you need to consider jet lag?	
What time zone is the training taking place in? How can you accommodate people attending from different time zones if the training is virtual?	
Are there any safety or access considerations?	
What should you consider in terms of dietary accommodations?	

Chapter 8
Doing Your Own Work

I grew up in the suburbs of Detroit. Our home was in a small, safe neighborhood that was mostly White, middle class, and Christian. The ethnic diversity that existed on our block included the Chens, who were Chinese-American, and the Kalias, who had emigrated from India. Beyond that, my family was probably next in line in terms of diversity because my father was foreign-born and spoke with an accent.

My parents were teachers at Finney High, a public high school in Detroit. When I visited their school, it was like I was traveling to a new country. The vast majority of the students were Black and from working class families. They spoke differently. They walked differently. The cadence of their conversations was different. The way they interacted with the adults was different.

My family had a circle of friends of diverse ages, religions, races, and nationalities. When my parents hosted dinners at our house, we were accustomed to seeing Mr. Johnson in his dashiki chatting with Uncle Hrayr and his Argentine wife, Maria Rosa. They sat next to Mrs. Murray, a retired ballerina and refugee from Greece who wore a black wig, deep purple eyeshadow, and flowing dresses, and her husband, John, an Irish-Scottish man in his 70s, resplendent in a three-piece suit and pocket watch. Then there were my two aunties and my grandmother, dressed like they had stepped out of the 1930s and speaking a mixture of Armenian and Spanish, alongside my mother's blond, blue-eyed sister,

Kathy, and her husband, Gene, who equally loves deer hunting and sewing and objectively has the best mustache in Michigan. Our meals were filled with a variety of flavors from our different ancestries, from imam bayildi (a vegetable dish like ratatouille) with pilaf, to charnina (a Polish soup), to ropa vieja (a popular Cuban dish).

The richness and mixing of these different customs and cultures was my norm. Yet it didn't preclude me from an early education in racism and privilege. There were the explicit messages from my parents, like the warning to make sure the car doors were locked when we drove into certain neighborhoods where the people we passed on the street were mostly Black. My parents had a code word, "sev," the Armenian word for the color black, which they used in public settings if they wanted to make a derogatory remark about a person of color. They would recount stories of their students, mocking their names or the way they spoke.

Then there were more implicit messages. There was gang violence that sometimes infiltrated the school, and several shootings that took place in the school while my parents were there. They made light of these events, so as not to frighten us. But in doing so, I never heard them utter any concern for the students' safety or for the condition of the injured teens. When I was old enough to go to the mall with my friends, we were encouraged to go shopping at the mall that was farther away in a more affluent (Whiter) area that they said would be safer, rather than the mall that was close by but in a less safe neighborhood (where mostly people of color resided). Although it wasn't explicitly stated, we read between the lines of our parents' comments. My brain stored those messages away in my unconscious mind.

My parents were my role models. I revered them. They taught me to be curious about the world, to fight for equality, and to treat others with respect and compassion. They were also a product of their upbringing and their environment. They were largely unaware of the impact of their explicit and implicit biases on their own behaviors. I was largely unaware of how their biases filtered into my brain.

It was and continues to be painful for me to acknowledge these contradictions, to recognize the prevalence of racism in my life and upbringing, and own my role (however unconscious I was to it) in perpetuating a system and culture of oppression and inequality.

I cannot in good conscience do the deep work of diversity, equity, and inclusion if I hold these topics at arm's length. The work begins and ends with self-reflection, and a willingness to expose myself to my own biases and unearned advantages. The purpose of this self-reflection is not to drown myself in guilt or shame, or to ridicule my family for the biases they had. It's quite the opposite. My stories are multifaceted, and it is only by holding them up to the light and examining both the beauty and the blemishes that I can see myself for all that I am.

What dimensions of your identity may influence your work as a DEI trainer? What implicit biases might you carry? What automatic advantages or disadvantages impacted your place in society? How does your personal story of identity influence the way you approach DEI work?

Looking Inward

In a podcast interview with the journalist Ezra Klein, Bryan Stevenson (2020), author of *Just Mercy* and founder of the Equal Justice Initiative, said:

> I think it's really important that people understand that if you're genuinely engaged and recovering from human rights abuses, you have to commit to truth-telling first. You can't jump to reconciliation. You can't jump to reparation or restoration until you tell the truth. Until you know the nature of the injuries, you can't actually speak to the kind of remedies that are going to be necessary.
>
> But until we tell the truth, we deny ourselves the opportunity for beauty. Justice can be beautiful. Reconciliation can be beautiful. Repair can be beautiful. It's powerful to actually experience redemption. And we deny ourselves that when we insist on denying our broken past, our ugly past, our racist past, when we insist on avoiding the truth.

It is only by having the courage to explore and own our full stories that we can begin to break the cycle of oppression and injustice. Trainers have to do the internal work in order to model what it takes to act inclusively with their learners. DEI work is deeply personal and can be emotional and raw. Trainers who are committing themselves to this work need to be willing to get vulnerable with their audience. It's not enough to rely on research and models. This work is about putting your full humanity on display. It is emotionally taxing, especially for trainers who come from nondominant or marginalized groups.

This chapter will prepare you as a training professional to effectively manage yourself when doing DEI training. It will provide opportunities for self-reflection. We will explore how your own identities and lenses influence your behaviors in the environment. We will also discuss ways to center yourself and engage in practices to maintain your mental, physical, emotional, and spiritual health. Two worksheets at the end of the chapter will help you explore your own identity and create a checklist for developing your skills as a DEI trainer.

Ask Yourself Why You Want to Do DEI

Diversity, equity, and inclusion training and facilitation require a deep self-reflection for practitioners to explore their own identity dimensions and the lenses through which they see and make sense of the world. You need to honestly explore your own blind spots, stereotypes, and behaviors in order to build the skills to manage yourself effectively in the learning space. This may seem simplistic, but it's important to begin with your "why."

If you are embarking on this journey to do DEI training, know your reason for getting into this work. If you are doing it right, it is exceedingly difficult. It is emotionally, physically, and even spiritually taxing. It requires complex skills and years of practice. Some of the people with whom you interact will respond with anger, resistance, or defensiveness. They may challenge you, blame you, or attack your credibility.

If you are part of one or more marginalized identity groups, your journey may be different than if you are part of one or more dominant or majority groups. Depending on your identity dimensions, you will face different opportunities and challenges when it comes to building trust, rapport, and credibility with your participants. You will also be emotionally triggered by different things. The extent of the emotional toll you will encounter will be different.

The work is intensely challenging but also intensely beautiful. You will learn so much from your participants and your co-facilitators. You will live for the moments when people experience catharsis in sharing their pain, when you find connection in hearing others' stories, and when you renew your own and others' hope in forging a better future.

DEI work requires an extraordinary amount of resilience, a sturdy spine, and endless stores of humility.

Explore the Dimensions of Your Identity

In chapter 3, we talked about the iceberg metaphor and the multiple dimensions of identity that form who we are. As a DEI trainer, it's important to be familiar with the various dimensions of your identity, and comfortable enough to share what's beneath the surface. It is important to consider how your identity lenses influence the way you see others based on what is visible about them.

First, consider what dimensions of your identity are visible to others (for example, skin color, hair style and texture, clothing, age, physical size, accent, physical ability). How do these dimensions that are visible influence your self-perception? How do they influence how others perceive and interact with you? What is the story that you believe you carry on the surface?

The reality is that, upon meeting someone for the first time, we all make instantaneous judgments about that person based on very little data—just what we can immediately see and hear. Research shows that when we even briefly encounter another person and have limited or ambiguous information, the parts of the brain that are activated are related to our emotions and values processing (Schiller, Freeman, Mitchell, Uleman & Phelps 2009). Our emotional memory of a person or group can still "stick" even when we are given new information that alters or contradicts that initial impression.

For example, I am a light-skinned female, petite in size, with medium-length blond hair. I speak with an American accent (and a hint of a Michigan twang if I get excited about something). In business environments, I wear relatively modest, tailored suits or dresses. I smile. A lot. (Again, from Michigan). When I walk into a room or show up on a webcam, these are the dimensions of my identity that are immediately observable and drive first impressions. When I have asked people to describe me based on first impressions, their responses are typically things like:

- "You are friendly and energetic."
- "You seem really nice and positive."
- "You work out a lot."
- "You are economically well off."
- "You are well educated."

I would not necessarily argue over the validity of these statements. However, they do not reveal much about who I am, about the experiences I have had, or about my core values and beliefs.

Also, the emotional response of each participant in my class based on first impressions will differ depending on their identity and experiences. Some may process the visible data about me and react with a positive impression. Others may take in the same visible data and react with a more negative impression of me based on their experiences and the identity groups I represent to them.

These immediate impressions happen subconsciously, but they are powerful. As a trainer, it is important to be familiar with the various dimensions of your identity that may immediately register emotions of trust or distrust, like or dislike, among different participants.

Because first impressions occur in an unconscious and involuntary way, we cannot necessarily change them. What we can and should do as trainers is be willing to share dimensions of our identity that are beneath the surface that give a more multifaceted view of our values, beliefs, and experiences.

In presenting the topic of dimensions of identity and the iceberg model, I will share my iceberg with participants to reveal more of my story.

Surface level:

- I am White.
- I am a cisgender woman.
- I am petite.
- I am blond (with some help from my hair stylist!).
- I have an American accent.
- I wear a sapphire ring on my left third finger.

When I discuss what is beneath the waterline, I invite participants to go snorkeling first by sharing aspects of their identity that are fairly easy and comfortable to talk about, even though they may not be immediately visible. These dimensions begin to build a fuller story of the individual.

Snorkeling level:

- I love running.
- I am a big reader.
- I have two daughters.
- I am married to a cisgender man.
- I am Armenian, Cuban, and Polish and grew up in a multicultural, multilingual family.
- I feel like my fullest self when I'm traveling and exploring other cultures.

Then I invite participants to put on their scuba gear and dive down a bit deeper, to share dimensions of identity that are not only invisible but perhaps less easy or comfortable to share. These dimensions require us to really trust others so we can be vulnerable. They often are the stories about us that carry the deepest emotions, but reveal a great deal about our core values, our passions, our fears.

Scuba level:

I was 18 years old when my mom died of cancer. I was 31 when I lost my dad suddenly to heart failure. Although I had my parents through my childhood, living as an adult without their guidance and not being able to share my children with them is heartbreaking for me. I immediately gravitate toward people who have lost a parent because we share a grief that is impossible to know unless you have lived through it.

Although I present to the world an impression of positivity and confidence, I have been diagnosed with clinical depression and anxiety. These conditions run in my family, and for most of my life were something that nobody spoke of. For years, I went undiagnosed because I carried embarrassment, fear, and shame around my condition.

I deeply value community, and for me the concept of "family" goes far beyond the people who live in my house. Family includes close friends from all walks of life, colleagues and supervisors with whom I have developed a deep devotion, aunties and uncles and cousins and pretty much anyone with a surname that ends in "-ian" because they likely have Armenian ancestry. If someone in my extended family is in need, I will drop everything and go to their aid.

Some scuba level stories can be challenging for us to explore for ourselves let alone share with strangers. It is uncomfortable and even terrifying to be so open and vulnerable, to show our full humanity (warts and all) to others. Yet, what I have come to learn is that my scuba stories are the ones that most resonate with people. I have had beautiful conversations with people who are very different from me in terms of their beliefs and experiences, because they have a similar scuba story.

A word of caution. Only you can determine the scuba stories you are ready and willing to tell. As the trainer, the spotlight should not be on you for an extensive amount of time. The intent of telling your story is for you to model the power of sharing what is below the surface so that participants can learn and practice. We'll discuss this later in the chapter.

Get Acquainted With Your Biases

Dr. Rupa Marya, a physician who has conducted significant research on the intersection between colonization, racism, and public health, recounted a story in a speech in which she described a Black female patient who was complaining about chest pains but not receiving proper treatment for her symptoms. Dr. Marya described the process of having to check herself to recognize the potential biases that might influence her decisions. She now challenges herself to engage in self-inquiry and to talk with her colleagues to ask, what are we missing?

In chapter 3 we discussed bias as a topic to cover in training. It is also critical for you as a training professional to acknowledge and own your implicit biases. Just as first impressions will impact how others see and judge you as a trainer, you also need to be aware of how your first impressions of others influence your perspective and judgment.

As human beings, we all have implicit associations and hidden biases. Often, those biases are in direct opposition to what we consciously believe, and may even be oppositional to our values. The explicit and implicit messages we receive from those in our cultural identity groups, our families, our schools, the media, and our social network all influence our unconscious brain.

We carry positive as well as negative attitudes and biases, depending on the similarities we assume we have with a person.

As an Armenian, I feel an instant sense of solidarity when I meet someone else who is of Armenian heritage. It's like a mini family reunion, even if we have never met before. We immediately smile at each other with our whole being and greet one another with, *"Inchpes ek"* (how are you?) and *"Lav em"* (I am well). Beyond the shared language and food, there is a deeper bond that pulls people of Armenian ancestry toward one another. When we meet, we implicitly see in one another's eyes the shared story of trauma and genocide that went largely unacknowledged for a century. We know of the common stories passed from our parents and grandparents of family and friends who perished or witnessed unspeakable acts of violence against their kin. We are a generation or two removed from a people who survived only by leaving behind their lives, their land, and their loved ones, and being scattered across the Earth, holding desperately to their language and customs. Much to my grandmother's chagrin, my sister and I never learned the language of our ancestors.

As a Michigan native, I automatically feel a kinship with others from my state. We have a common dialect and shared nostalgia for local restaurant chains, games, and even television commercials from our childhood.

Since the state is shaped like a mitten, we use our hands as a map to ask "where are you from?" The connection with other people from my home state runs deeper than some common landmarks or cultural memes. There is an implicit sense of familiarity, the comfort of knowing that someone "gets" me in a way that non-Michigan people don't.

Finding commonalities can be powerful for building connection with others. Because of that similarity and positive bias, we are often more patient, compassionate, and encouraging with people with whom we share some identity dimension.

On the other hand, even positive biases can be challenging or potentially harmful. We may overestimate the similarities we share with a person, or we may project our own experiences, values, and beliefs on someone who has a very different story, even if we do have something in common.

As a trainer, I need to consider which participants I may offer some additional encouragement or attention to simply because we share a common identity dimension. I may automatically feel a kinship with women of my age who have children like I do. There is nothing wrong with this affinity, but I need to be conscious that I:

- Don't assume similarity in values, beliefs, or life experiences simply because we share that dimension of identity. My experience as a mother is significantly different from that of a mother of a child with a disability, or a mother of a Black son, or a single mother, or an immigrant mother with children born in the US. Although we may share some common experiences, our interests, fears, worries, and expectations for our children are not universal simply because we share the identity of motherhood.
- Don't give an overabundance of positive attention to people of my identity group, which may send signals to other participants that their experiences or ideas are less important or valid to me. I may unconsciously engage in more micro-affirmations with people who are like me, encouraging their participation, calling on them more frequently, and agreeing with their views.

As a trainer, I need to model the intentionality of engaging with all participants equitably, not showing favor to those who are "like" me.

Take note of what you immediately see about each image in Figure 8-1. What is visible to you? What perceptions first float into your mind? What is the "story" you tell yourself about each person? Notice the automatic associations that you make in your mind when you see each image. This is not a judgment of yourself. It is an opportunity to become better acquainted with your implicit associations and prejudgments so you can recognize when they may be influencing your decisions.

To check your biases, ask yourself the following:

- What messages have I received in my life that may have influenced my perceptions?
- What identity groups do I have the most exposure to?
- What identities do I have the least exposure to? How does that lack of exposure impact my understanding of their customs, behaviors, and experiences?
- How can I check for blind spots?

Examine Systems of Oppression

In her recent book, *Caste: The Origins of Our Discontents*, Isabel Wilkerson describes examples of societal structures that are built and maintained to uphold a system of inequality, in which groups and individuals are assigned a place in the social hierarchy and expected to accept and stay in that order:

"A caste system is an artificial construction, a fixed and embedded ranking of human value that sets the presumed supremacy of one group against the presumed inferiority of other groups" (Wilkerson 2020).

Wilkerson goes on to state that for any of us who have been given unearned advantages because of the identity group to which we have been assigned, we have an important role that we must be willing to play to upend the very system that affords us the comfort and privilege of our place.

Figure 8-1. Visually Representing Diversity

"The price of privilege is the moral duty to act when one sees another person treated unfairly. And the least that a person in the dominant caste can do is not make the pain any worse" (Wilkerson 2020).

In her book *So You Want to Talk About Race*, Ijeoma Oluo (2018) gives a powerful analogy to describe the patterns that affect people of color:

> *Imagine if you were walking down the street and every few minutes someone would punch you in the arm. You don't know who will be punching you, and you don't know why. You are hurt and wary and weary. You are trying to protect yourself, but you can't get off this street. Then imagine somebody walks by, maybe gesticulating wildly in interesting conversation, and they punch you in the arm on accident. Now imagine that this is the last straw, that this is where you scream. That person may not have meant to punch you in the arm, but the issue for you is still the fact that people keep punching you in the arm.*

Oluo goes on to explain that the challenge we face in our society is that people want those who are being punched to "prove" the number of times they have been purposely punched, rather than listening to the individual who has experienced the pain too many times to count (Oluo 2018).

When someone's story doesn't "compute" for us because it doesn't match our own experience, we tend to devalue or invalidate the other person's experience simply because we can't understand it. Yet ironically, we all want our own experiences to be validated by others.

This is the case not only with racial identity, but also with gender, socioeconomic status, disability, sexual orientation, religion, and any other major dimension of identity that may lead to societal advantage or disadvantage.

For example, many men were stunned in 2017, when the #MeToo movement picked up steam, to hear their girlfriends, wives, sisters, mothers, and friends disclose their own experiences of being discriminated against, harassed, assaulted, and violated. Men could not understand how they hadn't known. Furthermore, men found it hard to accept that these experiences were not anomalies but were commonplace and deeply embedded in women's daily lives. It's not that men were uncompassionate or uncaring about the marginalization and oppression of women. It just didn't compute because it was not their experience. Even when the problem became something closer to them, when they saw it through the eyes of women they knew and cared about, it was still difficult to process.

To effectively conduct DEI training, you need to do your own research, to understand the history and socialization of inequalities that permeate our systems and cultures. It is impossible to know every detail, but start by acquainting yourself with the basics and be in constant learning mode.

One of the reactions I often hear in my training when we talk about the history of oppression in our society is, "Why didn't I learn this in school?" The simple reason is that if we were born into some automatic advantage, we didn't need to. The more privilege we have, the less informed we need to be to survive, because the system and the rules are set up for us. It is only when we are part of a marginalized or oppressed identity group that we must be educated about the systems because we are more likely to be punished if we step outside the lines that have been painted for us. The system continues so long as everyone upholds it. Thus, those whose identities place them higher in the social order are blinded to the existence of their advantage, and those who are oppressed must obey the rules or face punishment. In fact, calling attention to their oppression or the unearned advantages of their peers often leads to dire consequences for the oppressed. They are labeled as whiners or troublemakers. They are told that their story of oppression is unfounded, that they are looking for excuses when in reality their situation must be their own doing.

To examine systems of oppression, ask yourself the following:
- What is your understanding of and exposure to systemic inequality? What identity groups do you belong to that have given you unearned advantages?

- What identity groups do you belong to that have disadvantaged you or led to unfair treatment for me or people like you?
- What are some of your earliest memories around your identity? What messages did you receive that let you know where you fit in the social hierarchy?
- How did the people in your social network (family, friends, religious leaders, teachers) talk about or behave around people in your identity group? How was that similar to or different from the way they talked about or behaved around other identities? (For example, what messages did elders or leaders in your faith community send around the role of women versus men?)
- What immediate reactions do I have when someone from a different identity group talks about oppression? (For example, if I am White and I hear a POC talk about their experience with racism?)

Explore Your Automatic Advantages and Disadvantages

As we discussed in chapter 3, privilege is an automatic, unearned advantage that an individual receives based on some aspect of their identity, typically one over which they have little or no control.

In *Beyond Inclusion, Beyond Empowerment*, Leticia Nieto and her colleagues describe how within systems of human social hierarchy there are two roles: Agent and Target (Nieto et al. 2014).

The Agent group is the social group that is overvalued and seen as the "norm." People who are part of the Agent group receive unearned advantages and privileges, and consistent messages affirming their existence. They find it easier to get jobs and promotions, see more positive representations of their identity in the media, and expect that their needs will be taken seriously by institutions.

People who are part of the Target group are devalued and marginalized. They are seen as the "other," and find many more restrictions to access opportunities in society, education, and work. They see less representation overall in the media, and representation is more negative or stereotyped. Their needs are often not addressed adequately by public institutions.

People can belong to a combination of Agent identity groups and Target identity groups. See some examples in Table 8-1. Some of us belong to a large number of Agent identities, which afford us status and opportunities that we may not even realize. Some of us belong to several Target identities, which might compound to create additional barriers for us in our personal and professional lives.

Table 8-1. **Agent and Target Groups**

Examples of Agent Identities in US	Examples of Target Identities in US
• White • Male • Heterosexual • Christian • Able bodied • English speaking without foreign accent • Wealthy, middle or owning-class	• POC • Female, transgender, intersex, gender nonbinary • Gay, lesbian, asexual, queer, pansexual, bisexual • Non-Christian religions (Jewish, Muslim, Hindu, Sikh, etc.) • Non–English speaking/English with foreign accent • Poor, working class or nonowning class • Disabled (mental or physical)

For people who have experienced disadvantages in their lives because they belong to one or more Target identity groups, it can be profoundly frustrating when people from Agent identity groups are unable or unwilling to acknowledge the impact of privilege on their lives.

For anyone who is part of one or more Agent identity groups, it is important to acknowledge your automatic advantages. Acknowledgment does not negate the hard work you had to do to get where you are today, nor does it diminish your stories of grief, pain, trauma, or perseverance. It simply unmasks the advantages you have been afforded.

For example:

- A White woman shopping at a clothing store is not likely to be worried about being followed by a clerk who assumes she is going to steal something.

- A White man may be anxious or annoyed if he sees the flashing red lights of a police cruiser in the rearview mirror of his SUV, but he doesn't automatically feel a twist of terror and worry about whether he'll be shot for reaching for his wallet to show his ID.
- An elderly Christian woman walking up the street to the grocery store to get a gallon of milk is not looking around wondering if she will be harassed or even beaten for wearing an article of clothing that identifies her religion.
- A store owner who does not have a disability or a loved one with a disability doesn't necessarily notice the peril of a wheelchair ramp that has obstacles or hasn't been shoveled after a snowstorm.
- Parents of able-bodied children do not consider that wood chips on a playground make the space safer for their kids but preclude a child in a wheelchair from being able to join the fun.

If you belong to one or more Target identity groups, DEI work may carry an additional element of emotional labor. You may find yourself frequently expected to be the sole representative of that identity group, answering questions to "explain" your identity group or responding to stereotypical comments from people in the Agent identity group. You may feel like you have to prove your credibility more than others in order to be taken seriously. You may share a personal story of pain and hardship only to have someone from the Agent identity group dismiss the legitimacy of your experience. You may become disillusioned or impatient when progress is stalled due to a lack of commitment from leadership. You may very likely find yourself burning out if you are tasked with leading DEI efforts on your own.

For example:
- A woman of color may be more frequently expected to engage in DEI-focused activities than her White colleagues and may feel frustrated or overwhelmed by the frequent requests to serve as the in-house DEI "expert."
- A White man may feel like he is primarily seen by colleagues only for the privilege his race and gender afford him, and does

not feel comfortable sharing that he grew up in poverty and lives with post-traumatic stress disorder (PTSD) and a hearing impairment from serving in active military duty.

You can use the stories of both your Agent and Target identities to build connections with your participants.

As a woman, especially one of smaller stature, I know the pain of being treated with less respect. I've been talked down to, literally from taller people and figuratively from people who talk to me as though I'm a child. I have been called "cute" and referred to as "the baby" by colleagues. I have been sexually harassed and propositioned for sex by men in professional settings. I am always on high alert when walking alone in a parking garage or down a deserted street in the dark, with the numbers 9-1-1 already dialed into my cell phone, ready to hit the send button if I am attacked. I have learned how to be just the right amount of courteous and friendly without potentially giving off the wrong "signal" to men at conferences or work events. I am exceedingly cautious about my clothing choices to appear stylish yet modest, for fear of my curves distracting people from my intelligence or expertise. I have experienced significant personal trauma and loss in my life. I am very familiar with the shape and depth of my stories of pain.

Yet I move through my daily life not having to feel burdened by or fearful because of my White identity, my heterosexual and cisgender identity, my socioeconomic identity, or my physical and mental ability.

I wake up every day without fear of my daughters being treated by their teachers or friends' parents as though they were far older than their actual years, as girls of color are often treated. I don't live in fear when my husband goes out for a run or a drive that he might not come back. I don't worry about which utility bills we will be able to pay at the end of the month. I don't have to wonder how I will cope with chronic pain, or debilitating disease. I don't have to worry that because of my weight I will be judged for eating a cupcake. I don't have to fear that members of my family may be deported. I don't wonder if I'll lose out on a promotion because of my sexual orientation.

These are all facets to my story—the pain and the privilege. One does not negate the other. They coexist. If I discount or ignore my privilege, I am not revealing the entirety of my story. Not only that, but I will not be able to build trust with colleagues or participants as a DEI trainer if I don't examine my privilege.

To acknowledge the impact of your Agent and Target identities, ask yourself the following:

- What are the Agent groups to which I belong? How does my membership to those groups influence my daily life?
- What are the Target groups to which I belong? How does my membership to those groups influence my daily life?
- When I look at the number of Agent groups versus Target groups to which I belong, what picture emerges? Do I belong to more Agent groups or Target groups in society?
- What daily activities can I engage in without fear and how might that be different for other identity groups?
- When I turn on the TV or open a book, what representations do I see of my different identity groups (such as race, gender, age, citizenship, sexual orientation, religion)?
- Who are the leaders, role models, superheroes, and other sources of inspiration I most commonly hear about? What dimensions of identity do they represent? Are those the people I think of? Why or why not?
- When others talk about their disadvantages, or their experience of discrimination, harassment, or exclusionary treatment because of their identity, what is my reaction?
- Whose stories do I find it hardest to connect with? Whose stories do I find harder to accept?
- Do I ever feel frustration or skepticism when someone talks about the disadvantages they have experienced? How come?

Develop Your Skills for DEI

Let's revisit the Intercultural Development Continuum from chapter 3, this time through the lens of personal skills development for people with Agent and Target identities. We will continue to use the language from the IDC, but will apply Nieto et al.'s Agent and Target skills models to the IDC framework (Figure 8-2).

Figure 8-2. **Stages of Development for DEI**

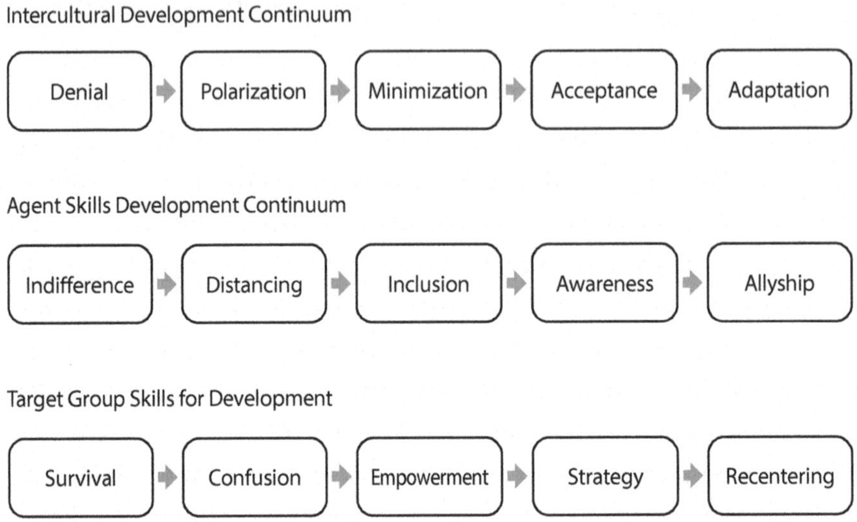

Intercultural Development Continuum

| Denial | ➡ | Polarization | ➡ | Minimization | ➡ | Acceptance | ➡ | Adaptation |

Agent Skills Development Continuum

| Indifference | ➡ | Distancing | ➡ | Inclusion | ➡ | Awareness | ➡ | Allyship |

Target Group Skills for Development

| Survival | ➡ | Confusion | ➡ | Empowerment | ➡ | Strategy | ➡ | Recentering |

IDC Stage: Denial

In denial, Milton Bennett and Mitchell Hammer describe that individuals are removed from exposure to different identities. They are disinterested or actively avoidant and have little to no ability to process or respond to differences. Their lack of interest and exposure leads to sweeping generalizations and stereotypes when they do consider different identity groups.

Agent Skills: Indifference

If you are a member of the Agent group, you are unaware of and thus indifferent to systems of oppression and the impact those systems have on Target groups. In this stage, you simply don't notice the existence of Target group members. That group is so far out of your range of vision that they are quite literally invisible to you and other members of your Agent group.

Target Skills: Survival

Members of the Target group are in survival mode, and respond only with the behaviors that are permitted within the system. If you are part of a Target group, your main focus is on making members of the Agent group comfortable by either being invisible to or "blending in" with the Agent group to the extent that is possible, or "fitting" the stereotype of your Target group, and presenting an exaggerated version of the Target group that fits the Agent group's expectations. You may not even realize you are doing this.

It comes from our basic survival instincts. We will adapt (or hide) our voices, words, actions, expressions, and appearance to align with the views and expectations of the dominant group. For example, a woman in a heavily male-dominated environment may either "act like a man" or judge herself by how well she fits the cultural expectations for female behaviors. A gay man might hide his sexual orientation from friends and even go so far as to "gay bash" to maintain his membership in the Agent group. Members of Target groups may even become mouthpieces for Agent groups in this stage, publicly stating "I don't experience oppression," or "I don't know what those other folks are complaining about."

IDC Stage: Polarization

In polarization, people seek to divide one identity group from another, typically with a value judgment applied where one identity group is superior to the other (or to all others).

Agent Skills: Distancing

If you are a member of the Agent group, this takes the form of distancing. You may distance out by pushing the identity group to the perimeter of your life ("I don't a have a problem with them as long as they don't move to my neighborhood or flaunt their lifestyle in my face"). Or, you may distance down by negatively evaluating, blaming, or openly hating the Target group ("They are the problem in this society," "They should go back to where they came from"). Distancing down can sometimes take a less hateful but no less harmful approach when members of the

Agent group label themselves as the saviors of a Target group and treat the group members as though they are incapable of helping themselves. This often occurs in service-oriented professions like education, religious missions, international development, and mental health or social services.

In polarization there is the phenomenon of reversal, where we exoticize or hold up another identity group as better than our own. In Agent identity groups, this is where cultural appropriation often occurs, or where you may romanticize or admire a group based on limited understanding of the group. Although it appears positive on the surface (for those in the Agent group at least) it can leave members of the Target group feeling tokenized or, worse, treated as a product for the consumption of the Agent identity group (Nieto et al. 2014).

Target Skills: Confusion

If you are a member of the Target group, you may experience a state of confusion at this stage. You may vacillate between wanting to value and honor your Target identity group and wanting to distance yourself from that identity. You are increasingly aware of the systems of oppression that are harmful to your identity group, but are conflicted and hesitant to speak out against those systems.

Tiffany Jana refers to this as attributional ambiguity, where a member of a Target group experiences a negative or exclusive message from a member of the Agent group but is unsure of whether the act occurred because of their Target identity or not. *Did he interrupt me because I am a woman of color? Did I not get the promotion because I am genderqueer? Did the boss really not hear me or was she ignoring my idea because I'm young?*

This stage is the point at which so many of us get stuck. When we are in polarization, especially as a member of the Agent group, we react to feedback with defensiveness. This is also the point at which DEI work can go awry. If we feel we're being labeled as mean-spirited, ignorant, callous, or selfish, that hardly encourages us to change our views. When we're part of the Target group, we may not have the language to articulate what we are experiencing, or we are fearful of "rocking the boat."

IDC Stage: Minimization

Minimization is the point at which we begin to evolve from "us vs. them" thinking. Minimization emphasizes what people perceive as core human needs and universal values. In minimization, we often downplay or ignore differences and reinforce perceived commonalities.

Agent Skills: Inclusion

If you are part of the Agent identity group, the concept of inclusion takes on a superficial form. You may downplay differences or engage in a simplistic celebration of differences. This is where we often hear members of the Agent group say things like, "I don't see color," or "If we all act with respect toward each other then we won't need to dwell on these issues."

To be clear, this is an important and sometimes necessary stage to bring people from a monocultural mindset to a multicultural mindset. When folks are in polarization, when Agent members are diminishing the experiences of those they perceive as the "other," minimization can be a valuable tool to build a common bond, to establish a sense of unity and hope. However, it can be destructive to progress if we stay in minimization without pushing ourselves and others to engage in the far less comfortable conversations around the existence and maintenance of oppressive systems.

Target Skills: Empowerment

For the members of the Target identity group, minimization can take a couple of forms. If you are still in survival mode in a space that is Agent-group dominant, you may fall into minimization to "go along to get along," because it is exhausting to feel like you are constantly fighting battles to be seen, heard, and valued.

Nieto et al. also point to a different set of skills for members of the Target identity group. This is the stage of empowerment, which occurs when members of the Target identity group create spaces solely for the Target group. They come together to seek support, advice, encouragement, and confirmation of their shared experiences. A more formal example is affinity groups or employee resource groups. The act of gathering can provide collective clarity and strength to address systems of oppression (Nieto et al. 2014).

Empowerment is a powerful skill set that can be used to demand that members of the Agent group recognize and take action toward dismantling inequalities.

We can be part of a Target identity group or believe ourselves to be part of a Target identity group without realizing or acknowledging the differences between ourselves and others.

IDC Stage: Acceptance

Bennett refers to the next stage of the continuum as acceptance, where people appreciate and understand identity differences. They are open to learning more about cultural differences, and willing to reflect on their own cultural identities. However, they may not have the skills or willingness to adapt their behaviors to other cultural identity norms.

Agent Skills: Awareness

Members of Agent identity groups practice the skill of awareness, in which you recognize systems of oppression and your own unearned advantages. This can be a painful process, as it requires you in your Agent identities to sit with the discomfort of your privilege. You may feel guilt or shame for your past blindness or for your unintentional contributions to oppression through your actions (or inactions). You may be compelled to "fix" the problem and seek out immediate, superficial, overly simplistic solutions. The challenge is to sit with the discomfort. The longer you do, the more you will learn.

Target Skills: Strategy

If you are a member of a Target identity group, you have moved from empowerment to strategy. This is the skill set that helps you know when and how to respond to incidents of inequality or oppression. We acknowledge oppression and the impact it has on us and others. We are intentional about where we expend our mental and emotional energy, realizing the potential consequences to our own mental health, our relationships with others, and the probability and extent to which our actions will enact change.

Nieto et al. (2014) describe strategy skills in the following way:

> We start to see the common ground we have with other Target groups, and to understand how systems of oppression operate in general. Our analysis becomes more sophisticated and less personal. We think about how systems of oppression operate and how to maximize anti-oppressive possibilities. When using Strategy skills, we tend to focus less on addressing Agent group members and Agent consciousness, and more on changing policies, developing organizations that have larger benefits over time, and creating systems that support Targets.

IDC Stage: Adaptation

People in the adaptation stage are able to shift their own perspectives to understand others' experiences, and have the skills to adapt their behaviors to best fit different cultural contexts and situations.

Agent Skills: Allyship

For members of the Agent identity group, you practice allyship skills, in which you have the capability and willingness to use your privilege "on behalf of justice and liberation for everyone" (Nieto et al. 2014). You are willing to stay in the discomfort of acknowledging systems of oppression as a person who benefits from that system, and you are willing to challenge others in your Agent identity group to do the same. You do not take action as a savior of members of the Target group, and you don't expect recognition or reward.

Target Skills: Re-Centering

For members of the Target identity group, you are able to move from strategy into re-centering. The process of re-centering is one in which you and other members of the Target group define your own identity, rather than accepting the story that was written about you by members of the Agent identity group. You also request and expect members of the Agency group to engage in allyship behaviors, and you hold people in the Agency group accountable for their actions. When re-centering occurs, people are able to tap into the internal energy and power of their identity.

When allyship and re-centering occur in synchrony, powerful change can happen. For example, when men and White women step back, listen, and encourage women of color to take the lead in presentations, protests, or meetings, those women of color who now have the microphone become more vocal and confident to share their true stories.

To assess and build your DEI skills for your Agent and Target identities, ask yourself the following:
- Which Agent identity groups do I belong to and how does that impact my daily life?
- Which Target identity groups do I belong to and how does that impact my daily life?
- What skills do I need to develop in my Agent identities? What do I need to do to practice allyship?
- What skills do I need to develop in my Target identities? What do I need to do to practice re-centering?
- As a trainer, how can I support people who share my Agent identities to develop their skills?
- As a trainer, how can I support people who share my Target identities to develop their skills?

Manage Your Desire to Prosecute, Preach, or Politicize

In *Think Again*, Adam Grant explores the challenges we face in trying to challenge our own and others' beliefs. He explains that when we encounter people with whom we disagree, we often fall into one of three different roles—that of the prosecutor, the preacher, or the politician. (Spoiler: None of them is very effective!)

When we are in preacher mode, we are focused on convincing the person to believe what we believe. We often engage in preacher behaviors when we think our beliefs are endangered in some way. We lecture passionately about the merit of our beliefs, advocating for others to follow us.

When we are in politician mode, we are invested in being liked and accepted by others. We will ingratiate ourselves and seek approval to gain favor. We may engage in politicking when we are eager to prove ourselves or to maintain our status within a certain identity group.

When we are in prosecutor mode, we are invested in telling the person with whom we disagree why our view is right and theirs is wrong. We may debate the merit of the other person's beliefs or even engage in cross-examination, where we ask questions with the intent to trap them or point out the flaws in their thinking. Our focus is on winning the argument, and we are not interested in exploring the other person's view (Grant 2021).

What this looks like in DEI work:

DEI trainers sometimes fall into preacher tendencies when they spend more time lecturing to participants about the merit of DEI, and judge or shame those who do not hold the same beliefs. This can even happen in situations where participants are invested in DEI, but perhaps their practices are different. Trainers may be so locked into a certain philosophy or approach that they judge those who do not practice the same way.

DEI trainers may fall into politician tendencies if in their desire to develop rapport with an audience or maintain their standing with a particular identity they will avoid conflict even when it is necessary. They may not challenge or call out microaggressions or stereotypes.

DEI trainers may fall into prosecutor tendencies if they fall into debate mode with participants who do not share their beliefs. In their book, *Thanks for the Feedback*, Sheila Heen and Doug Stone refer to this as "wrong-spotting," where we will fixate on the elements of another person's opinion we want to invalidate rather than zooming out and listening to the individual's full message. We often miss valuable opportunities to engage participants when we fall into "wrong-spotting," which is a surefire way to shut down a dialogue.

Anytime we fall into the role of preacher, politician, or prosecutor, we diminish our role as facilitator. We place ourselves as a subjective party in the group dynamic. We become a participant rather than a conductor of the conversation.

As a DEI trainer, I will admit I have played all of these roles in different situations. I am probably most likely to engage in preacher mode, so convinced that my view is right and that if I deliver my message in an impassioned way, others will set aside their deeply held beliefs and join me. The challenge then is that I lose my curiosity and my openness to appreciate and explore the validity of others' experiences. I fall into "I'm right, you're wrong" thinking, and become unwilling to acknowledge my own blind spots. I have to manage that preacher voice and acknowledge the existence of multiple realities.

To manage your inner preacher-politician-prosecutor, ask yourself the following:
- Which of these roles am I drawn to most often?
- What situations trigger these roles for me?
- What is the potential impact for me and others in a learning environment if I step into one of these roles?
- What can I do to maintain my openness and also open others up to new ways of thinking?

Craft and Share Personal Stories

For a trainer, storytelling can be a powerful method for building trust, illustrating key concepts, and engaging people at the emotional as well as intellectual level. In DEI training, the stories you share with participants will impact their perception of you as well as their understanding of the subject matter. Your stories tell a great deal about your identity, values, and even privilege. Therefore, it is important to take time to craft stories that will support your training goals.

The personal stories of identity that you share with your learners will also potentially evoke strong emotional memories in you. Not every story is ready to be shared. Take time to prepare, refine, and practice the delivery of your stories, especially those that require more vulnerability and may have an emotional pull. You want your emotions to be genuine but not to overtake you and your ability to tell the story and connect with participants.

Your stories will also be received differently by participants depending on their identity dimensions. If you represent an Agent identity group and share a story acknowledging your privilege, people from your group may gain new awareness and feel more inclined to express their own privilege. However, if they are still uncomfortable acknowledging their privilege, they may seek other identity dimensions that distance you from them. People from the Target group may feel surprised and pleased to hear someone in an Agent position acknowledge the inequities they have long felt. They could also be irritated or offended if they believe your intention is to engage in performative allyship.

For example, let's say in a DEI training I decide to tell a story about being a heterosexual female who takes my young children to celebrate Pride every year with my LGBTQIA+ friends. My children since birth have known same-sex couples and LGBTQIA+ adults as unofficial aunties and uncles. I've read books on the experiences of transgender people to understand their lives better. My husband and I regularly read our children books that feature characters who have same-sex relationships and families.

The following reactions may all simultaneously occur:

- A heterosexual female with children smiles, nods with approval, and shares her own stories of educating her children on LGBTQIA+ issues.
- A heterosexual woman with a deeply held religious faith who does not believe in same-sex marriage may actually experience great discomfort or disapproval with my story. She distances herself from me, emphasizing how we are different because we

do not share the same religious beliefs. She withdraws from the conversation.

- A genderqueer participant feels a sense of connection and happiness that I shared the story and opened up a conversation around allyship. This person is hopeful to see an example that normalizes LGBTQIA+ lives and is approving of the actions I take to educate my children and myself.
- A gay man is irritated by the story. His family disowned him when he came out of the closet, and he feels like my story creates a glossy, superficial image that does not understand or acknowledge the deep-seated trauma that LGBTQIA+ people experience.

The intention of this hypothetical scenario is not to dissuade you from telling your story as either an Agent or a Target identity. Rather, it is a reminder to be conscious of how your stories will be received by people of various identity dimensions, and not assume a story will resonate the same with everyone.

Similarly, a story you tell from a Target identity perspective may land differently with diverse participants. For example, when I share stories of my Target identity as a woman and the times I have been treated disparagingly, I will also acknowledge how my identity as a White woman is different from the experiences of people of color.

When training in a globally diverse or multicultural environment, consider how appropriate and relevant your story will be to the audience. Often, US trainers will tell stories or provide examples that work quite well in US environments but are lost on or even offensive to an international audience.

Some tips for crafting stories for DEI training:

- Identify stories that clearly model or exemplify a concept.
- Know why you are telling the story. It should be to benefit the learning experience for the participants. It's not for your own benefit, pride, or need for approval or counseling.
- Think through how people from different identity groups may react emotionally to your story.

- Consider how to blend in stories from both your Agent and Target identities and provide the proper balance between the two. The more Agent identities you have (for example, White, cisgender, able bodied, male, and so forth), the fewer Target stories you should tell.
- Use culturally appropriate and relevant language.
- Balance the emotional arcs of your stories. It can be most effective to weave in stories that are humorous and light as well as stories of anger, pain, or loss.
- Show your full humanity. Share stories of both successes and mistakes. If you only share stories about when you did things right or successfully acted as an ally, it may seem like you are humble bragging and unwilling to acknowledge your imperfections.
- Be authentic. Don't make stuff up.
- Keep your stories simple. The most powerful stories are often those seemingly small moments or interactions that have a lasting impact. They don't need to all be huge life-altering events. They should represent our daily human experiences.
- Practice your stories before going live with them. Ask colleagues or friends from other identity groups to listen and give you feedback on your stories.

Self-Care, Renewal, and Healing

DEI training is uniquely challenging work. It requires you to be aware of your various dimensions and how they influence the way you show up and how others experience you. You are expected to make yourself open, transparent, and vulnerable to a group of strangers with no guarantee that they will practice care or compassion with you. DEI work requires immense stores of energy and focus to tune in to the emotional reactions of individual participants and the changes in group dynamics. You will be expected to empathize and connect with people whose beliefs and behaviors are opposed to yours. You will be questioned and challenged. You may be the target of others' anger.

You will be summoned to emotionally empathize with people who have experienced deep pain, and you may internalize their emotions in doing so.

Even the most emotionally intelligent, experienced DEI practitioners can struggle with maintaining their agility to manage the needs of the learning environment. Not only that, but we may experience different types of frustration and fatigue depending on the Agent and Target identity groups we represent.

For DEI practitioners who belong to one or more Target identity groups, a deep fatigue often comes from experiencing repeated patterns of little to no progress with DEI initiatives. They may find themselves having to continuously educate and re-educate people about stereotypes, exclusionary behaviors, and disparate policies that impact members of their Target identity. They may be frequently put upon to convince people in power of the "business case" for DEI, to prove that their experiences and those of others in their identity group are valid.

In her book *Black Fatigue*, Mary-Frances Winters (2020) recounts her own fatigue having been a leader in DEI work for many years:

> It is fatiguing for me after all these years to hear about the same lack of progress toward racial equity decade after decade and have White people respond with the same ignorance or lack of interest in the topic or by not acknowledging the profound impact of their racial identity. I sometimes do not know whether to scream, cry, or just give up.

Trainers and practitioners who are members of one or more Agent identity groups often experience frustration borne out of internal conflict as they wrestle with the role they unintentionally have in maintaining the oppressive systems to which they are so opposed. They may become frustrated with (even embarrassed by) people in their identity group who don't "get it." In *White Fragility*, Robin DiAngelo (2018) describes how in her early years as a DEI practitioner, she was surprised by the anger and defensiveness many White people showed.

> *I couldn't understand their resentment or disinterest in learning more about such a complex social dynamic as racism. . . . I assumed that in these circumstances, an educational workshop on racism would be appreciated. After all, didn't the lack of diversity indicate a problem or at least suggest that some perspectives were missing?*

As a DEI trainer, knowing your Agent and Target identities is an important starting point, but you also need to consider how to care for yourself and rebalance your own energy if you are committed to this work.

In *Resonant Leadership*, Richard Boyatzis and Annie McKee describe a phenomenon that causes even the most emotionally intelligent leaders to derail—the "Sacrifice Syndrome." The Sacrifice Syndrome occurs when leaders face ongoing challenges or crises day in and day out:

"We give a lot, strive for excellence, and we use our power for the greater good," Boyatzis and McKee explain. However, they argue that, "in the process of giving of ourselves, we give too much, leading us to ultimately become ineffective" (Boyatzis and McKee 2005).

DEI trainers often fall prey to the Sacrifice Syndrome, because we care deeply about contributing to positive change in the world. Yet we may fall into the trap of believing that by stepping back and taking a break we will lose the precious ground we have gained in our organizations and our society. This false narrative causes us to go at a pace that is unsustainable.

Anyone who chooses to do this work after all the cautions I've laid out in this book is obviously strong, resilient, and willing to take more than a few hits on the chin. However, we may also suffer from some hubris, believing that we are indestructible. We may ignore or discount the pain or exhaustion we feel because we have convinced ourselves that we have bottomless stores of battery life.

Preparing for DEI Work

Mindfulness is a critical practice for DEI trainers, not only to engage in self-care but to be able to show up as your best self in training. Mindfulness is the practice of being fully present to internal and external forces. Mindful practices help you to observe and tune in to your current internal state—physical, mental, emotional, and spiritual—as well as to be more fully aware of your external surroundings, including the space you inhabit, the people who engage with you, and the natural environment around you. Mindfulness practices are important for us to conduct before, during, and after DEI training experiences.

Mind

In the days and weeks preceding a DEI training event, you will likely take time to review materials, read up on additional content as needed, and prepare the examples and stories you want to share with participants.

We often default to mental preparation and sometimes it's the only preparation we do, which is not always enough to adequately ready ourselves for a potentially taxing DEI training experience.

Emotion

What emotions do you experience in your preparation? Are you excited? Anxious? Afraid? Tired? Have a conversation with yourself about what you are feeling and what is causing the emotional reaction.

Body

Focus on what you observe in your body prior to the training. Where are you holding tension? What parts of your body are activated as you think about the upcoming training? How is your current physical energy level? Are you getting enough rest, nutrition, exercise? Taking care of your body is an integral part to having the stamina for DEI work.

Spirit

Spirituality in terms of mindfulness relates to any practices that connect you to something greater than yourself. Spirituality may be related to your faith, or to your sense of oneness with humanity, the planet, and the universe. How connected are you feeling with your spiritual self?

Practices for Renewal

Find a mindfulness practice or routine that is in alignment with your needs, and that supports your individual physical, mental, emotional, and spiritual being. Here are some common practices to consider:

- **Journaling.** Taking time to engage in written reflection is a powerful way to get your thoughts and emotions out. It also provides a documented journey for you to reflect on in the future. Take a few minutes at a quiet time of your day. Notice what thoughts, ideas, questions, or feelings come into your mind and write them down.

- **"To Be" vs. "To Do" lists.** Many of us have "to-do" lists filled with all the tasks we must complete. We are sometimes so trapped in thinking about what we have to do that we don't give time to consider who we need to be. Consider your most deeply held values. Tap into your sense of purpose. Think about the different roles you play in your life. Consider your talents and strengths, the elements of your personality that bring value to others. Your "To Be" list is about living every day with an intention.

- **Meditation.** A daily meditation practice can be not only a way to feel calm and centered and alert, but also provide immense, long-lasting health benefits. Engaging in mindfulness meditation lowers our blood pressure and can help heart health. Meditation has been shown to improve our immune system and actually reduce cell aging. Meditation also has immense psychological benefits, helping us manage stress and experience an increase in general well-being.

- **Inhale and exhale.** Deep breathing is so beneficial to helping us calm our nervous system. As a natural empath, I take in people's emotions and feel with them, which is an incredible gift but also can be harmful if I don't consciously let those emotions go. I have found I need to visualize myself having inhaled the painful stories, harsh words, fears, anxieties, and insecurities that people brought with them into the learning space, and then exhale them out of my body so that what is left is memories of others' compassion, kindness, and light.

- **Connect with your people.** In DEI training you have to be constantly alert to the needs of others, taking in perspectives and stories, being thoughtful and intentional when choosing words and actions. You are managing the time and the agenda while also improvising and moving with the needs of the group. It's important to give yourself space and time to be with those who speak the same "language," with whom you can be your unvarnished self, where you do not need to be in the spotlight. Connecting with family and friends who know you deeply is an important part of renewal.

- **Hold the long note.** I heard this analogy several years ago and it has been a guide for me ever since. Anyone who has ever sung in a choir or played in a musical group has probably practiced staggered breathing. When a musical note needs to be held for a long time, musicians and vocalists will sometimes take turns holding the note so others can take a breath. None of us can hold those long notes by ourself, so we let someone pick up the note while we take a breath, and then we pick the note back up for others to breathe. As DEI trainers, we need to see ourselves as part of a collective. We know someone will be there to pick up the work when we need to step back and breathe. And we will do the same for them.

LOVING-KINDNESS MEDITATION

A particularly helpful practice for me as a DEI practitioner includes loving-kindness meditation, which is centered on sending unconditional love to every living being. For me, this includes the following thoughts:

- I send loving-kindness to myself (I wish for myself peace, happiness, and freedom from suffering)

- I send loving-kindness to people I love (I send light, peace, happiness, and freedom from suffering)
- I send loving-kindness to a difficult person or someone who has hurt me (I think of them with gentleness and forgiveness, and send peace, happiness, and freedom from suffering)
- I send loving-kindness to all sentient beings (I feel connected to all humanity, and wish peace, happiness, and freedom from suffering)

Summary

DEI training requires more than subject matter expertise and good content design. To create transformational experiences for others, you must be willing to transform yourself. DEI training is an emotional journey. It requires vulnerability, humility, and courage to look inward at your own life experiences and identity, which permeate your daily life. As a DEI trainer, be willing to acknowledge your innate biases, own your privilege, and share your personal stories to drive connection with your participants. Be kind to yourself and build in time for self-care and renewal to continue to provide meaningful learning experiences.

Worksheet 8-1. Exploring Your Identity: Surface, Snorkel, Scuba

Consider the dimensions of your identity that impact who you are, what you believe and how you live.

Surface	What dimensions of your identity are immediately visible to others? How do these dimensions impact the way you are judged? How do these dimensions influence the way you are treated, or the way you are able to move through your day? What assumptions may people have about you based only on what is above the surface?
Snorkel Level	What dimensions of your identity are not immediately visible, but are fairly easy for you to share with others and give further insight into your interests and behaviors? These are dimensions of your identity you would not be hesitant to share with co-workers or acquaintances.
Scuba Level	What dimensions of your identity are deeply connected to your core being, and may have a powerful influence on your values, beliefs, and reactions to people or situations? These are stories that tell a lot about you, and require a deeper level of trust to share with others.

Reflection:
- What do these stories reveal about you?
- How might these stories impact how you are perceived by others?
- How might these stories impact how you perceive others who are either similar to or different from you?
- How might these stories impact the way you show up as a DEI trainer?

Worksheet 8-2. Checklist for Developing Your Personal Skills as a DEI Trainer

To check your biases, ask yourself the following:

- What messages have I received in my life that may have influenced my perceptions?
- What identity groups do I have the most exposure to?
- What identities do I have the least exposure to? How does that lack of exposure impact my understanding of their customs, behaviors, and experiences?
- How can I check for blind spots?

To examine systems of oppression, ask yourself the following:

- What is my understanding of and exposure to systemic inequality? What identity groups do I belong to that have given me unearned advantages?
- What identity groups do I belong to that have disadvantaged me or led to unfair treatment for me or people like me?
- What are some of your earliest memories around your identity? What messages did you receive that let you know where you "fit" in the social hierarchy?
- How did the people in your social network (family, friends, religious leaders, teachers) talk about or behave around people in your identity group? How was that similar to or different from the way they talked about or behaved around other identities? (For example, what messages did elders or leaders in your faith community send around the role of women versus men?)
- What immediate reactions do I have when someone from a different identity group talks about oppression? (For example, if I am White and I hear a POC talk about their experience with racism)

To acknowledge privilege, ask yourself the following:

- What are the Agent groups to which I belong? How does my membership to those groups influence my daily life?
- What are the Target groups to which I belong? How does my membership to those groups influence my daily life?
- When I look at the number of Agent groups versus Target groups to which I belong, what picture emerges? Do I belong to more Agent groups or Target groups in society?
- What daily activities can I engage in without fear and how might that be different for other identity groups?
- When I turn on the TV or open a book, what representations do I see of my different identity groups (such as race, gender, age, citizenship, sexual orientation, religion)?
- Who are the people I most commonly hear referred to as leaders, role models, superheroes, and other sources of inspiration? What dimensions of identity do they represent? Are those the people I think of? Why or why not?
- When others talk about their disadvantages or their experience of discrimination, harassment, or exclusionary treatment because of their identity, what is my reaction?
- Whose stories do I find it hardest to connect with? Whose stories do I find harder to accept?

- Do I ever feel frustration or skepticism when someone talks about the disadvantages they have experienced? How come?

To assess and build your DEI skills for your Agent and Target identities, ask yourself the following:

- Which Agent identity groups do I belong to and how does that impact my daily life?
- Which Target identity groups do I belong to and how does that impact my daily life?
- What skills do I need to develop in my Agent identities? What do I need to do to practice allyship?
- What skills do I need to develop in my Target identities? What do I need to do to practice re-centering?
- As a trainer, how can I support people who share my Agent identities to develop their skills?
- As a trainer, how can I support people who share my Target identities to develop their skills?

To manage your inner preacher-politician-prosecutor, ask yourself the following:

- Which of these roles am I drawn to most often?
- What situations trigger these roles for me?
- What is the potential impact for me and others in a learning environment if I step into one of these roles?
- What can I do to maintain my openness and also open others up to new ways of thinking?

Some tips for crafting stories for DEI training:

- Identify stories that clearly model or exemplify a concept.
- Know why you are telling the story. It should be to benefit the learning experience for the participants. It's not for your own benefit, pride, or need for approval or counseling.
- Think through how people from different identity groups may react emotionally to your story.
- Consider how to blend in stories from both your Agent and Target identities and provide the proper balance between the two. The more Agent identities you have (for example, White, cisgender, able bodied, male, and so forth), the fewer Target stories you should tell.
- Use culturally appropriate and relevant language.
- Balance the emotional arcs of your stories. It can be most effective to weave in stories that are humorous and light as well as stories of anger, pain, or loss.
- Show your full humanity. Share stories of both successes and mistakes. If you only share stories about when you did things right or successfully acted as an ally, it may seem like you are humble bragging and unwilling to acknowledge your imperfections.
- Be authentic. Don't make stuff up.
- Keep your stories simple. The most powerful stories are often those seemingly small moments or interactions that have a lasting impact. They don't need to all be huge life-altering events. They should represent our daily human experiences.
- Practice your stories before going live with them. Ask colleagues or friends from other identity groups to listen and give you feedback on your stories.

Acknowledgments

I am eternally grateful to the many people who have helped shape my journey and given it wondrous color, texture, depth, and light.

First and foremost, to Charlie Meisch, my partner in life, love, and laughter, who spent many weekends over the last year ferrying our girls around to give me space to write. I am supremely grateful for every moment I get to spend with you.

To Rosie and Lilia, who own my heart. Every day you inspire me, fill me with joy, and make me want to be the best possible human I can be for you.

To Joni and Val Morukian, the parents everyone wishes for. All that I am is because of you, and I miss you fiercely every day. I hope you are leading conga lines and polka dances in Heaven.

To Laura, my sister and best friend, who keeps me grounded and laughs at me and with me at exactly the right times. You know how to be my fiercest critic and most loyal cheerleader. I am deeply proud and grateful to have you, *mi hermana.*

To the Bruski women, who from one generation to the next share infinite strength, fierce love, and sharp wit. The matriarch, Verna, who at 105 years old can still beat anyone at Pinocle and pie crusts. Kathy and Carol, loving aunts and second mothers to me. Christy and Emily, cousins, sisters, accomplices in goofy pranks. The next generation: Augusta, Alexa, Kasia, and Hannah.

To the Bruski boys, merciless with their teasing and hilarious in their jokes, whose tough exteriors never fully mask their generosity and sensitivity.

To my loving aunties, Meline and Susana, who treated me as a daughter and taught me to embrace my inner *gitana*, to read people's fortunes in the grounds of a coffee cup, and to live every day with passion. To my Mezmairik, who continues to be the inner voice of stillness and serenity in my heart.

To all my beautiful Armenian aunties, uncles, and cousins who inspire me to share our ancestors' story and treat *everyone* as family.

To all my adopted aunts and uncles from Finney. You have been there for me since I can remember, and you have always kept Joan and Val alive in your stories.

To "Mean Old" Aunt Carole, who has been a constant source of love and learning since I can remember.

To my beautiful friends who inspire me and enrich my life with their laughter, wisdom, and humor: Alison, Angela, Fletcher, Kerri, Kim, Liz, Maren, Melissa, Mercedes, Netanya, Rachel, and Sweet V.

To the Meisch family, Debbie, Charlie, Lindsay, Laura, and Craig. Thank you for embracing me as one of you. To my nieces, Gia and Meghan, I treasure being your Aunt Maria. Thank you for your love and trust. I can't wait to see the next steps in your journeys.

To ATD Press for taking a chance on me to write this book, and the wonderful new colleagues who supported me every step of the way on the production of this book: Eliza Blanchard, Alexandria Clapp, Suzy Felchlin, Sarah Halgas, Kay Hechler, Kathryn Stafford, and Hannah Sternberg. And special thanks to Rob Halgas for sharing my TEDx talk, which helped launch this whole journey!

To my numerous colleagues who have provided endless encouragement, support, wisdom, and chuckles through the years. You make this work challenging, fun, and fulfilling.

Special thanks to the MSM Global Gang:

Shilpa Alimchandani, I am deeply humbled to call you my colleague and friend. You have helped me to challenge my own identity biases when I have been too blind to see them. Thank you for your endless encouragement and generosity.

Gwen Crider, my unending gratitude for your friendship and partnership in this work. I have grown and deepened in this work because of you. You bring infinite patience and positivity, and you always know the right thing to say in the moment.

Dr. Carmen Foster, who brings wisdom, spirituality, and a whole lot of fun into every conversation we have. I have gained so much learning from your ability to weave complex concepts with personal stories and historical facts.

Chris Haigh, who has not only been a colleague and dear friend, but has also mentored me on my journey to exploring whiteness and privilege. You serve up plates full of knowledge, free of B.S. and full of heart.

Melissa Graetz, my appreciation for you is boundless! You make every workday easier and more lighthearted, with sparkles, cats, and musical metaphors. You bring such creativity, flexibility, and thoughtfulness to your work.

Timothy Kane, your ability to connect with people is magical. I have learned so much from you about the intersection of faith and identity, and your calming presence is like a balm to my soul.

Dr. Zimife Umeh, you are like a fresh spring breeze. Your thoughtfulness and calm, logical approach make every project we collaborate on feel easy even when it's complicated and messy!

Sika Dunyoh, my amazing marketing expert who keeps me focused and informed. You have helped us create a vision for MSM Global's future.

To my former MC colleagues, the best team ever—Lahaja Furaha, Natalya Pestalozzi, Anna Mauldin, and Kathy Johnson. Although our time together was too short, it was so full of creativity and growth, and taught me a great deal.

To my NMCI colleagues and mentors, thank you for teaching me the foundations of DEI. I was young and inexperienced and absurdly overconfident. You took that all in stride and challenged me to be curious. You gave me the chance to mess up and learn from my mistakes. Thanks to my dear colleagues and friends, Bev-Freda, Audrey, Kelly, and Laura; and my amazing mentors, Liz Salett, Evelyn Boyer, Nancy Di Dia, Rohini Anand, Eva Young, Ruth Littlejohn, Karyn Trader Leigh, Tod Ewing, Cheryl Gardner, Martha Miller, Emilio Williams, Juan José Callejas, Dolores Fridge, and the dearly missed Manny Brandt.

To my friends from the Foreign Service Institute, thank you for the friendship and fun during our years together. I'm grateful that our bonds continue. Thanks to my wonderful colleagues, Matt DeMarco, Steve Whearty, Stephen Moles, Susan Luck, John Pettit, Cathy Raines, Max McLaughlin, Duane Karlen, Kerry Molinelli, Rondalyn Kane, Gail Neelon, Laura Miller Smallwood, my dear surrogate work mom Nancy Rosenshine, and the very much missed Charlie Peacock.

Special thanks to Ray Leki, who has been my mentor, advocate, and friend for many years. I am forever grateful for your endless willingness to listen and offer gentle guidance.

Gratitude to those whose expertise and research helped shape and enrich my writing: Minal Bopaiah, Tiffany Jana and Michael Baran, Jim Kirkpatrick, the Intercultural Development Inventory Team, the Centre for Global Inclusion, Howard Ross, Mary-Frances Winters, Annaliese Singh, Jamil Zaki, Erin Meyer, Adam Grant, Amy Edmondson, Ibram X. Kendi, Ijeoma Oluo, Kimberlé Crenshaw, Letitia Nieto and Margot Boyer, to name just a few.

To the teachers, professors, and mentors who inspired me, awakened me, challenged me to see the world from multiple realities: Christine Chin, Peggy Means, Barbara Moran, Mark Mizruchi, Lyrae Myxter, Gary Weaver, and Sandy Zuk.

To all of the people who have taken a chance on me, who have given me permission to coach and train them, who have opened themselves up so we could share and grow together as a learning community, I am deeply humbled for your trust. I have learned so much more than I ever imagined because you were willing to engage with me.

Recommended Resources

There are many additional resources for further learning about DEI. Here are a few to consider as you continue your learning journey.

Organizations

Catalyst.org: A global nonprofit organization dedicated to workplace inclusion for women, addressing intersectional differences and sharing leading practices to advance women. Catalyst provides rich research and resources on issues related to women's rights and needs in the workplace.

Human Rights Campaign (HRC): A nonprofit organization dedicated to advocating for freedom and equality for LGBTQ+ people. HRC provides resources, tools, and research to support understanding and support for LGBTQ+ communities in the workplace and society.

Equal Justice Initiative (EJI): An organization committed to fighting racial and economic inequality and injustice by ending mass incarceration and supporting human rights. In addition to its advocacy work, EJI provides reports and research on racial injustice, criminal justice reform, and education, and runs two historical sites dedicated to telling the story of terrorism and human rights violations committed against African Americans.

The Centre for Global Inclusion: The Centre for Global Inclusion's mission is to serve as a "resource for research and education for individuals and organizations in their quest to improve diversity and inclusion practices around the world." It is also the home of the Global Diversity, Equity & Inclusion Benchmarks (GDEIB), which provides a set of standards and practices for sustainable DEI in organizations.

Podcasts

Scene on Radio: This is a series created by Duke University's Center for Documentary Studies. In season 2, Seeing White, host John Biewen explores the creation and perpetuation of the social construct of race. Season 3, Men, provides deep insights into the history of patriarchy, male dominance, and sexism in our society. The website provides study guides and bibliographies to support ongoing learning and dialogue.

NPR's Code Switch: Hosts Gene Demby and Shereen Marisol Meraji explore challenging topics and conversations around race and intersectionality.

Forum on Workplace Inclusion: The Forum on Workplace Inclusion provides global conferences, events, webinars, and resources on DEI. It also has a podcast with DEI practitioners focusing on specific topics related to organizational DEI programs and initiatives.

Culture Stew: This podcast, created and hosted by Maria Morukian, is dedicated to exploring diversity, equity, and inclusion in its many dimensions. Through interviews with scholars, practitioners, journalists, and leaders, Culture Stew delves into concepts of cultural identity and seek ways to learn and build bridges across our differences.

Books

Baran, M., and T. Jana. 2020 *Acts of Exclusion*. Oakland, CA: Berrett-Koehler.

Kendi, I. 2016. *Stamped From the Beginning: The Definitive History of Racist Ideas in America*. New York: Nation Books.

Kendi, I. 2019. *How to Be an Antiracist*. London: One World.

Livingston, R. 2021. *The Conversation: How Seeking and Speaking the Truth About Racism Can Radically Transform Individuals and Organizations*. New York: Random House.

McGhee, H. 2021. *The Sum of Us: What Racism Costs Everyone and How We Can Prosper Together*. New York: Random House.

Oluo, I. 2018. *So You Want to Talk About Race*. New York: Seal Press.

Singh, A. 2019. *The Racial Healing Handbook: Practical Activities to Help You Challenge Privilege, Confront Systemic Racism & Engage in Collective Healing*. Oakland, CA: New Harbinger Publications.

Wilkerson, I. 2020. *Caste: The Origins of Our Discontents*. New York: Random House.

Winters, M. 2020. *Inclusive Conversations: Fostering Equity, Empathy and Belonging Across Differences*. Oakland, CA: Berrett-Koehler.

Zinn, H. 1980. *A People's History of the United States*. New York: Harper & Row.v

Assessment Tools

Intercultural Development Inventory (IDI): Provides insight into an individual's ability to accept, understand, and adapt to different cultural perspectives and behaviors.

Intercultural Conflict Style Inventory (ICS): Explores four conflict styles that are representative of different communication styles and cultural identity values around emotional expression and directness.

GlobeSmart Profile: A self-assessment tool that explores an individual's cultural identity based on five dimensions: egalitarianism, independence, risk taking, directness, and relationship orientation.

Inclusive Behaviors Inventory (IBI): Assesses an individual's competence and comfort with engaging and communicating across differences. It includes five dimensions: learning about bias, building key skills, working across boundaries, becoming a champion, and getting results.

Global Competencies Inventory (GCI): Measures leadership and management skills in diverse settings. The GCI looks at three areas: perception management, relationship management, and self-management.

Glossary

allyship. The continuous process in which someone with privilege and power seeks to learn about the experiences of a marginalized group of people and empathize with their challenges, build relationships with that group of people, and use their privilege and power to promote fair treatment and respect for that group of people.

antiracist. Engaging in behaviors that actively challenge and work to disrupt systems of racism in society. Ibram X. Kendi, one of the foremost thought leaders in antiracism, defines an antiracist as "One who is supporting an antiracist policy through their actions or expressing an antiracist idea" (Kendi 2019). Antiracism challenges individuals to go beyond a passive response to inequality. Saying, "I'm not racist" does not make us antiracist, because racism itself is more than an individual belief. Antiracism requires one to recognize and work to dismantle racist systems and institutions.

belonging. A sense of comfort, safety, and support, where individuals feel a deep connection and membership within a group. When people feel like they are accepted by a group, they are more likely to be engaged and motivated to contribute to the group's shared purpose.

cisgender. A term used to describe a person whose gender identity is the same as that assigned to them at birth.

diversity. The unique constellation of dimensions of human identity that make us who we are. Diversity includes all characteristics that shape our identity "lenses"—our beliefs, values, worldviews, and perceptions—which thus influence our communication, our behaviors, and ultimately our relationships with others.

Diversity includes characteristics like race, skin color, ethnicity, gender, national origin, sexual orientation, religion, physical or mental ability or disability, socioeconomic background, academic background, profession, family and relationship status, language, habits and activities, and personality traits.

equity. Fair treatment, access, and opportunity for all people. Equity promotes fairness by addressing injustice and creating a level playing field for those who have been marginalized or oppressed because of some dimension of their identity.

equity versus equality. Equality aims to give everyone the same thing. It can only work if everyone is starting from a level playing field and needs the same things to have full, healthy lives. Equity is distinct from equality in that it requires us to acknowledge that systemic barriers have impeded opportunities for fair and just treatment for some members of society.

ethnicity. The way in which an individual affiliates with a particular group that shares a common identity, including shared language; national, regional, or tribal background; religious beliefs; and cultural origins and norms. Although race and ethnicity are often intertwined, they are not synonymous. For example, a person's race may be Asian because their family is from Japan, but if they were born and raised in Paris they may identify as ethnically French.

expansion. The practice of immersing oneself in the lived experiences of others, broadening one's social networks beyond the comfortable "us" group, and building community across the broad landscape of our differences. Expansion requires individuals, especially those in positions of privilege and power, to actively seek out and elevate the voices of groups who are often marginalized or disadvantaged because of their identity; to challenge existing schemas and blind spots; to shift power toward those who have been systematically targeted, disenfranchised, or oppressed; and to co-create a new culture with shared purpose and power for all.

gender expression. External appearance of one's gender identity. This may be shown with the choice of nonverbal behaviors, clothing, haircut, or voice. One's gender expression may or may not conform to socially defined behaviors typically associated with being either masculine or feminine.

gender identity. One's innermost concept of self as male, female, a blend of both, or neither. Gender identity relates to how individuals self-identify. One's gender identity can be the same or different from that assigned to them at birth. For example, a person may have been labeled a girl at birth based on their anatomy, but may identify as a boy or as nonbinary.

harassment. Unwelcome conduct that is based on race, color, religion, sex or gender, pregnancy status, national origin, age (when targeting those 40 or older), disability, or genetic information. Not all disrespectful or unwelcome behaviors may rise to the legal definition of harassment. To be unlawful, the conduct must create a work environment that would be intimidating, hostile, or offensive to the targeted people. Sexual harassment refers to unwelcome sexual advances, requests for sexual favors, or other verbal, nonverbal, or physical conduct of a sexual nature (EEOC n.d.).

implicit association. Mental shortcuts based on internalized messages and mental conditioning that lead a person to automatically associate one thing with another. Implicit associations may cause us to automatically assign people with certain characteristics a social role, job function, or anticipated behavior (for example, associating men with work and women with family obligations).

implicit bias and unconscious bias. Attitudes or prejudices that affect our understanding, actions, and decisions in an unconscious manner without awareness, intention, or control. Implicit biases are often in opposition to one's consciously held beliefs, and are very difficult for a person to identify in themselves.

inclusion. An environment in which everyone is welcomed, respected, and encouraged to fully participate. An inclusive environment is one in which everyone is valued for their unique individual characteristics.

intersectionality. The confluence of multiple social identity dimensions (such as, race, economic background, gender identity, sexual orientation, religion, or physical or mental ability) that creates overlapping and compounding systemic disadvantages or barriers for individuals. For example, a Latina woman who is an amputee and identifies as lesbian has multiple identity dimensions that may often be marginalized or othered in society. Many people who belong to multiple identity groups that are disadvantaged or marginalized say they feel like they have to work twice, three, or four times as hard as people who come from dominant identity groups to achieve the same results, due to structural and cultural obstacles.

micro-affirmations. Subtle or small acknowledgments of a person's value and accomplishments. Micro-affirmations are akin to small positive energy jolts. Over time, they make the receiver feel respected, supported, and encouraged.

micro-messages. Small, subtle messages we send and receive verbally and nonverbally, which can have a cumulative impact on who feels respected and valued.

micro-inequities. Subtle, often unconscious and involuntary messages that transmit a devaluing message to the receiver, typically connected with a dimension of their identity that has been marginalized or targeted (for example, gender, race or ethnicity, national origin, or physical or mental disability). They are conveyed through facial expressions, gestures, tone of voice, choice of words, nuance, and syntax.

microaggressions. Subtle messages or behaviors that cue a sense of inequality or subordination toward a person based on a dimension of their identity that is often marginalized or targeted (such as, gender, race or ethnicity, national origin, or physical or mental disability).

privilege. In the context of DEI work, privilege refers to the unearned societal advantages afforded to people from a certain identity group, often an identity over which they have little control. Privilege occurs for people who belong to a dominant identity group, where systems are set up to normalize and cater to their lives and needs, often to the detriment of others. People can have privilege based on some dimensions of identity but not in others. For example, a White man with a physical disability who comes from a lower income economic background has a great deal of privilege because of his racial identity but has likely faced disadvantages in society because of his disability and economic status. A Black straight cisgender woman with a doctorate from a wealthy suburb has experienced privilege because of her economic status and education, but has likely experienced a great deal of oppression because of her race. Privilege can be fluid and is not one-size-fits-all. However, it is important to recognize that in different societies, certain identity dimensions carry significant automatic privileges over others. In the US, racial identity privileges bring powerful advantages to people, even when they have experienced disadvantages because of other identity characteristics (including economic background, national origin, and sexual orientation).

race. A concept used as a classification system to categorize groups of human beings based on factors such as observable traits, ethnicity, and geographic ancestry. The concept of race morphed into a means of exploitation in the 16th and 17th centuries with European colonization. The ideology of race became a means of maintaining a social system that stratified people based on physical appearance and assigned individuals from each racial group with inherent cognitive, emotional, physical, behavioral, and moral characteristics, which were ultimately adopted as societal beliefs. For example, the Atlantic slave trade further incentivized a social construct of race to justify the enslavement of Africans and their descendants. Race is a social construct in that there is no genomic difference to separate people along racial lines. However, the ideology of race is deeply ingrained in our human social experience and has become a crucial means of self and other identification.

racism. Prejudice, discrimination, oppression, or violence targeting people who have been categorized in a particular racial identity group, based on a socially constructed racial hierarchy that stratifies racial identities. Racism typically stratifies White, Anglo, and European identities as the dominant racial group. Racism can occur at the individual, group, and systemic levels. Individual acts of racism support and perpetuate structural racism. In fact, race scholars argue that the lack of action to disrupt or challenge racist policies or behaviors is in and of itself inherently racist.

sexual orientation. A person's inherent emotional, romantic, or sexual attraction to other people. Sexual orientation is distinct from gender identity.

stereotype. A widely held but fixed and oversimplified idea of a particular type of person or thing. Stereotypes are often negative or demeaning in their description of a targeted group. For example, "women are emotional," "Muslims are violent," or "evangelical White Christians are racist." These stereotypes, many based on biases against an identity group that are intended to perpetuate "us vs. them" thinking, are problematic because they narrow the view of an individual to one dimension of their identity, and within that narrow view label the person based on a false narrative. Stereotypes are universal by design, characterizing anyone belonging to an identity group as the same in terms of their behaviors, beliefs, and characteristics.

Stereotypes can at times appear to be positive. For instance, "Asians are good at math." However, even "positive" stereotypes can be problematic in that they label an individual without evidence and prohibit the person from being seen or valued for their unique identity. They can be challenging for individuals who identify in that group but do not fit the stereotype and thus feel like an outlier.

systemic racism. A combination of structural and cultural systems, policies, and institutions that continue to provide automatic advantages to one racial identity group, often at the expense or exploitation of other racial identity groups. Systemic racism typically stratifies and provides systemic privileges to White, Anglo identities as the dominant racial group.

transgender. An umbrella term for people whose gender identity and/or expression is different from cultural expectations based on the gender they were assigned at birth. Being transgender does not imply any specific sexual orientation. Therefore, transgender people may identify as straight, gay, lesbian, bisexual, asexual, pansexual, or any other orientation.

References

Chapter 1

AAAED (American Association for Access, Equity, and Diversity). 2021. "More History of Affirmative Action Policies From the 1960s." American Association for Access, Equity, and Diversity. aaaed.org /aaaed/history_of_affirmative_action.asp.

ADL (Anti-Defamation League). 2021. "A Brief History of the Disability Rights Movement." Anti-Defamation League. adl.org/education /resources/backgrounders/disability-rights-movement.

Anand, R., and M.F. Winters. 2008. "A Retrospective View of Corporate Diversity Training From 1964 to the Present." *Academy of Management Learning & Education* 7(3): 356–372. wintersgroup .com/corporate-diversity-training-1964-to-present.pdf.

Brewer, M.B. 1991. "The Social Self: On Being the Same and Different at the Same Time." *Personality and Social Psychology Bulletin* 17:475–482.

Crenshaw, K. 2006. "Framing Affirmative Action." *Michigan Law Review First Impressions* 105:123.

Dixon-Fyle, S., K. Dolan, V. Hunt, and S. Prince. 2020. *Diversity Wins: How Inclusion Matters.* McKinsey & Company, May 19. mckinsey .com/featured-insights/diversity-and-inclusion/diversity-wins -how-inclusion-matters.

Eisenberg, B., and M. Ruthsdotter. 1998. "History of the Women's Rights Movement." National Women's History Alliance. national womenshistoryalliance.org/history-of-the-womens-rights -movement.

Shelby County v. Holder, 570 U.S. 529. 2013.

HRC (Human Rights Campaign). 2021. "Fatal Violence Against the Transgender and Gender Nonconforming Community in 2021." Human Rights Campaign, July 7. hrc.org/resources/fatal-violence -against-the-transgender-and-gender-non-conforming-community -in-2021.

Hsu, H. 2018. "The Rise and Fall of Affirmative Action." *The New Yorker*, October 15. newyorker.com/magazine/2018/10/15/the-rise -and-fall-of-affirmative-action.

Krentz, M., J. Dean, J. Garcia-Alonso, M. Tsusaka, and E. Vaughn. 2019. "Fixing the Flawed Approach to Diversity." Boston Consulting Group, January 17.

Mohr, T. 2014. "Why Women Don't Apply for Jobs Unless They're 100% Qualified." *Harvard Business Review*, August 25.

United Nations International Forum for Social Development. 2006. "Social Justice in an Open World: The Role of the United Nations." New York: United Nations.

Vaughn, B.E. 2007. "The History of Diversity Training & Its Pioneers." *Strategic Diversity & Inclusion Management Magazine* 1(1): 11–16.

Ward, M. 2021. "There's a Key Difference Between 'Equity' and 'Equality'—and You Need to Understand It to Help Dismantle Systemic Racism in America." *Business Insider*, February 2. businessinsider.com/racial-equity-equality-definition-systemic -racism-2021-2.

Chapter 2

Useem, J. 2017. "Power Causes Brain Damage." *The Atlantic*, July-August. theatlantic.com/magazine/archive/2017/07/power -causes-brain-damage/528711.

Chapter 3

Banaji, M., and A. Greenwald. 2011. "Culture, Cognition, and Collaborative Networks in Organizations." *American Sociological Review* 76(2): 207–233. doi.org/10.1177/0003122411399390.

Banaji, M., and A. Greenwald. 2013. *Blindspot: Hidden Biases of Good People*. New York: Delacorte Press.

Bloom, B.S., M.D. Engelhart, E.J. Furst, W.H. Hill, and D.R. Krathwohl. 1956. *Taxonomy of Educational Objectives, Handbook I: The Cognitive Domain*. New York: David McKay.

Ceron, E. 2015. "Nicki Minaj Perfectly Articulates Her Problem With Miley Cyrus and Cultural Appropriation." *Teen Vogue*, October 7. teenvogue.com/story/nicki-minaj-miley-cyrus-cultural-appropriation.

Dastin, J. 2018. "Amazon Scraps Secret AI Recruiting Tool That Showed Bias Against Women." Reuters, October 10. reuters.com/article/us-amazon-com-jobs-automation-insight/amazon-scraps-secret-ai-recruiting-tool-that-showed-bias-against-women-idUSKCN1MK08G.

Haidt, J. 2012. *The Righteous Mind: Why Good People Are Divided by Politics and Religion*. New York: Vintage.

Jana, T., and M. Baran. 2020. *Subtle Acts of Exclusion: How to Understand, Identify, and Stop Microaggressions*. Oakland, CA: Berrett-Koehler.

Klocke, C. 2018. "I Am a Man VR Civil Rights App." NC State College of Design Blog, January 25. design.ncsu.edu/blog/2018/01/25/i-am-a-man-vr-civil-rights-app.

Lavietes, M. 2020. "U.N. Warns COVID-19 Could Wipe Out Gains in Equality for Women at Work." Reuters, June 30. reuters.com/article/us-health-coronavirus-usa-women-labor-tr-idUSKBN2413L6.

Meigs, D., and M. Baw. 2021. "Finding Refuge in Omaha: The Karen Community's Perseverance Through War, Displacement, and Pandemic." *Omaha Magazine*, February 15. omahamagazine .com/2021/02/15/347618/finding-refuge-in-omaha-the-karen -community-s-perseverance-through-war-displacement-and -pandemic.

Morukian, M. 2020. "Connecting Cultures: Luby Ismail." Culture Stew With Maria Morukian, Season 2, Episode 1. Shelby Row Productions. directory.libsyn.com/shows/view/id/culturestew.

National Partnership for Women & Families. 2021. "Fact Sheet: Quantifying America's Gender Wage Gap." National Partnership for Women & Families, March. nationalpartnership.org/our-work /resources/economic-justice/fair-pay/quantifying-americas -gender-wage-gap.pdf.

Nieto, L., and M.F. Boyer. 2007. "Understanding Oppression: Strategies in Addressing Power and Privilege." *ColorsNW*, March. evergreen .edu/sites/default/files/writingcenter/docs/cv/Nieto_Ask%20 Leticia.pdf.

PBS. 2017. "What I Hear When You Say Viewing Guide: Cultural Appropriation." PBS Viewing Guide. bento.cdn.pbs.org/hosted bento-prod/filer_public/whatihear/9-Cultural_Approp-Viewing _Guide.pdf.

Pronin, E., D. Lin, and L. Ross. 2002. "The Bias Blind Spot: Perceptions of Bias in Self Versus Others." *Personality and Social Psychology Bulletin* 28:369-381. DOI: 10.1177/0146167202286008.

Roberts, M. 2020. "Marking the Deadliest Year on Record, HRC Releases Report on Violence Against Transgender and Gender Non-Conforming People." The Human Rights Campaign. hrc .org/press-releases/marking-the-deadliest-year-on-record-hrc -releases-report-on-violence-against-transgender-and-gender -non-conforming-people.

Rowe, M.P. 2020. "Barriers to Equality: The Power of Subtle Discrimination to Maintain Unequal Opportunity." *Employee Responsibilities and Rights Journal* 3(2): 153-163.

Schein, E. 2010. *Organizational Culture and Leadership*, 4th ed. San Francisco: Jossey-Bass.

Turner, A. 2018. "HRC Report: Startling Data Reveals Half of LGBTQ Employees in the U.S. Remain Closeted at Work." The Human Rights Campaign. hrc.org/news/hrc-report-startling-data-reveals-half-of -lgbtq-employees-in-us-remain-clos.

Weaver, G.R. 1986. "Understanding and Coping With Cross-Cultural Adjustment Stress." In *Cross-Cultural Orientation: New Conceptualizations and Applications*, edited by R.M. Paige. Lanham, MD: University Press of America.

Chapter 4

Celis, L., and V. Keswani. 2020. "Implicit Diversity in Image Summarization." New York: Association for Computing Machinery, October. dl.acm.org/doi/10.1145/3415210.

Grant, A. 2021. *Think Again: The Power of Knowing What You Don't Know*. New York: Viking.

Heumann, J. 2019. "Road Map for Inclusion: Changing the Face of Disability in Media." Ford Foundation. fordfoundation.org /media/4276/judyheumann_report_2019_final.pdf.

Kang, S.K., K.A. DeCelles, A. Tilcsik, and S. Jun. 2016. "Whitened Résumés: Race and Self-Presentation in the Labor Market." *Administrative Science Quarterly* 61(3): 469–502.

Kruse, K. 2012. "100 Best Quotes on Leadership." *Forbes*, October 16.

O*NET OnLine. "Survey Report for: 25-9031.00—Instructional Coordinators." onetonline.org/link/summary/25-9031.00.

Prevent Blindness. n.d. "Eye Diseases and Conditions: Color Blindness." preventblindness.org/color-blindness.

Schrupp, L. 2019. "Why We Created a Gender-Inclusive Stock Photo Library." *Vice*, March 26. vice.com/en/article/qvyq8p /transgender-non-binary-stock-photos-gender-spectrum -collection.

Smith, D.G., J.E. Rosenstein, and M.C. Nicolov. 2018. "The Different Words We Use to Describe Male and Female Leaders." *Harvard Business Review*, May 25. hbr.org/2018/05/the-different-words -we-use-to-describe-male-and-female-leaders.

Soundview Executive Book Summaries. 2020. "The 25 Best Leadership Books of All-Time." *Soundview Magazine*, December 10. summary .com/magazine/the-25-best-leadership-books-of-all-time.

TED. n.d. "The Most Popular Talks of All Time." TED.com. ted.com /playlists/171/the_most_popular_talks_of_all.

U.S. Bureau of Labor Statistics. 2021. "Labor Force Statistics from the Current Population Survey." BLS, January 22. bls.gov/cps/cpsaat 11.htm.

U.S. Social Security Administration. 2021. "Top Names Over the Last 100 Years." ssa.gov/oact/babynames/decades/century.html.

Chapter 5

Bohm, D. 1996. *On Dialogue*. New York: Routledge.

Chapman, S., P. McPhee, and B. Proudman. 1995. "What Is Experiential Education?" In *The Theory of Experiential Education*, edited by K. Warren, 235-248. Dubuque: Kendall/Hunt Publishing Company.

Covey, S. 1989. *The 7 Habits of Highly Effective People*. New York: Free Press.

Dweck, C.S. 2006. *Mindset: The New Psychology of Success*. New York: Random House.

Edmondson, A. 2019. *The Fearless Organization: Creating Psychological Safety in the Workplace for Learning, Innovation, and Growth*. Hoboken, NJ: Wiley.

Glaser, J. 2016. *Conversational Intelligence: The New Psychology of Success*. New York: Random House.

Kolb, D. 1984. *Experiential Learning: Experience as the Source of Learning and Development*. Englewood Cliffs, NJ: Prentice-Hall.

Leonard, K., and T. Yorton. 2015. *Yes, And: How Improvisation Reverses "No, But" Thinking and Improves Creativity and Collaboration*. New York: HarperCollins.

Parker, P. 2018. *The Art of Gathering: How We Meet and Why It Matters.* New York: Penguin.

Schein, E.H. 2013. *Humble Inquiry: The Gentle Art of Asking Instead of Telling.* Oakland, CA: Berrett-Koehler.

Steele, C. 2010. *Whistling Vivaldi: How Stereotypes Affect Us and What We Can Do.* New York: W.W. Norton & Company.

Chapter 6

Chang, E.H., K.L. Milkman, L.J. Zarrow, K. Brabaw, D.M. Gromet, R. Rebele, C. Massey, A.L. Duckworth, and A. Grant. 2019. "Does Diversity Training Work the Way It's Supposed To?" *Harvard Business Review*, July 9. hbr.org/2019/07/does-diversity-training -work-the-way-its-supposed-to.

Dobbin, F., and A. Kalev. 2016. "Why Diversity Programs Fail." *Harvard Business Review*, July-August. hbr.org/2016/07/why-diversity -programs-fail.

Kirkpatrick, W.K., and J.D. Kirkpatrick. 2016. *Kirkpatrick's Four Levels of Training Evaluation.* Alexandria, VA: ATD Press.

Molefi, N., J. O'Mara, and A. Richter. 2021. *Global Diversity, Equity, and Inclusion Benchmarks: Standards for Organizations Around the World.* The Centre for Global Inclusion. centreforglobalinclusion .org/wp-content/uploads/2021/04/GDEIB-APRIL-2021-2.pdf.

Stillman, J. 2017. "Google's Tiny Secret for Actually Impactful Employee Training." *Inc.*, December 21. inc.com/jessica-stillman/googles -secret-for-employee-training-people-actually-use-shrink-it.html.

Chapter 7

Baudh, S. 2021. "Demarginalizing the Intersection of Caste, Class, and Sex." *Journal of Human Rights*, 20(1): 127-142.

Benhabbib, S. 2002. *The Claims of Culture: Equality and Diversity in the Global Era.* Princeton, NJ: Princeton University Press.

Dlabaja, C., J. Hofmann, and A. Knecht. 2016. "Inequality, Poverty and Prosperity in Austria." *Global Dialogue* 6(2). globaldialogue .isa-sociology.org/inequality-poverty-and-prosperity-in-austria.

Gundling, E., and A. Zanchettin. 2007. *Global Diversity: Winning Customers and Engaging Employees Within World Markets.* Boston: Nicholas Brealey Publishing.

Hofstede, G., G.J. Hofstede, and M. Minkov. 2010. *Cultures and Organizations: Software of the Mind*, 3rd ed. New York: McGraw Hill.

Meyer, E. 2014. *The Culture Map: Breaking Through the Invisible Boundaries of Global Business.* New York: Public Affairs.

Petroff, A. 2015. "U.S. and Israel have worst inequality in the developed world." CNN Business, May 21. money.cnn.com/2015/05/21 /news/economy/worst-inequality-countries-oecd.

United Nations. 2016. *Living Free and Equal: What States Are Doing to Tackle Violence and Discrimination Against Lesbian, Gay, Bisexual, Transgender, and Intersex People.* New York: United Nations. ohchr .org/Documents/Publications/LivingFreeAndEqual.pdf.

Chapter 8

Boyatzis, R., and A. McKee. 2005. *Resonant Leadership: Renewing Yourself and Connecting With Others Through Mindfulness, Hope and Compassion.* Boston: Harvard Business Review Press.

DiAngelo, R. 2018. *White Fragility: Why It's So Hard for White People to Talk About Racism.* New York: Penguin Random House.

Jana, T., and M. Baran. 2020. *Subtle Acts of Exclusion: How to Understand, Identify, and Stop Microaggressions.* Oakland, CA: Berrett-Koehler.

Klein, E. 2020. "Bryan Stevenson on How American Can Heal." Vox, July 20. vox.com/21327742/bryan-stevenson-the-ezra-klein-show -america-slavery-healing-racism-george-floyd-protests.

Institute for the Study of Societal Issues (ISSI). 2018. "Beyond Identity: Building Collective Struggles for Racial and Health Justice." ISSI YouTube Channel, July 16. youtube.com/watch?v=wjq_xgptEuo.

Schiller, D., et al. 2009. "A Neural Mechanism of First Impressions." *Nature Neuroscience* 12(4): 508–514.

Wilkerson, I. 2020. *Caste: The Origins of Our Discontents.* New York: Random House.

Winters, M.-F. 2020. *Black Fatigue: How Racism Erodes the Mind, Body, and Spirit.* New York: Penguin Random House.

Glossary

Kendi, I.X. 2019. *How to Be an Anti-Racist.* London: One World.

Index

Page numbers followed by *f* or *t* refer to figures and tables, respectively.

About the Author

Maria Morukian is a recognized organization development practitioner specializing in training, coaching, and facilitation with a focus on diversity, equity, inclusion, and intercultural competence. Maria is the president of MSM Global Consulting and an adjunct faculty member at American University's School of International Service. She previously served in leadership and organization development positions at the US Office of Personnel Management's Federal Executive Institute and the US Department of State. She has also served in leadership positions at Management Concepts and the National MultiCultural Institute.

Maria has trained and coached thousands of individuals around the world to build practices for better communication, foster competent and respectful workplaces, and navigate conflict for meaningful culture change. She has worked with such diverse clients as PBS Distribution, the National Park Service, National Institutes of Health, the World Bank, and the Association for Animal Welfare Advancement.

Maria is a sought-after speaker and has presented at numerous events, including TEDx, the Forum on Workplace Inclusion, the Association for Talent Development, Blacks in Government, and Ellevate Women's Network. Her work has been published in *Forbes* and the Association for Talent Development's *Public Manager*, and she is the co-author of

Designing & Implementing Diversity Initiatives: A Guide for Organizational Culture Change.

Maria is host of the podcast Culture Stew, which focuses on the multidimensionality of identity and best practices in diversity, equity, and inclusion.

Maria earned a dual bachelor's degree from the University of Michigan in organizational studies and Spanish, and a master's degree from American University in international communication. She lives in Washington, DC, with her husband and two daughters. She is an avid runner, dancer, reader, traveler, and lover of theatre.